Anglo-Saxon Burial Mounds
Princely Burial in the
6th & 7th Centuries

Stephen Pollington

BY THE SAME AUTHOR

Meadhall
Wordcraft
Leechcraft
The Warrior's Way
The English Warrior
Rudiments of Runelore
First Steps in Old English
An Introduction to the Old English Language & its Literature
Old English Poems, Prose & Lessons – 2CDs – read by S Pollington
Anglo-Saxon FAQs

Published 2008 by

Anglo-Saxon Books
www.asbooks.co.uk

25 Brocks Road
EcoTech Business Park
Swaffham, Norfolk PE37 7XG

PL

ISBN 978 1 898281 51 1

Contents

Illustrations

Unless otherwise indicated -
Photographs by Stephen Pollington
Drawings by Lindsay Kerr

Foreword

The inspiration for this book is twofold. Firstly, I have been researching the contents and construction of graves from Anglo-Saxon times in connection with another project for some years now, and have been struck by the lack of a good, clear guide to the types of high-status burial available to the Anglo-Saxons at the point when their heathen religion was most threatened by the march of Christianity through northern Europe. Secondly, both Lindsay Kerr and I have developed a considerable interest in the details of feasting gear, weapons, brooches, jewellery and the other physical remains of the early English past, and we wanted to provide a handy guide to set Sutton Hoo and the other sites into their proper context. So many of our English sites seem strange, both weird and splendid at once, but this is a false impression to some extent, since very little in the English material is without parallel: it is simply that the parallel finds occur on the far shores of the North Sea.

The mound burials fall into two main groups: those with a chamber or internal room in which the deceased was displayed, and those with a simple grave-cut. The chamber graves were in many ways the more interesting and elaborate burials, since the opportunities for conspicuous display of wealth were so much greater in an open space such as the chamber provided, but some of the less pretentious mounds actually contained the more interesting burials – the youth and his horse beneath Mound 17 at Sutton Hoo being an obvious example.

The first part of the present book contains an overview of mound burial in general and chamber burial in particular against its Germnic background. I have contrasted some English finds with each other and with Continental graves for the sake of providing a context. I have also looked at the part which barrows played in Anglo-Saxon literature and in later folk tradition.

The book's second part is a compilation of information about the burial mounds known from Anglo-Saxon England. The listings of mound burials by area include both chamber burials and the more mundane mound burials. This is partly to show that inhumation (and cremation) within a barrow was not an unusual Anglo-Saxon practice, although it varied from region to region, and where prehistoric barrows were common it was considered perfectly acceptable to re-use them – indeed, it may have been desirable to do so for reasons connected with displays of political power.

As with so much early English material, there is a great deal of information which can be gleaned from a close study, especially when comparable sites in northern Europe are taken into account. It is hoped that this book will enable others to undertake and further this work.

A Note on the Quest for Barrows

The barrow-hunter's lot is not always an unhappy one, but it can be quite varied. In the course of preparing this text for publication, I have visited many of the sites mentioned and the experiences differ greatly. I offer here just a small sample, and what they can teach us.

Probably the most vivid experience to be had by the modern seeker after Anglo-Saxon mounds is at Sutton Hoo, where the barrowfield has been carefully preserved and Mound 2 has been recreated at something approaching its original size. The on-site National Trust visitor centre offers a good basis for interpreting the monuments – as well as refreshments and the usual facilities catering for the needs of visitors - and the attached museum holds many of the original treasures and some fine reproductions, including the entire chamber with its contents. A short introductory filmshow offers a glimpse into the world of the Anglo-Saxons and the circumstances of the discovery and excavation of the treasures. Periodically, themed events are held on the site as well as educational seminars in Tranmer House (the home of Mrs. Pretty, who owned the land) and informal talks by costumed interpreters. The visitor experience at Sutton Hoo is second to none. It is, however, a planned and shared experience, not usually a quiet or solitary one.

Taplow has less of an 'Anglo-Saxon' atmosphere due to the proximity of the rather grand Taplow Court, which is now a Buddhist retreat. There is a small themed exhibition in the main building, as well as visitor facilities. Taplow village is pretty, and Bapsey Pond at the foot of the hill is allegedly the site of the first Christian conversions in the area in Anglo-Saxon times. The views from the top of the barrow over the Thames landscape are worth the effort of seeking it out.

The Asthall barrow has no facilities at all. It sits in a field adjacent to the A40 and is a fine example of a barrow which has retained some of its former grandeur even without the isolation it was erected to enjoy. The traffic on the modern road passing a few yards from the mound does not assist quiet contemplation, but the barrow itself sports a thicket of vegetation which gives it an imposing air.

At the other end of the scale are the Roundway Down barrows. Having visited Barrow I with Mike McGuinness in late spring 2008, I was intrigued to discover that the local area was the site of a major battle of the English Civil War. The barrow was quite invisible beneath a vigorous crop of rape; the fluorescent yellow flowers and dark green stalks masked any suggestion of a tumulus, which presumably survives only to a height of a few centimetres.

Even looking down from the summit of Kingsplay Down, nothing could be seen of the mound. From this perspective, the only enjoyment to be gained from visiting the site is the satisfaction of ticking another one off the hit-list. Barrow II, by contrast, we found quite easily as the footpath runs slightly south and downhill of the monument, so that it is silhouetted against the sky effectively. While no longer a striking feature of the landscape, it is nevertheless in good order and worth the short walk from the parking area.

The visitor seeking Plumberow Mount will find it quite visible, although carefully tucked away behind a modern housing estate in a nature conservation area screened by trees. If the mound itself were not plain enough, a circular railing now encloses it to prevent erosion by dog-walkers and stunt cyclists. In good weather and with the monument to yourself, it is a remarkably quiet place in the busy south Essex landscape.

No such problem disturbs the barrows at Yatesbury, which sit in a field behind the modern hamlet. Originally these mounds were 20' (6m) high, and a local labourer was employed to reduce them so that effective modern ploughing could take place: he took the top 11' off, and discovered the burials in the process. Today they stand at perhaps 3' or 4' and look rather forlorn, like once-proud ocean-going liners reduced to hulks in some tidal creek.

For a perfectly dispiriting barrow-hunting experience, Prittlewell is hard to beat. The pleasant recreation space of Priory Park is bounded to the north by a modern road which rises to the bridge crossing the Southend-to-London railway line. Due to chronic traffic congestion in this part of the south-east, the local council plans to widen the road; local residents and environmental campaigners have resisted this idea, which would involve cutting down some ancient trees and destroying the tranquillity of the park. It is hard to see how the needs of the motorist and the conservationist can both be met, unless an alternative route can be found for the road. A protest camp has been set up on the very site of the mound, with a few people in permanent residence there. The council, to its credit, seems keen to house the Prittlewell artefacts in an appropriate visitor centre, but at the time of writing has no firm plans as to location or design. The barrow is to be effectively obliterated – whether by further landscaping or by the road remains to be seen.

Steve Pollington, Essex, 2008

Glossary

accompanied burial	A burial with which there are some detectable grave-goods such as beads, brooches, a buckle, a knife, weapons, drinking vessels, etc.
angon	A spear with a long shank and small, barbed head, used as a javelin
Ælfric	English homilist of the 11th century
ASC	Anglo-Saxon Chronicle
barrow	A large earthen mound covering a burial
cloisonné	Style of jewellery in which the surface is covered with cut stones in metal cells; in Anglo-Saxon contexts, these are usually red garnets in gold, with occasional pieces of millefiori glass to lighten the pattern
cremation	A burial in which the body is burnt; usually the bones are collected and placed in a specially decorated ceramic container, which is later buried
Final Phase	The period of the last accompanied Anglo-Saxon graves, coincident with the rise of kingship and the conversion to Christianity
francisca	Archaeological term for a kind of small axe with a curved head, which could be used for throwing as well as hewing
furnished	Alternative name for "accompanied", q.v.
Fürstengräber	(German) 'princely' or leaders' burials
Gewissæ	Early Saxon settlers in the Thames Valley; the nucleus of the later West Saxons
Hallstatt Culture	Culture of central Europe from ca. 750 to 400 BC, usually associated with early Celtic societies
Ibn Fadlan	Arab diplomat whose account of meetings with the Rus in the early 10th c. offers an interesting perspective on social structure, customs, burial rites, etc.
inhumation	A burial in which the body is laid in a grave, sometimes in a coffin

kontos	A long lance used by horsemen
meadhall	A hall used for feasting, law-making, ceremonies and rituals
Middle Saxon Period	Period ca. 650 to 850 AD in which Christianity established itself in England, involving also consolidation of settlements and economic re-alignment
Oiscingas	The ruling family of Kent in the 7th century
ring-ditch	Circular ditch enclosing a piece of land, from which the removed soil goes to form a barrow
Rus	Scandinavian traders on the Volga in the 10th century
Sleddingas	The ruling family of the East Saxons in the 7th century
seax	A single-edged sword or long knife
spatha	A long, straight-edged sword
Thuringia	Area of western Germany
tumulus	A burial mound
Wuffingas	The ruling family of the East Angles in the 7th century

Map

Main chamber graves & tumuli discussed in the text

1		Saltwood	13			Lowbury Hill
2	■	Broomfield	14			Scutchamer Knob
3	■ Π	Prittlewell	15	■		Taplow
4		Bloodmoor Hill	16			Rodmead Hill
5	■ Π	Coddenham	17	Π		Roundway Down
6		Lakenheath	18	Π		Swallowcliffe Down
7	Π	Shudy Camps	19			Benty Grange
8	Δ	Snape	20			Caenby
9	■	Spong Hill	21			Loveden Hill
10	■ Π Δ	Sutton Hoo	22			Newhaven Low
11		Asthall	23			Wollaston
12		Cuddesdon	24	Π		Lapwing Hill

Key

Δ	Ship burial
■	Chamber burial
Π	Bed burial

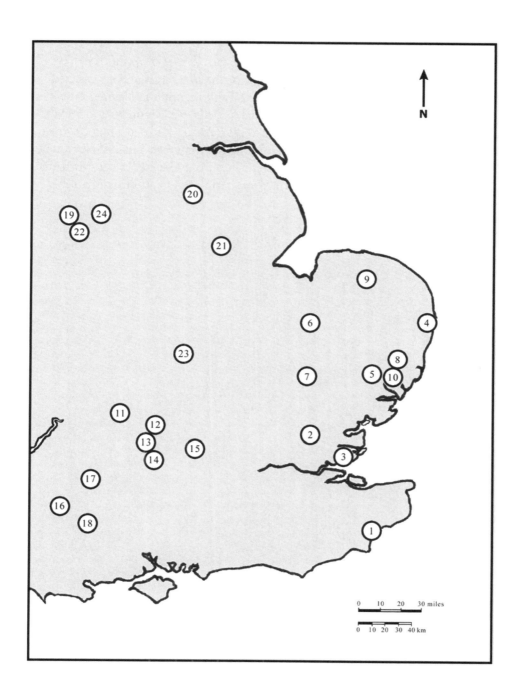

N

0   10   20   30 miles

0 10 20 30 40 km

Acknowledgements

Thanks are due to Peter Horn, for assistance with details of mound construction and the attendant engineering problems. Lindsay Kerr assisted with much material on the still unpublished Taplow mound. Wayne Letting generously made his picture archives available. Mike McGuinness provided much interesting material relating to the West Country and the Thames Valley. Janai McKenna assisted with very useful research materials. Hilary Strongman very kindly assisted with Northumbrian information. Marilyn Bruce-Mitford, Angus Wainwright and Kate Sussams provided much useful information concerning Sutton Hoo.

Introduction

Most of us have heard of the magnificent royal burial in Mound 1 at Sutton Hoo, the East Anglian king laid out in his ship with all his treasures and weapons around him, and the whole grave covered by a massive earthen mound. Many of us probably know that there were other mounds nearby, and that they all once contained rich graves. Perhaps less well-known is the fact that the Mound 1 burial was far from unique, and was in fact simply the most splendid so far discovered of a series of noble or kingly graves of the same general period, all sharing one feature: the large grave mound with its internal wooden chamber in which were both human remains and a selection of 'royal' treasures.

The burial of nobles of both sexes in purpose-built mounds or *tumuli* was a long-standing practice in barbarian Europe and, although it was not one specifically associated with Anglian or Saxon culture before the transfer of power to Britain, it was quickly adopted as part of the rites of high-status burial in the later 6th c. Mound burials were probably reserved for people of note in their communities – not necessarily the wealthiest, but perhaps the most important, the spiritual and temporal leaders of the settlements. These were people whose physical presence was important to their successors, who took comfort from the knowledge that they were physically still close at hand, a resource on which the living could draw for comfort and for authority.

Mound-burial was apparently not forbidden for Christians in the 7th c., but it soon fell out of favour. This must be linked to the spread of the idea of 'consecrated ground' found next to churches, in which the power of the holy spirit was understood to permeate the vicinity and thus to protect the building and its contents, and the enclosure in which it stood.

This book is an attempt to bring together some of the evidence from Sutton Hoo and elsewhere in England for these magnificent burials and to set them in their context: a society on the cusp of great internal upheavals as it abandoned centuries-old traditions and developed newer and more complex structures – social, political, ideological, bureaucratic and religious. The first section will look at the physical construction and symbolic meaning of these monuments. The second section will offer a listing of known Anglo-Saxon barrows with notes on their contents and the circumstances of their discovery. The appendices deal with some literary evidence from later centuries.

KINGSTON, KENT, FROM THE SITE OF THE TUMULI, 1855.

A mid-19th century engraving of Kingston Down, Kent,
with the barrowfield in the foreground

Barrow and Chamber Burials

1. The Mound and its Context

Background

The background to the Sutton Hoo burials concerns the early history of England. In fact, when the Sutton Hoo burials took place, 'England' was only just coming into existence. Britain, the Roman provinces of *Britannia*, long dominated by Roman power and ideology, had suffered the effects of the 4th c. AD economic downturn and had been effectively left to its own devices. The various 'Counts of the Britains' (the four or five provinces into which the lowlands were divided) and their field armies saw the opportunity to seize power, although there was little enough real authority to seize. The early 5th c. saw the emergence of new power blocs, many based on the harnessing of manpower from outside Britain. Settlement of prisoners-of-war in Britannia had been a Roman policy which had allowed the army to divert its shrinking man-power to more pressing needs: these included the defence of Rome itself. These prisoners were forced to become low-status settlers, *læti*, who were spread across the south and east of Britain and included able-bodied men drawn from a variety of defeated foes, some Germanic as well as Sarmatians and probably others. Their function was intended to be more economic than military, but their skills in war may have given them a significance that their numbers never would have.

Elsewhere, whole groups were transported and settled on deserted estates under the terms of a treaty (*foedus*) which granted them virtual autonomy in return for military service and payment of taxes. These *foederati* or 'federates' included groups from northern Germany who were persuaded to repopulate the eastern midlands of Britain, which had apparently been depopulated in the 4th c. It is among these groups that the East Angles had their origins, being the eastern group of Anglian descent.[1]

The backgrounds of the many groups were diverse, but the group identities chosen were mainly 'Saxon' from the homelands between the Elbe and Weser rivers in northern Germany, or 'Anglian' from further north into Jutland. These identities came to dominate the thinking and traditions of the settlers as they formed into larger units while post-Roman control weakened. In contrast to the British of the west and the Scots of the northwest, the

---

[1] Henson, 2006; Pollington, forthcoming

Germanic-speaking areas eventually characterised themselves by the hybrid term *Angulseaxe* 'Angle-Saxons' or as we now call them 'Anglo-Saxons'.

By the mid-6th c. new religious impulses arriving from Scandinavia were bringing novel ideas about leadership and social structure: instead of temporary alliances of chiefs, based on personal allegiance, more stable groupings were forming, which in time would lead to kingdoms. In the closing years of the 6th c., the formation of kingdoms was underway, and the noble families around whom these units developed felt the need to express both their new-found importance and their territorial claims through the building of large and highly visible structures. Among these were the mound burials, and especially the chamber burials, which are the subject of this book.

The Anglo-Saxons built burial mounds, but they buried people in other ways also; the mounds they used were not always new creations; they were not the only people among the Germanic nations to make use of burial mounds. Therefore, while burial mounds and Anglo-Saxons go together, the presence of the one does not necessarily point to the presence of the other. Why some groups chose mound burial and others did not is an important question, because it leads unavoidably into a discussion of the kind of legacy these people expected to leave.[2] We shall examine this issue below.

The Grave in the Mound

Burying people inside mounds, or building mounds over the graves of people, was not a new idea in Anglo-Saxon England. Many societies of ancient Europe (and elsewhere) had seen the benefit of making a large and emphatic monument out of a grave – perhaps the initial hump caused by the displaced earth when the burial was fresh suggested the idea of using this feature for grave-side rites, and when the hump subsided and settled, it was felt necessary to supplement it to preserve the physical location. The practice of adding earth to the grave may even have become part of the ritual of remembrance. Constant augmentation would necessarily result in a small mound. The creation of the impressive structures we see today would involve much time, effort and planning and certainly required a knowledge of engineering principles far in excess of those normally ascribed to 'barbarian' peoples.

The location and distribution of barrows can disclose quite a lot of information about the people who were enacting this rite.[3] In Britain, burial

---

[2] Carver, 2002, p.132

[3] Carver, 2002, p.133-5

mounds of the conical-to-hemispherical type first appeared in the Bronze Age, when they were just one of a variety of monuments available. In the pre-Roman Iron Age, they were not a common form of monument, although they were perhaps never totally unknown especially in Essex and in east Yorkshire (the Arras culture). In the Roman Period, mound burial was still not common, but some imposing examples do survive. The immediately post-Roman mounds are generally small, and are found in Anglo-Saxon contexts as well as in parts of Wales and eastern Scotland. The Anglo-Saxon examples are the focus of this book.

There are two kinds of Anglo-Saxon barrow by distribution: in the south-east, mainly Kent and Sussex, we find whole cemeteries consisting of small-to-medium sized mounds; many of these have since been ploughed flat, but some were still recognisable in the 18th c. and records exist of them. (see engraving p.16) Elsewhere, in the midlands, the west and the north, isolated barrows are more usual – not always isolated from other graves, which often cluster round them, but isolated from other barrows. This type is found most often where barrows were already common – for example, in parts of the West Country and the Peak District, where previously built monuments were ready for re-use. In the south-east there are exceptions – the barrows at Broomfield, Taplow and Clacton were apparently isolated from any other graves, for example, while Sutton Hoo's numerous and large barrow cluster is unusual by any standard.

What is a Princely Burial?

The class of graves known as "Princely Burials" appears in the Later Roman Iron Age and is widely diffused by the end of the 6th c. in northern and western Europe; in a wider sense, such high-status mound burials are of great antiquity and certainly extend back to the European Bronze Age. We shall consider the early history of the monument type below (Origins of Chamber Burial, p. 23). The Late Roman and post-Roman manifestations of the monument in Germanic Europe became standardised around a few indispensable fixed-points, although local tradition was also maintained in many respects. This no doubt involved a tension between the must-have ingredients for an authentic high-status funeral and the strong emotional pressure exerted through the expectations of the mourners.

"Princely Burials" in Anglo-Saxon contexts are distinguished by provision of a very large burial mound, often exceeding the height of a person and up to 20 yards (18 metres) across. As such, they are too large for the enactment of simple, intimate graveside burial rites because the mourners involved would not be able to see and hear all the other participants. More likely is the idea that the mourners enacted their rituals while the grave was open and before the mound itself was constructed, or at least before it was completed. Perhaps on completion of the interment they either filed past the mound to make their last farewell, or circled round it as the warriors did in *Beowulf* at their lord's funeral. (See Appendix 2)

Another characteristic of these graves is that they include very high-status, imported objects, mostly connected with the preparation and serving of food and drink. These items of feasting-gear were very important to their owners because of the opportunity they afforded to show membership of an international, long-distance circulation of prestige goods which were not commercially available. Guests were honoured by being offered the opportunity to dine from silver plates, drink from glass goblets, and be served from fine bowls and platters; all such treasures showed respect for the guest and enhanced the prestige of the host and his people. We shall return to these aspects below.

Some Princely Burials were also Chamber Burials and/or Bed Burials, each of which will be dealt with separately below. However, there are surprisingly many important graves of the later 6th and early 7th c. which were neither, and comprised nothing more than a grave-cut, a ring-ditch and a low mound, despite the inclusion of high-status grave-goods.

The presence of prestige objects within high-status graves implies that a great deal of effort went into the construction of the burials, but the physical grave was itself only one aspect of a probably lengthy burial rite which is invisible to archaeology. Early mediaeval funeral rites are generally understood to have been determined partly by family tradition and partly by the need to provide a unique and splendid event which would stay in the memories of all who saw it, or who heard about it afterwards. In this way, the memory of the individual being buried was kept alive within the community down the generations. The time, effort and expense devoted to the funeral were all resources which could be brought to bear on the problem of prolonging the tale of the deceased, giving him or her a place in posterity. A memorable funeral was a good guarantee of this.

Many of the larger grave mounds were sited prominently, near or overlooking a place where many passers-by could be expected. It is not unusual for such burials to have attracted attention and for other graves to cluster round them, as if in doing so their occupants could gain some of the glory of the first grave on the site, the 'founder burial'. The site by a much-used path would also preserve the name of the occupant as successive generations refered to the monument as "so-and-so's barrow".

The designation "princely" is in some respects inappropriate to the monument class as a whole. A 'prince' must mean a young, high-ranking male within a ruling family but many of the tumuli contain females and older males, and we have no direct information about their 'rank' or social class, only the access that their family or mourners had to expensive resources. Mound 17 at Sutton Hoo might be termed a "Princely Grave" with good reason, but the title hardly fits the Swallowcliffe Down barrow or even Sutton Hoo Mound 1. The English phrase is a calque on the German term *Fürstengrab* 'leader's grave' which better captures the notion of status and authority for the deceased without assigning rank (although *Fürst* is often translated as 'prince' in the more general sense of a male member of a royal family). What we seem to be looking at in these male burials are persons who, in OE, would have been called *æðelingas* 'athelings, male members of the royal family' without further subdivision. A king's brother or uncle was no less an *æðeling* than his son or grandson. The females were presumably *idesa* 'ladies of rank, powerful women' with a hint at both religious and secular authority.

What is a Chamber Burial?

In the context of Germanic funerary tradition, a 'chamber burial' or 'chamber grave' is a grave within a mound, whereby an internal cavity was timber-lined to form a free-standing small room or 'chamber'. Usually, within the chamber, the body was laid out supine along with a quantity of rich grave-goods, set out in a tableau or formal display. (There is however some evidence for cremations placed under large mounds, for which the opportunities for display were different, perhaps centred on the short-lived spectacle of the pyre.)

The chamber can sometimes be viewed as a substitute for (or extension of) the meadhall, which was the central place of Anglo-Saxon community life, presided over by the noble, wealthy and powerful – the kinds of people who are believed to have been given chamber burial. The high-seat in the feasting-hall was the stage on which their power and authority were displayed in life, and it seems natural that a transformed meadhall should have formed the backdrop against which their worth continued to be displayed in death.[4] The provision of drinking vessels, cauldrons, cups, harps and gaming pieces all evoke the pleasures of the hall as a public place for entertainment and enjoyment. Some are quite modest in size: St Dizier (France) featured two male chamber graves, each 2.8m x 1.6m in plan. The largest known example is Prittlewell (Essex) at 4m x 4m, the size of a small modern living-room.

---

[4] Pollington, 2003

Not all chambers are feasting-halls however. A few are bedrooms, complete with beds and bedding, drinking vessels and textiles, as well as weapons and other rich items.

As the area available for display was so much greater in a chamber than in a standard grave, even one with a substantial coffin, it was possible to include very large objects with the deceased: not only the weapons, small vessels and personal jewellery which feature in standard high-status graves but also items of furniture, large feasting cauldrons and complete sets of tableware. There is often good evidence for textiles lining the walls and floor. Most examples appear to have had a lot of empty space which, it may be speculated, was deliberately made available to allow the mourners to view the dead person and the funeral tableau before the chamber was closed forever.

The display may have been the culmination of the funeral, but it is likely that the process of construction and arrangement was more important: the visiting friends, family and peers all bringing their own contribution to the display, enjoying food and drink at the grave-side and performing the appropriate rites. Only once all these activities had ceased could the chamber be closed and roofed over, and the mound be constructed over it.[5]

Sometimes barrows are built in lonely, highly visible places where they act as landmarks, but more often they are the richest and most prominent burials in larger graveyards. Kemble's *Codex Diplomaticus* cites 150 cases where an estate boundary is defined in relation to a barrow.[6] There are probably ideological reasons for choosing one location over another: either the dead person wanted to remain with the companions of lesser rank who served him or her in life, and so chose a spot within the existing graveyard; or the person wanted to be remembered as a significant and formidable personality whose memory should remain with the community forever, kept alive by the presence of the prominent mound. In some cases both ideas are present: the chamber burial was sited in a lonely spot, but subsequent burials were made around its perimeter and it became the founder's grave for a large cemetery. This practice gives rise to the so-called primary barrow cemeteries of southern and eastern England, where a whole series of barrow burials may be concentrated in a small area.[7]

---

[5] Williams, 2006a, p.31-5

[6] Ellis Davidson, 1950, p.173-4

[7] Ellis Davidson, 1950; Halsall, 1995, p.7

Origins of Chamber Burial

The term 'chamber burial' is sometimes used to describe Neolithic forms of interment in which human remains are deposited in a stone-lined cavity covered with an earthen mound, often in bundles of assorted bones. The relationship of such burials to the Iron Age wooden chambers is not certain, but a direct derivation seems unlikely.[8]

Burials in a wood-lined cavity covered by a mound have been employed in various parts of the world and most should probably be seen as independent inventions. Burial mounds known as *kurgans* have been recognised as a diagnostic type of field monument in the spread of Indo-European language and culture, although this idea has not gone unchallenged.[9] Kurgans originate between the River Dnieper and the Ural Mountains, and the 'Kurgan Theory' suggests that the spread of these burial mounds accompanied the movement of horse-borne pastoralists, who were vectors in the diffusion of certain technologies such as stock-breeding, agriculture and bronze-working. The early adoption of bronze technology and horsemanship among the Indo-Iranian peoples of the southern steppe is crucial in understanding how the cultural expansion took place. Almost nothing that can be said about the 'kurgan culture' in relation to both technology and the Indo-European languages is uncontroversial, and there are several alternative models for this diffusion, which differ in many respects and which have proven irreconcilable with present knowledge of the evidence, linguistic and archaeological.

In Bronze Age Greece, it was sometimes customary for the dwelling of a hero (a posthumously deified warrior or leader) to be demolished after his death and, after some elaborate rituals had taken place within the ruins of the house, his body to be buried on the site and a mound of earth raised over the whole site.[10] This gave rise to a tradition of the 'house of the dead' within the earth-mound, and to a tradition of veneration of the mound as a vestige of the ancestral dead.

The Qäwrighul Culture of the Konchi River region in the western end of the Gobi Desert has an exceptionally good presence in the archaeological record, due mainly to the arid conditions in which the graves of this society were constructed leading to remarkably good preservation of organic remains. The graves are timber-lined pits dug into the sandy soil, into

---

[8] Svanberg, 2005

[9] Mallory & Mair, 2000, p.128-60; Mallory & Adams, 2006, p.452 discuss the Yamna and Timber Grave Cultures briefly. Anthony, 2007, p.245ff

[10] Svanberg, 2005, p. 75-6. Kaliff, 2007, p.85 suggests a similar image for inhumation in northern Europe within the Indo-European tradition.

which the bodies of the dead were placed, then covered with 'coffins' of Euphrates poplar wood, and the top then sealed with animal skins, woven textiles or a basketwork cover. Some of the more remarkable male graves had an unusual surface feature: seven concentric rings of timber stakes radiating out from the tomb in a 'solar' configuration up to 60m (nearly 200') across. Some kind of cosmological statement appears to have underlain this practice. The people of the Qäwrighul Culture are one of several Central Asian groups associated with Indo-European-speaking polities of Central Asia, loosely known as Tokharians; their language, which is recorded in two dialects, shares some features with the languages of western Europe and some of the technologies used, such as the weaving of 'tartan' fabrics, are also closely associated with historical European culture groups. The physical remains of the dead were also of a 'European' rather than Mongolid appearance. Among the variant burial traditions of the region are some interesting practices: bed-burials, for example at Jushi; barrows into which upright posts had been inserted, the tops painted red (Lopnur region); life-sized wooden anthropomorphic figures accompanying the mounds (Lopnur region); boat-shaped coffins (Sampul). The origins of Asiatic chamber burials appear to lie in the construction of a simple shaft-grave which developed into a more elaborate structure over time, including multiple layers of coverings with wood, fabrics and skins.

Some of the earliest forms of wooden chamber burial with historical links to Central Europe are ascribed to the Pazyryk culture, a horse-borne nomadic Iron Age culture of Central Asia which has reasonably been identified with the people known to history as the Scythians.[11] These people lived in the period 500 to 300 BC in the foothills of the Altai Mountains on the border between present-day Mongolia and China. The typical burial consisted of a mound of earth within which was a rectangular 'tomb shaft', and the chamber was built within this cavity; the body was placed within on the south side, lying with its head to the east. The outer facing of the chamber was made from roughly-hewn logs, but the inner facing was carefully dressed and smoothed. The roof was covered with bark, moss and vegetation. Horses were buried in the northern portion of the chamber, also facing east; sometimes a waggon was included.

Pazyryk bodies were embalmed after removal of the brain and entrails, but such practices are not known in Europe. The purpose of embalming appears to have been preservation of the skin, which was clearly of great significance:

---

[11] Parker Pearson, 1999, p.61-7; Mallory & Mair, 2000, p.142-3, 160-3; Allan, 2004. Whether these people called themselves Scythians or were assumed to be Scythians by their neighbours is a moot point.

some of the male burials were covered in tattoos showing animal designs. These tattoos appear to have been a mark of nobility, a permanent outward display of rank and honour, and probably the preservation of the skin intact was bound up with ideas of continuity of existence. Leather grave-goods were included in the tombs, among which were cut-out shapes of animals, some of which were applied to the coffin as decoration. When horses were included in the graves, sometimes they wore a leather mask over their heads as if a second, protective layer were needed.

In Latium in the early Iron Age, so-called trench-graves occur in which a spacious but shallow grave-cut was made into which were put the dead person along with weapons, personal ornaments, pots and ewers, bronze feasting vessels and sometimes a chariot, e.g tomb 15 at Castel di Decima (Italy).[12] Some of these ingredients (shallow grave, chariot) recur in certain specific contexts such as the Belgic areas of Britain and the northwest Continent, while others (vessels, feasting equipment, weapons, personal decorations) are more widespread. The rise of the trench-grave is usually seen against the background of increasing social stratification in the late 8th century BC.

The idea of the burial chamber spread over the centuries. The Hallstatt Culture of Central Europe, which ran from ca. 750 to 400 BC, also developed or adopted chamber burial for members of its upper social levels.[13] With the Celtic love of display, the opportunity for offering an idealised image of the deceased leader in his fictive feasting chamber surrounded by his wealth and opulence was too good to miss. The famous burial at Hochdorf (Germany) of about 550 BC featured a wooden chamber, the walls of which were draped in fabrics and hung with feasting equipment such as cauldrons and drinking horns.[14] This burial of a chieftain included a four-wheeled waggon, as well as gold dress accessories, weapons and a large gold neck-ring. The couch on which he lay was supported by cast bronze anthropoid figures.

A Belgic burial tradition called the 'chambered grave' is known from southern England, from the Catuvellaunian and Trinovantian regions extending roughly from Colchester in the northeast to St. Albans in the southwest.[15] They resemble the Continental graves in that a square subterranean enclosure has been created, in which some rich remains are deposited. The human remains are always cremated, however, and only one example seems to have been covered by a mound – the Lexden tumulus, near Colchester (Essex). The

---

[12] Bietti Sesteri & de Santis, 2000

[13] Ellis Davidson, 1988, p.4

[14] Ellis Davidson, 1988, p.41; Parker Pearson, 1999, p.79

[15] O'Brien, 1999, p.15-6; Crummy, Crummy, Jackson & Schädler, 2008

chambers are vast – often in excess of 50m square - and contain multiple burials. They date from the late years BC, e.g. Hertford Heath (Hertfordshire) 30-15 BC, and extend into the beginnings of the Roman Iron Age, e.g. Colchester and St. Albans dated to around 75 AD at the latest.

The Arras complex of late Iron Age cemeteries in the area of Garton Station and Kirkburn (Yorkshire) feature large square grave-cuts, but whether these should be termed 'chambers' or not is debatable. They are unlike the Belgic graves, being inhumations in barrows accompanied by wheeled vehicles; they resemble the Hochdorf type rather more.

A form of chamber burial continued in Trinovantian territory into the Roman period, with multiple examples from Kelvedon (Essex) and Colchester (Essex). The 'chambers' are timber-lined grave-cuts, around 2.5 x 1.5m and 1m high. There are occasional finds outside the region, as at Holgate Bridge (Yorkshire) and beneath Wells cathedral (Somerset).

Germanic chamber graves were constructed occasionally throughout the Roman Iron Age, but by the later Roman period they were not common in southern and western Scandinavia: the only known example from the whole of Jutland is at Neudorf-Bornstein in Schleswig (Germany), which is possibly an Anglian royal site from the period before Anglian political authority moved across the North Sea. However, the lack of recognised similar sites of the same period (3rd and 4th c.) in this area may rather indicate that the Angles were centred on the adjacent island of Funen (Denmark) at this time.

The origins of the Germanic chamber-grave and *Fürstengrab* have been investigated by Fischer, who looks to the Late La Tene period (up to circa 100 AD) in Central Europe for the ultimate source, augmenting Sarmatian (Indo-Iranian) traditions brought from western Asia.[16] It is certainly the case that La Tene culture had influence in areas such as Slovakia and Moravia, and this may have extended into neighbouring Germanic cultural zones such as the Przeworsk, Wielbark and Cherniakhov Cultures which united eastern Europe with the Ukraine and the western steppe. Furthermore, in Late Roman contexts, Sarmatian settlements in Gallia are documented, centred around Reims. It is possible, as Fischer notes, that the earliest examples are those of returning Germanic military personnel who chose to show their wealth and status with a display of Roman materials and objects. Roman ideas about burial and status certainly influenced the chamber-grave tradition.

---

[16] Fischer's paper is available at www.arkeologi.uu.se/ark/projects/ Luciasymposion/ Kammargrav02_Luciasymposion.pdf

A distinction has been made between the chamber-grave, with its wooden lining and role as a fictive bedroom or meadhall, and the simpler 'princely grave' which in Continental contexts is usually distinguished by the presence of quantities of Roman tableware and especially glass vessels. These attributes of the highest status gradually spread into less wealthy burials – either as an aspirational statement by lower-status groups, or as a less important factor of burials of high-status persons.

At about the same time as chamber burial was starting to be practised in England, the late 6th c., it was also being promoted in other Germanic-speaking areas as the burial rite for the wealthy and successful. These areas included Thuringia, where there have been several spectacular finds. Perhaps the most remarkable from an English point of view is the cemetery at Trossingen (Germany) where a small chamber grave (number 58) was found with spectacularly good wood preservation – something almost universally lacking among English finds.[17] The grave's contents were lifted in a soil block and excavated under laboratory conditions, which allows for even tiny shreds of evidence to be detected and recorded. The grave dates to ca. 580 AD, based on the felling date of the timber; the occupant was a man of between 30 and 40 years of age, born around the middle of the 6th c.

The grave chamber was formed from oak planks and was in the form of a large, canopied bed or platform, 2.8 m long by 1m wide, with a roof formed with gables and decorated with interlaced carving. The grave included weapons: a *spatha* in its sheath, and a 3.6m long horseman's lance with its shaft made from hazelwood (presumably a *kontos*, an Avar weapon at this time). A saddle was also preserved in the burial, as well as a wooden container for liquids, and a dinner service consisting of lathe-turned wooden plates and a carved dish. A small circular table with three lathe-turned wooden legs and a backrest was an unusual find, and an oaken candlestick. There were no dress accessories present in the grave but a small bone comb was placed near the head, and there were copious textile and leather remains in the body area, and leather strips on the lower legs which probably represent leg-bindings (OE *windingas*) which held the trousers close to the leg. Some small leather strips may be the remnants of a pair of leather gloves. A fine decorated harp was the most spectacular find.

The mention of this German grave brings us to an important point in the history of the chamber burial, which is the role played by the Franks in the evolution of this rite. The Merovingian ruling line had spent most of the 6th c. establishing its authority over large parts of the post-Roman western

---

[17] Theune-Grosskopf, 2006

European world. The core territory was bounded by the royal seats of Paris, Rheims, Soissons and Orleans, with border states including Austrasia (the lower Rhineland), Alamannia (southern Germany) and Burgundy (south-eastern France and Switzerland).[18] The central relationships in the Frankish world, inherited from their Germanic past, were between lord and underling, and among lordly peers, and these relationships were kept alive by the regular exchange of gifts – tribute offered by clients, diplomatic gifts between equals, rewards from lords to underlings; marriage alliances were another aspect of this exchange mechanism, since they bound together the leading families of whole regions. The gifts could be exotic items which were only available to members of the exchange network (e.g. Coptic bowls) or they could be symbolic gifts which identified the user as a member of a particular social group (e.g. ring-hilted swords).

By the later 6th c., only two areas of Europe were regularly using mound burial accompanied by lavish gifts as a burial rite: one was northern Scandinavia (where the rite was a continuation of Iron Age practice) and the other was centred on the lower Rhine and the Frankish realms.[19] Probably the burial of the Frankish king Childeric at Tournai (Belgium) in 481-2 was the model used by later Merovingian kings, and the notion spread from the Frankish core to the peripheral states. It is nevertheless curious that at the same time as the Merovingian Franks were adopting mound-burial (the mid-5th c.), it was also (re-)surfacing in south-west Norway in an apparently totally different social, ideological, religious and political climate.

In time, due to Francia achieving dominion over Kent, sealed with a marriage alliance between the two ruling families, the practice of accompanied barrow burial was adopted in southeast England and with Kentish wealth forming an important part of relations among the Anglo-Saxon kingdoms, Kentish practice was adopted north of the Thames. Access to those products which only Kentish favour could provide was an important part of demonstrating that an Anglo-Saxon ruler or leader was a person of stature in the western European world.[20] Paradoxically, by the time that the rite had been generally

---

[18] Parker Pearson, van de Noort & Woolf, 1993

[19] Parker Pearson, van de Noort & Woolf, 1993 fig.1; Carver, 2002, p.134

[20] Parker Pearson, van de Noort & Woolf, 1993, p.33 note the work of Huggett, 1988, in demonstrating that a certain Kentish range of grave-goods was adopted, including specific types of glassware, wheel-turned pottery, crystal balls and amethyst beads. Many of the burials considered in this book will be shown to have included such items. However, these are confined to a group whose northernmost and westernmost member is the Taplow barrow: chamber burials and high-status burials north and west of Taplow apparently did not have access to these items. It appears then that an important political frontier was marked by such access.

adopted in England, Frankish rulers were already electing to be buried in sarcophagi inside churches, and the Anglo-Saxon chamber burials probably seemed rather outdated to Frankish eyes. Nevertheless, for the smaller kingdoms and chiefdoms of the Anglo-Saxons, access to the network of gifts and the opportunity for lavish display were no doubt impressive to people who were certainly in touch with their distant Scandinavian kinsmen, who themselves had never abandoned the rite.

The English barrows, from the later 6th and early 7th c. also appear to be earlier than the corresponding mounds in Sweden although the close dating evidence needed to establish this is presently lacking: perhaps we can assume that the English and Swedish traditions evolved side-by-side and possibly developments on one side of the North Sea exerted an influence over the rites of kinsmen on the other side.[21]

Construction of a Chamber and Barrow

The process of mound construction was just one element in a series of funerary acts which included the construction of the grave, the burial of the deceased, probably processions of mourners and a formal meal near the grave, the performance of songs of remembrance, rituals and prayers, then covering the grave and erection of the barrow. All this work would have taken quite some time to plan, organise and execute and the whole funeral rite must therefore have lasted at least a week, and probably much longer. While it may not be directly relevant, Ibn Fadlan noted that the Scandinavian Rus mourners on the Volga placed the dead leader's corpse in a special chamber for ten days, accompanied by ale, fruit and a musical instrument, while they made the arrangements for his funeral. A ten-day period of preparation would have been reasonable for such a large undertaking as barrow construction.

The first act in constructing a mound was the cutting of a circular patch into the topsoil, the perimeter of which was dug out into a ditch. This initial act of separation provided a symbolic inner and outer zone, and enabled the mound-builders to deal with the inner zone as sacred space cut off from the secular world.[22] Within the reserved area, a grave-cut was made of sufficient size to allow the planned burial to take place. When this was to include a chamber, the dimensions of the planned space would have to include opportunities for viewing down into the room. In the case of an inhumation straight into the soil, a step or platform was usually cut into one end of the grave, on which one or more mourner could stand or kneel to arrange the

---

[21] Carver, 2002, p.134
[22] Ellis Davidson, 1988, p.27

body and grave-goods. If the offerings and gifts were only being assembled at this time, it may have been the case that one mourner stood on the platform and accepted the gifts from a file of people who had come to say farewell to the deceased.

The grave-cut was often sealed with clay, or a layer of clay was added to the grave's lower area, before the body was introduced. The laying of the body into the grave-cut would have taken at least two strong individuals to manage, passing it from the grave-side into the hollow; in the case of a chamber, in which both a body and a quantity of valuables were to be manhandled, this might have been managed using wooden stakes as a ramp.

After completion of the rituals and the consumption of a graveside meal (see p.31), the chamber was closed by a timber roof; in the case of soil-based graves, a covering was placed over the body, often textile but sometimes hazel poles or stakes.[23] At a certain point, the grave was considered complete and the process of mound-building began. The earth from the ring-ditch provided the base structure, and the height of the mound would have depended largely on the local availability of usable soil, and on the amount of time and size of workforce available for the task.

The chamber's structure must have been immensely strong, since the roof had to bear the weight of the soil above it. Wet soils vary between 1500 and 2000 kg per cubic metre, depending on the type of soil and how finely it has been broken up or sifted. Even the smaller chambers therefore had to support a soil weight of several tonnes and for the larger ones the load must have been very considerable indeed. The wooden components must have been carefully chosen, because decay is inevitable - no matter how large the cross-section of the timbers used, they will rot and give way eventually. The weak part of each horizontal beam would be the unsupported centre, especially if it is not square in section and has been used flat rather than on edge. However, not all the weight of the earth would be borne by the timber structure – some would be displaced sideways, down the mound, and not all vertically on the wooden chamber. A simple method for displacing the weight sideways would be to use short rafters above the chamber (as the Anglo-Saxons did on their house buildings): the more rafters used and the closer together they are spaced, the greater the strength. These rafters were then covered by boards to form the roof of the chamber. If all the rafters were fixed to cross-beams, then a very strong construction would result.

---

[23] Bedwin, 1986

Another strengthening factor would be the earth mound itself. Techniques may have been used which would result in a support for the timber chamber: for example, progressive consolidation of earth around the sides of the chamber as work proceeded, so that the chamber would be stabilised and reinforced by the earth surround.

The Funeral Rites

The construction of the barrow was one part of a lengthy process, in which several individuals would have taken part and it may be that the erection of a prominent monument was a deliberately collaborative effort designed to involve the whole community. The following sequence is adapted from Williams's suggestions:[24]

- the grave is dug into the ground surface
- the grave-cut is lined with timber, reinforced with corner posts and caulked with clay
- a temporary cover is raised over the grave-cut while the initial funerary rites take place
- the body is prepared (washed and dressed)
- the chamber is decked out with textiles and other decorations
- the bier/bed and other fittings are lowered into the chamber
- the body is passed down into the chamber and arranged appropriately
- grave-goods and other deposits are passed into the grave and arranged around the body
- further rites take place including sacrifices of animals for the graveside feast, singing of funeral songs, rites transferring power and possessions to the successor(s), procession of the mourners around the grave-chamber to witness the tableau
- the chamber is roofed over
- the grave-cut is back-filled
- the mound is erected over the chamber
- a large timber post is inserted into the top of the mound to mark the burial

---

[24] Puhvel, 1983; Williams, 2006a, p.31 The specific example chosen by Williams is Swallowcliffe Down, a later 7th c. bed-burial, but the process must have been essentially similar for all mound burials, allowing for detailed variation.

All this activity at and around the grave means that there must have been considerable traffic to and from the grave-side, of both builders and the procession of mourners paying their last respects, and undertaking the final rites of closure.[25]

Mound Markers

The presence of the post above the mound is interesting. On flat-graves, a wooden stake acting as a grave-marker was a common Germanic tradition: for example, when Queen Rodelinde of the Lombards ordered a church built at Pavia, outside the city walls, the building was afterwards known as *Santa Maria ad Perticas* "Holy Mary at the Stakes", these being the grave-markers for fallen warriors.[26] Modification of the post to identify the deceased seems likely, although this may have been no more than a simple runic inscription of the name or an identifying mark.

A cremation burial beside Lake Dalstorp in Västergötland (Sweden) was spread on an existing barrow of Migration Period date; the circle of ashes was then pierced by five spears which penetrated far into the barrow's fabric and the heads were deformed in the process. The remains were those of a 10th c. female with moderately wealthy grave-goods (beads, combs, brooches, knives).[27] It is likely that these five spearshafts marked the burial spot of this lady, but they may have been intended to hold her firmly in the grave. Fear of the revenant dead was common in Scandinavia and elsewhere.

In parts of the Baltic regions – where Christianity and western ways were enforced only in the later mediaeval period – burial customs are very conservative. Here, it was until the mid-20th c. customary to plant a tree on the grave of a loved one; at holiday festivals, the family would gather at the graveside to eat a special picnic meal, being careful to leave some food for the deceased, and they would touch and embrace the tree as if it were the dead person. In this way physical contact could be maintained with the ancestors.[28]

---

[25] Ellis Davidson, 1950. In the example of Beowulf's funeral, the mourners rode round the barrow reciting his great deeds, much as Jordanes said that Attila's followers did for him.

[26] Schutz, 2001, p.125; Todd, 2004, p.236. The presence of the post was of course a great help to tomb-robbers who were thus able to target their efforts more effectively. Bruce-Mitford, 1978, p.363 illustrates the Uncleby (Yorkshire) whetstone which was set up at the foot of the grave with the (possibly runic?) text visible.

[27] Artelius, 2005

[28] Valk, 2007, p.144 A small wooden cross has now largely replaced the grave-tree.

In Yorkshire a barrow called *Stang Howe* (see below, p.226 *Loftus*) 'stake mound' retains an important place in local tradition. The reference to a stake or post in connection with this cairn may be relevant in this context.

The place-name *Throckley* appears to be from *þrocc hlaw* 'post- barrow, barrow marked with a post' which supports this idea. The OE word *steapol* can apparently mean 'cairn' or 'grave-marker' and perhaps may refer to such a post; its later history refers to the highest point of a church tower, 'steeple'. A number of Anglo-Saxon barrows appear to have had a small depression in the top, sometimes lined with clay - see for example Coombe (Kent). It has been suggested that this feature was associated with the pouring of libations for the deceased and the veneration of the ancestors.

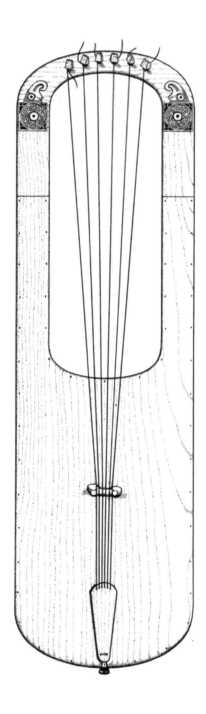

Reconstruction of a harp from Sutton Hoo

2. The Meaning of Chamber Burial

*When burial mounds were used by individual families, they
meant just what those families wished them to mean, neither
more no less. Such a code may be very difficult to crack.*

Carver, *Reflections on the Meanings of Monumental Barrows
in Anglo-Saxon England*

Houses of the Dead

What purpose did chamber burial serve, and what did this form of disposal
of the dead offer which was not available from other rites?

On one level, the burial chamber was an idealised portrayal of the 'house of
the dead', the last resting place of the deceased into which they would
welcome those who sought them out through spirit travel. Also, the journey
into the Otherworld could be perilous, as Beowulf found out when he
entered both the underwater lair of Grendel's mother and the dragon's
treasure cave.[29] This appears to have been the traditional view among the
Anglo-Saxons, the later Scandinavians and the Irish, at least, all of whom
have stories of deceitful or vindictive barrow-dwellers.

More pragmatically, mound burial and chamber burial were a means of
making a permanent mark on the landscape, of claiming the territory and the
right to hold it. It was for this reason that secondary inhumation in Neolithic
and especially Bronze Age round barrows was so prevalent. There is no real
doubt that the Anglo-Saxons knew what Bronze Age mounds were for –
similar monuments were already in existence in their southern Scandinavian
homelands, for example. Nor do the Anglo-Saxons seem to have been
obliged to re-invent their entire barrow-building tradition out of nothing
more than legend, even in a land where such rites had not been generally
practiced for centuries. It may be, as Carver implies, that re-adopting their
own traditional rite of barrow burial was a way for newcomers to bind
themselves into the fabric of Britain.[30] Interestingly, at about the same time
as the Anglo-Saxons were developing barrow-burial as a marker of territorial
ownership, in parts of Wales inscribed stones were being used for much the
same purpose, and in connection with Bronze Age barrows.[31]

---

[29] Williams, 2006a, p.172.

[30] Carver, 2002, p.134-5; Aspeborg, 2005

[31] Knight, 2001

The thorny question of identity raises itself here: to what extent were the Anglo-Saxons 'newcomers' and to what extent were they simply a continuation of the pre-existing population? A great deal has been written on this subject and Carver is surely right to stress that "explanations of change due to popular movement have been questioned, and the dearly held idea that finds, particularly grave-goods, are indications of ethnicity is, in Britain, extremely unfashionable and often challenged. The problem for archaeological scholarship of the early Middle Ages is that the equation between cemeteries and ethnic groups is widely accepted on the Continent and used as the basis for writing historical geography. The distribution maps of brooches and burial practices which provide the staple data-set of central and eastern Europe are, it is fair to say, largely interpreted as due to the migrations and settlement of social entities. Other explanations, which adapt current non-diffusionary models from prehistory, oblige us to believe that a whole people suddenly decided to adopt an exotic burial rite."[32] The barrow is certainly a means used to assert territorial claims, but it does not of itself assert ethnicity since it is not a specifically Anglian, Saxon or even Germanic form of burial – there are parallels among the Picts, British, continental Gallic peoples and the Slavs of eastern Europe. To this extent it signals something new in the landscape, but not necessarily a new model of expressing ethnicity.

Sentinel Burials

The protection of a heroic leader could be extended beyond the grave by burying his body in a symbolic position of guardianship, controlling access to the land. In the *Historia Brittonum*, Vortimer is made to express this intention: having routed the English, he asks to be buried by the coast in the port from which his defeated foes had fled, so that they could be prevented from returning. Ignoring this advice, they buried him in Lincoln and the English returned in force.[33]

Large and symbolic monuments such as the barrows and chamber graves acted, in part, as a reassuring demonstration that the life of the society was not to be interrupted; chaos would not return. They may also have acted as a means of keeping the Ancestors present in the everyday life of the community: many folktale heroes who were expected to return from death are described as sleeping beneath their mounds awaiting the nation's need.[34]

---

[32] Carver, 2002, p.136

[33] O'Brien, 1999, p.55-7; Aspeborg, 2005

[34] Simek, 1993, s.v. *burial mound;* Kershaw, 2000, p.26-30

The siting of the barrow or chamber in a prominent position above a major road or waterway and on the border of the territory was an important factor in maintaining social order and territorial cohesion: the burial of the king or chief with his armour and weapons could act as a symbolic 'sentinel' or guardian of the paths into the realm.[35] Indeed, all weapons burials may have acted as symbolic protection for the individual interred, and for the graveyard as a whole.

Arnold attempted to relate the positions of barrows with the foci of Anglo-Saxon kingdoms, and thus to map out the territories to which the barrows belonged. In this he overlooked the fundamental importance of placing barrows on the borders of kingdoms rather than at the centre.[36] Barrows acted as foci for local activity – they were often the site of moots in English hundreds – and there is some evidence for external structures on some Continental examples, suggesting some form of monument or cult site.[37]

In mythological terms, according to Weston Wyly, the burial of an individual is a form of symbolic planting of the human seed back within the earth; within this interpretative model, the barrow can be seen as the pregnant belly of the earth waiting to give rebirth to the soul in a new human life.[38]

Statements of Status?

As to the meaning of chamber burials, there is room for considerable debate. It seems clear that the provision of a quantity of high-status goods in a large grave must be saying something important about the individual. The obvious statement is that of social position or 'status' within the community, and indeed this does appear to have been the dominant aim in erecting chamber graves: to show power and access to resources.[39]

However it should not be forgotten that we do not know for sure the history of any assemblage. The goods in the Sutton Hoo Mound 1 chamber are impressive and form a credible set of statements about a powerful individual, but we have no means of knowing whether the armour, weapons, feasting equipment and so on were the deceased's personal items or whether they

---

[35] Dickinson & Speake, 1992, p.122-3; Price, 2003; Effros, 2003, p.148; A. Haymes pers.comm.

[36] Arnold, 1997; Carver, 2002, p.139

[37] Effros, 2003, p.200. It is tempting to speculate that the Sutton Hoo ship's prow and stern-post might have remained visible, protruding from the mound as a marker and reminder of the king's burial.

[38] Weston Wyly, 2007, p.323-4

[39] Chaney, 1970, p.96-104

were brought together for the first time for the purpose of the burial. Indeed, Parker Pearson has warned that "(a)ssociations with certain and copious grave goods may have less to do with wealth and more to do with the mourners over-compensating for an untimely death with abnormal expressions of grief and loss."[40]

Given that the dead do not bury themselves, the choices made in the funeral rites and grave goods are those of surviving family, friends, allies, supporters and well-wishers – and perhaps of those who saw an opportunity to claim membership of such a group, and to bathe in the reflected glory of contributing to the costly funeral of an important member of the community.

The provision of a lavish funeral and of a permanent monument such as a barrow must be seen as an attempt to transcend the confines of the immediate situation and perhaps to manipulate memory in the community through an event which controls both the past and the future – the story of the individual's past life and how he or she should be remembered by future generations.[41] The social position of the deceased was displayed in the chamber or grave and the rites (based on the evidence of literature such as *Beowulf*) probably included recitations of personal biography and of the history of the kindred and the broader group, including information about the genealogy and mythical ancestors of the group.[42] This establishment and reinforcement of historical identity was intended to manipulate the past to the service of the future, to stake a claim in posterity for the deceased's successors and heirs. The selection of an appropriately prominent position for the grave may not have been determined by the existence of a mound, but it seems that any pre-existing structures were not regarded as a barrier.[43]

It is also recognised that in pre-capitalist societies, the notion of 'status' is not based solely on wealth or access to resources, and that the word need not refer to ranked social class but rather to membership of a closed social group which displays its position within society through various badges or markers forming insignia of prestige, independent of personal wealth.[44] The marking of one individual's identity prominently on the landscape through a barrow served not only to underscore the authority of the burying folk, but also to exclude others; this must have been a factor in the decision to re-use existing (mainly Bronze Age) structures.

---

[40] Parker Pearson, 1999, p.77

[41] Carver, 2002, p.135-6; Williams, 2006a, p.33-5, 145; Pedersen, 2007, p.351-2

[42] Puhvel, 1983

[43] Chaney, 1970, p.97; Pedersen, 2007, p.351

[44] Dickinson & Speake, 1992, p.121; Parker Pearson, 1999, p.83-5; Williams, 2006a, p.172

However, the early mediaeval construction of large and impressive tombs is normally considered to be associated with the transition from a kin-based social order to one based on ownership or control of territory, in which boundary markers took on a new importance; and indeed the display associated with a large funeral may have been of value in providing an opportunity for a display of cohesion and solidarity in times of instability and rapid change.[45] While historians today do not normally look to individuals (or even individual families) for the causes of far-reaching change in the societies they inhabit, it is beyond question that some individuals certainly do have a profound effect upon those with whom they interact, and that social upheavals are often initiated by these effects and the reactions to them.[46] An appropriately volatile political or religious environment can give the words or deeds of one man a vast range of ramifications, intended and unintended. To this extent, some people's lives may have been worth celebrating – in story or song or architecture, as we still do today. That said, we must not lose sight of the fact that in almost no case can we do more than guess at the identity of any barrow's occupant; the tales of the heroes and leaders of old are still with us vestigially, but we cannot match physical remains to these tales.[47] The temptation to see the graves of the *Wuffingas* at Sutton Hoo is strong, but not entirely irresistible: there is no single object in the mounds or flat-graves which can be unquestionably linked to the East Anglian royal house and no other, despite a considerable weight of circumstantial evidence pointing to this conclusion.[48]

Shephard suggested that the very highest social rank could be assigned to just three barrows: Sutton Hoo Mound 1, Taplow and Broomfield.[49] (Today, Prittlewell would presumably have to be added to this list.) However this group is quite diverse in its contents, and does not form a cohesive set; there is no single item in the grave-goods, possession of which would admit the holder to the top rank. Indeed, the mourners showed considerable inventiveness in their collection of assemblages. Perhaps this free reign of imagination was itself part of the tradition for the very highest status burials: certainly, no two burials at Sutton Hoo appear to have received exactly the same treatment.

---

[45] Hedeager, 1992

[46] Carver, 2002, p.135-6

[47] But see *Lilla Howe* below, p.224

[48] Parker Pearson, van der Noort & Woolf, 1993, challenged the East Anglian link and suggested instead an East Saxon origin for the Mound 1 burial. Despite some interesting correspondences between aspects of Mound 1 and known East Saxon regnal data, the idea has not been generally accepted.

[49] Dickinson & Speake, 1992, p.112

Bauschatz noted the recurrence of certain types of grave-goods in the higher-status mounds (and especially the chamber graves seem to be intended in his study).[50] These include:

- woven textiles, and articles for producing them such as combs, tweezers, shears (and occasionally looms in Scandinavia)

- weapons and armour

- containers, especially those for liquids

The weaving items symbolise the weaving of human life and secular time (in ON, *Urðr* or in OE, *wyrd*). The weapons, especially the shield, symbolise the personal vigour and identity of the male. The containers may include the cauldrons, hanging bowls, glass beakers, wooden tubs and buckets, strainers and spoons, glass bowls and jars, drinking horns and cups; all are associated with the containment and free flowing of liquid. The idea of containment is suggested to relate to the notion of the spring or well as the source of space-time in Germanic cosmology.

Mound burial is usually deemed an extreme form of inhumation, which ties in with Ellis Davidson's binary scheme whereby the dead either dwell in the earth (inhumation, which binds the soul to the soil) or move on into the realm of the gods (cremation, which releases the soul into the Otherworld).[51] Mound burial not only holds the dead person's soul in the earth, it also provides a focus for veneration. Bede's account of the conversion of the English to Christianity holds examples of both models: Fursey's vision (book 3:19) is of a vertical ascent to heaven, based on older sources, while the account of Drycthelm's vision relates to horizontal wandering in the Otherworld.

The most obvious feature of chamber burial, as against other forms practiced at that time, is the opportunity for displaying the deceased in his or her finery, with all the valuable and symbolic possessions and gifts arranged around the body in a 'tableau' of death.[52] This tableau may have been intended to fix a certain image of the deceased in the memory of the viewers, and if so, then the image selected for presentation was the choice of the mourners. It was the mourners' traditions, aspirations and preferences which determined the details of the scene presented for public view before the chamber was closed. The choices of objects for inclusion (and no less for exclusion) would have highlighted some aspects of the life of the deceased while suppressing others.

---

[50] Bauschatz, 1982, p.34ff;

[51] Ellis Davidson, 1943; Wellendorf, 2007

[52] Williams, 2006a, p.42-3

Indeed the construction of a chamber within the barrow was itself a choice, and one with strong implications of élite membership.

If this reading is correct, then the emergence of the larger and more lavish forms of mound burial, including the chamber burial, must be seen in the context of an increased stratification in society at some point in the later 6th c., which would coincide with the concentration of power in fewer hands and the emergence of 'mediaeval kingship' as the dominant social model.[53]

Display Value

Taking the most completely recorded published excavations as the starting point, being Mounds 1 and 17 at Sutton Hoo, it is possible to see the contradiction, the two sides of kingly life, represented in the furniture: these are war and peace.

War

A mediaeval king had to be able to inspire his supporters and to frighten his enemies. There are several aspects to the Mound 1 and Mound 17 treasures which reflect this aspect of royal responsibility. It should be noted that the Mound 17 burial was focused rather more on hunting than on warfare; this may be due to the dead nobleman being younger and keener for the hunt as practice for war, than on actual warfare itself.

Mound 17

Shield	Without the leather and wooden components, the shield is not now a very impressive item, but if it was originally large and decorated with painted patterns it would have served well to identify the bearer on the battlefield to friend and foe.
Sword	The sword was pattern-welded and apparently very well made, but the organic fittings of the hilt have not survived. We thus have no means of knowing whether it was plain or ornate, but the evidence of other burials suggests that decoration would have been used wherever possible.

continued

---

[53] Carver, 2002, p.137-9 The objection remains that social hierarchy can be expressed in many ways, of which burial is one of the more attractive because of its permanence.

Horse	The horse, which was probably sacrificed to go off to the Otherworld with its master, was a respectable 17 hands (68", 170cm) high at the shoulder. The decorated bridle and a bran bucket were included in the human's grave. (There are close parallels to this at Lakenheath, also in Suffolk.)
Spears	The spears were the first items placed in the grave, and symbolised the owner's readiness to use force. In a hunting context, the spear was the first and main weapon for attack, with the knife used to despatch a wounded animal.
Knife	A *seax*, large dagger or hunting knife was part of the normal costume of noble Anglo-Saxon men in the 6th and 7th c.

Mound 1

Helmet	The helmet is unique among Anglo-Saxon finds. The closest parallels are found in Vendel Period Swedish royal graves, but the Swedish helmets are not constructed in quite the same manner as the Sutton Hoo example, do not feature a full face-plate and mostly have a mail curtain to protect the face, throat and neck. (However there is evidence for a face-plate helmet on Gotland from this period.)[54]
Shield	The shield's metal components survive quite well but the wood and leather elements remain only where protected by the presence of metallic corrosion. One unusual feature is the metal outer rim, held in place with clips; this allows the shape and size of the shield to be determined. The decorative scheme is highly complex and includes separate ornamental plaques in the shape of a winged dragon (?) and a bird of prey. It is very likely that the leather surface was painted or otherwise decorated, but this is speculation.
Byrnie	The mailcoat is unique in England: there is no other known early mailcoat with which to compare it, and very little mail of any kind. The byrnie is entirely mineralised so that none of the original ferrous metal survives, merely the corrosion products and some copper alloy components.

---

[54] Mortimer, forthcoming

Sword	The sword is a fine example of a pattern-welded blade of highly complex construction, which alone would make it one of the finest weapons of its time ever discovered. The pommel with its cloisonné garnets and gold settings is a lavish addition. The sword has few equals, but weapons of this general type are known from the Baltic to Italy.
	The sheath was bound with linen tape at the top, and the belt mounting and gold suspension system was ingenious and very flexible, being able to turn in all three planes.
Axe-hammer	This unique article, with its complex swivel mount, was an unlikely weapon; it would have suited a fast-moving horseman, but would be too unwieldy for fighting on foot. It is more likely that the axe-hammer was used to stun and despatch cattle at the major heathen sacrifices.
Standard	The standard is without exact parallels and several functions have been proposed for it, including a flambeau or fire-beacon. However, the standard is top-heavy and would be quite dangerous if used in this way. One proposal, which has been tested experimentally, is its use as a stand for weapons; once spears are rested in the crooks of the bulls' horns at the corners, the assemblage is very stable and offers a good platform for display of weapons and other items.[55]
Whetstone	This unique item has excited much speculation. The schist from which it was made occurs mainly in the north of England and southern Scotland, so it may have originally been a diplomatic gift. The eight impassive faces glare out from the ends of the stone, suggesting majesty and powerful hostility.
Spears	Spears of Swanton's groups D2 and E3 are present in the mound; the spear was symbolically the weapon of the freeman and was connected with the cult of Woden.

---

[55] Mortimer, forthcoming

Peace

Kingship was not only about cowing opponents, it was also about forming strategic alliances with potential foes and rewarding those whose support had already been given. For this purpose, the main instrument was the *symbel*, the ceremonial feast with religious and sacramental content. There are many treasures, especially in Mound 1, which refer to this important social event.

Cauldrons	A large cauldron and its magnificent suspension chain were among the more practical treasures in Mound 1
Hanging bowl	The bowl would have been used to serve food and drink in the king's hall. It had apparently never been used for cooking over a fire, so it is likely that the bowl was the container in which prepared food was displayed and kept warm in the hall.
Tableware	Silver bowls and a large silver dish were among the tableware items which would have been used to impress guests. The dish was an antique at the time of its deposition, and had been a diplomatic gift from the Byzantine Emperor Anastasius. How it came to East Anglia is unknown, but it is likely that it formed part of the currency of diplomatic exchange in the early mediaeval world.
Drinking horns	The huge horns were mounted with decorative plaques of gilt bronze, bearing symbolic birds' heads and other motifs of great complexity. Horns were highly symbolic and played an important part in the customary drinking rituals of the hall.
Wooden cups	The burrwood cups were mounted with small plaques, similar to those on the drinking horns. They would have been suitable only for serving small quantities: perhaps a distilled liquor, or even for salt and spices with which to flavour food.
Wooden pots	Tiny wooden pots may have been used for drinking spirits, or perhaps for pastes and salves.
Stave-built buckets	Stave-built buckets with metal hoops to hold the wooden components in place are a common grave-good of the 6th and 7th c., not confined to the very high-status burials

Spoons	The pair of spoons had religious overtones, one bearing the name 'Saulos' and the other 'Paulos'. They may have been a baptismal gift to the king.
Knives	A pair of knives were found in a leather sheath; they were too small for use in war or hunting, and may have been used at table.
Lyre and gaming pieces	The king's position as host meant that he was responsible for the entertainment of his guests. (There are five lyres from Anglo-Saxon England, three found in chamber graves and two in more humble burials.)

Female Graves

The high-status female graves are accorded equal attention with the male, and in most respects they are just as lavish in contents and monumental in execution. One notable feature of the female barrows is that they are in the main re-used existing structures, i.e. they are secondary burials.

Female barrow-burial also appears to have outlived its male counterpart, according to the admittedly imprecise dating techniques presently available. The latest female burials of this type continued into the later 7th c. and beyond, while no male example is certainly dated later than the middle 600s. (This excludes the small-scale local resurgence in barrow-burial in the later 9th c. in the east.)

Another feature of the female graves is that the barrows in which they are found are generally smaller in diameter than their male equivalents. This may be a mere statistical quirk based on a very small sample size, or perhaps it is due to the previously noted practice of more commonly re-using Bronze Age mounds for female burials, these being in general smaller than the Anglo-Saxon period versions favoured for males. Despite a disparity in average diameter, there is no sense in which the female graves were second-tier burials, since the association with pre-existing structures actually added to the prestige and glamour of the grave.

Prehistoric Mounds

Existing mounds attracted the attention of Anglo-Saxons, especially the typical round bowl barrows of Bronze Age date which resembled their own major funerary monuments. Naturally, these convenient structures were used for the placement of new burials, often disturbing the original occupant's remains. One

Bronze Age barrow at *Five Knolls*, near Dunstable (Bedfordshire) accommodated over ninety supine Anglo-Saxon burials.[56] Such 'secondary inhumation' was evidently a perfectly acceptable practice in those areas where round barrows were still visible.[57] Sometimes the burials were laid in pits dug into an existing barrow, while at others the new burials were laid on the existing ground surface and covered with a further layer of topsoil.

Re-use of existing monuments is a recognised phenomenon in intrusive communities.[58] It enables the incomers to show mastery of the land and domination of the previous inhabitants. It also allows them to acquire the protection of the existing supernatural powers, by claiming them as ancestral burials for their own culture. However, it should be noted that barrow re-use was no less a tradition in the southern Scandinavian area before the Anglian exodus, and it may have seemed perfectly natural to the newly arrived settlers to take over existing mounds for new burials.[59]

Relevant to the question of how the Anglo-Saxons regarded existing barrows are the names 'Wayland's Smithy' and the (lost) 'Giants' Barrow', *Enta hlæw*, at Overton (Hampshire).[60] An association with Welund the smith, with the *entas* responsible for large stone constructions, and with the marvellous output of their forges, may have fired the Anglo-Saxon imagination, and it is perhaps the enticement of such fabulous treasure which encouraged seekers after fortune to delve into burial mounds.

The Berkshire Downs seem to have been a centre for Welund traditions, according to place-name research by Huningford and Grinsell.[61] A barrow situated on the parish boundary between Woolstone and Compton Beauchamp was known as *beahhildæ byrigels* 'Beaghild's barrow'; this monument was dug in 1850 and yielded ornaments of jet, Kimmeridge shale and a bronze pin. The nature of the grave-goods means that an Anglo-Saxon date cannot be totally excluded, but the probability is that this is a Bronze Age barrow. Nearby, below Hardwell Camp, is another mound known as *hwittuces hlæw* 'Whittock's barrow'. It has been suggested that these personal names are garbled versions of *Beadohild* and *Widia*; the former was the lady whom Welund raped in the story of his capture and escape, and the latter was the

---

[56] Meaney, 1964, p.35-6

[57] Grinsell, 1936, p.29-30; Meaney, 1964, p.18-9; Hållans Stenholm, 2007

[58] O'Brien, 1999, p.60

[59] Pedersen, 2007

[60] Grinsell, 1936, p.41; 1991, p.50

[61] Grinsell, 1936, p.44, 154-62

child born from this union. *Idle Tump* (or *Idlebush Barrow*) on Woolstone Down was allegedly the tumulus known as *hafeces hlæw* 'hawk's barrow' in a charter boundary, and elsewhere *weardæs beorh* 'sentinel's hill' which could be a corruption of 'Wade's barrow', Wada being the father of Welund. Attractive and intriguing as these suggestions are, it hardly needs saying that *Beaghild* is not the same name as *Beadohild*, nor *Hwittuc* as *Widia*, nor *Weard* as *Wada*. The name 'Idle Tump' probably derives from the OE *idel* 'empty' and denotes a barrow which had previously been robbed.

It may be that the association of giants (*entas*) with barrows is ancient and derives from the practice of re-using existing tumuli: on opening such mounds, they were often found to contain the skeleton of a man of unusual height and stature.[62] This is probably due to displacement of the bones within a cavity which would allow them to spread and so appear to occupy a greater length and width than they did while the flesh was upon them.

---

[62] Grinsell, 1936, p.41

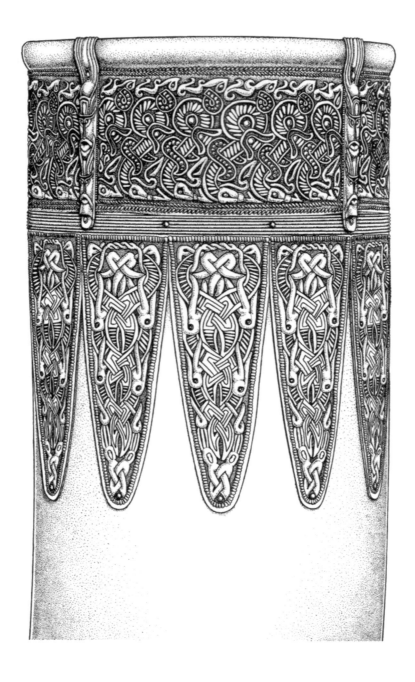

Rim of the drinking horn from Sutton Hoo, Mound 1.
One of a pair of magnificent feasting vessels made from the horns of an aurochs.

3. Chamber Burial Traditions

The development of the barrow as a burial structure was outlined in the early 20th c. by L.V. Grinsell in a series of publications, notably *The Ancient Burial Mounds of England* in 1936. Grinsell distinguished between 'grave-mound clusters' and 'barrows'.[63] The former are groups of grave-mounds spaced close together and often partially intersecting, typical of the British Iron Age and of the Anglo-Saxon graves with low mounds; the latter are single large mounds, or groups of such mounds with a large open space around them, such as are found in the Bronze Age and in some Anglo-Saxon contexts where more prestigious burials were being made. The Roman form of barrow was steep-sided and conical with a flattened top, and this profile was also used in some areas in the British Iron Age.

The Germanic Background

The emergence of 'princely burials' such as chamber tombs, ship burials, barrow burials and other means of interring high-status individuals is a striking element in the archaeology of early Anglo-Saxon England. However, the most splendid burials are rather a product of the Middle Saxon period, when states had already formed and 'royal' or 'noble' families secured their access to wealth and status.[64] Effros cites Arnold in seeing the emergence of the princely tomb in Kent as significant because this kingdom was richer and more densely populated than other areas of Britain at this time (6th and 7th c.). One result of this was a greater disparity in funerary deposits, with both very rich and very poor burials existing side-by-side.

The royal imposition of Christianity was an attempt to reorganise Kentish society, in order to avoid social and economic collapse due to the lack of opportunities for further territorial expansion. The later Anglo-Saxon kingdoms which were most successful – Northumbria, Mercia and Wessex – had British neighbours who could be subject to taxation or tribute as a means of gaining wealth without the necessity to indulge in production. Härke has nevertheless shown that regional variation in weapon burials does not necessarily correspond with the economic wealth of the region – the finest

---

[63] Grinsell, 1936, p.28-9

[64] Lutovsky, 1996; Arnold, 1997, p.162-3; Parker Pearson, 1999, p.74-7; Carver, 2000, p.35-7; Effros, 2003, p.91-2; Hinton, 2005, p.57. Hedges & Buckley, 1985, p.17-9 discuss possible construction methods.

weapons are not necessarily found where the wealthiest graves were located, nor the most productive land.

The immediate origins of this burial type for the Anglo-Saxons lie among the Alemanni in the regions of the Main and the middle Neckar river valleys in Germany. They developed the details of the chamber burial rite as it spread to western Europe, Scandinavia and the North Sea coasts. It extended, along with other elements of Germanic culture, into Gaul – now re-named *Francia* in deference to the change in political order - and thence across large areas of western Europe.[65] The famous German grave at Morken, published by Böhner in 1951, is a classic chamber burial with a wooden plank-built room containing the body, lying in state, and the rest of the space given over to offerings or grave-goods.[66] This fashion was adopted by Franks, Saxons, Angles and countless other groups all eager to make their mark in the new political order of the 7th c.

Chamber burials are found in Germany, such as the famous example from the cemetery at Krefeld-Gellep discovered in 1936.[67] The chamber grave was numbered 1782 in the grave-field and was excavated in 1962. At first it was identified as a warrior-grave due to the presence of many weapon types, but the later identification of some of the other items as horse-furniture and finely-made personal accessories prompted the promotion to *Fürstengrab* or 'princely burial'. The pit was roughly 4m x 5m in plan and about 2m deep; it was timber-lined and covered with tufa (stone). The grave contents are interesting for the parallels they offer to English graves, and for the contrasts. The dating is firmly 6th c. according to the chronology of local finds.

---

[65] Carver, 2005, p.289-92 offers reconstructions of Germanic coffins and chamber tombs.

[66] Doppelfeld & Pirling, 1966; Guillaume, Rohmer & Waton, 2004

[67] Doppelfeld & Pirling, 1966;

Krefeld-Gellep no.1782	Anglo-Saxon	Parallels / similar finds
Gold coin of the Byzantine Emperor Anastasius	Sutton Hoo Mound 1	Coins (and a large silver dish bearing this emperor's stamp)
Gold finger-ring with an insert of chalcedony carved in cameo style with a classical motif	Snape	Gold intaglio finger-ring with classical motif
Several saddle- and harness-fittings, including two garnet-and-gold D-shaped mounts for the saddle and garnet-and-gold mounts on the bit	Sutton Hoo Mound 17	Wooden and leather saddle
Two iron knives in gold-mounted sheaths	Sutton Hoo Mound 1	Two seaxes in a leather sheath
Silver Roman spoon	Sutton Hoo Mound 1 & Prittlewell	Silver Roman spoons
Pouch with garnet-and-gold fittings	Sutton Hoo Mound 1	Pouch with garnet-and-gold cloisonné fittings
Various bronze, silver and gold shield-on-tongue buckles and strap-ends	Sutton Hoo Mounds 1 & 17 & Taplow	Various bronze and gilded buckles and belt-fittings
Iron roasting spit		
Silver needle		
Iron firesteel and flint		
Two circular garnet-and-gold strap distributors and rectangular belt fittings	Sutton Hoo Mound 1	A set of rectangular garnet-and-gold strap distributors and belt fittings
Iron pattern-welded spatha with garnet-and-gold pommel, free-running hilt-ring and domed gold fitting	Sutton Hoo Mound 1	Iron pattern-welded spatha with garnet-and-gold pommel, and two domed gold fittings

Iron angon	Sutton Hoo Mound 1	Three angons
Iron thrusting-spear	Sutton Hoo Mound 1 & Prittlewell	Thrusting spear
Leaf-blade spear	Sutton Hoo Mound 1	Leaf-bladed spear
Francisca	Sutton Hoo Mound 3	Iron head of a throwing-axe
Roman glass flagon		
Roman glass bowl		
Bronze hanging bowl	Sutton Hoo Mound 1	Bronze hanging bowl
Bronze bowl on iron tripod		
Bronze flagon	Prittlewell	Bronze flagon
Bronze dish		
Wooden bucket with metal fittings	Sutton Hoo Mound 17	Iron-bound wooden tub
Short iron seax in a wooden sheath	Sutton Hoo Mound 17	Iron knife in scabbard
Gilded iron spangenhelm helmet with side-flaps	Sutton Hoo Mound 1	Ridge-helm with face-plate and side-flaps
Shield with iron boss and fittings	Sutton Hoo Mound 1	Shield with iron boss and gilded copper-alloy fittings

The gold coin of the Byzantine Emperor Anastasius is curiously coincidental, since a large silver dish bearing this emperor's stamp was found at Sutton Hoo. A gold finger-ring with an insert of chalcedony, carved in cameo style with a classical motif, was found at Krefeld-Gellep, paralleled by the gold intaglio finger-ring from Snape.[68] The chalcedony forms a contrasting image of dark blue on light blue. There were also several saddle- and harness-fittings in the grave, including two garnet-and-gold D-shaped mounts for the saddle and several buckles.

The Swedish site at Högom, Norrland, features a series of at least 12 burial mounds, after which it is named (*högom* 'at the barrowmounds").[69] Mound 2 contained a log-built chamber grave set partly into the ground surface and with a cairn of loose stones above it, over which the turf mound was raised. The grave chamber was richly furnished with weapons (sword, seaxes, shield, arrows, lance and spear) and feasting equipment (cone beakers, bronze vessel) and horse equipment (bridle, saddle).

Mound-Dwellers

The question has to be asked: who were the people in the chamber graves? And why were they accorded such high status? Working from Continental parallels, these graves are often called *Fürstengräber* meaning 'leaders' graves' or 'princes' graves', and the English term 'princely' is sometimes used, as for example in the titles of Tania Dickinson's report on Cuddesdon, *Cuddesdon and Dorchester-on-Thames: Two Early Saxon 'Princely' Sites in Wessex* and Martin Carver's long-awaited book on the Sutton Hoo excavations of the 1990s, *Sutton Hoo: A Seventh Century Princely Burial Ground and its Context*. It is unlikely that all the people in these graves were 'princes' in the modern sense but they were all *æþele* in the Old English sense, people of noble birth, of either sex, who had led their communities in life. Some were probably *cyningas* 'kings' or *dryhtenas* 'warlords' or *idesa* 'ladies' but few were monarchs in the modern sense, since power and authority resided more in the kindred rather than the individual at this time.

We must also not lose sight of the fact that people do not bury themselves, and that the display of wealth and power in these treasure-filled chambers was a decision taken by surviving relatives and mourners. The emphatic statement of access to luxury goods was as much for the benefit of the successors as for the well-being of the soul of the deceased.

Most chamber graves appear to us to be heathen burials, but this is a modern reaction to graves in which goods for the afterlife were prominently displayed. There is nothing inherently religious about these burials and it is highly likely that some of the people in them had been converted to Christianity in life.

---

[68] Doppelfeld & Pirling, 1966
[69] Ramqvist, 1988

This is especially true when we consider the probable dates of the burials (in the early 7th c.) and the kinds of people who were treated in this manner, being the royalty and the nobles who were among the first and most willing converts to the new religion.

Chamber burial has a handful of variant forms which we will discuss below. All are characterised by the presence of a chamber and by the opportunity for displaying the dead person lying in state.

Barrow Burial

Mound burial was not an innovation for the Anglo-Saxons, who had a tradition of cutting a ring-ditch for an important grave, and then scooping the soil up into a low mound above the completed burial. These early mounds were seldom large or imposing, and served mainly as place-markers for the remains of important or successful people; many of the barrows mentioned in Section II were never more than low hillocks. Barrow burial in the 7th c. was rather more impressive, with large mounds constructed to a height of 4 metres (13') or more, and with a considerable circumference.

Burial mounds were large engineering enterprises requiring considerable planning. Often the first phase was the cutting of a circular boundary trench which was then widened and deepened to form a 'quarry ditch', from which the excavated material could be piled over the burial chamber and built up as the ditch progressed. This is the most efficient method of construction, because it does not involve the movement of the earth outside the site, and the apparent height of the mound is increased by the fact that the ditch has lowered the starting level of the slope. Another method involved the digging of a series of pits and then hauling the displaced earth from these to a central point; this method was apparently used for Mounds 1 and 17 at Sutton Hoo.[70] The technique was not new. The original feature of the Tranmer House cemetery, adjacent to the Sutton Hoo mounds, was a Bronze Age burial within a ring-ditch. At West Heslerton (Yorkshire), one of the most expansive excavations of an Anglo-Saxon site, several Bronze Age barrows formed the nucleus of the later cemetery.

Such burial rites were not a male preserve. Females could be accorded chamber burial within a barrow – Mound 14 at Sutton Hoo had contained a high-status lady in an upholstered coffin with rich grave-goods, which were subsequently robbed.[71] The Norwegian chamber burial at Oseberg contained

---

[70] Hedges & Buckley, 1985; Carver, 2005, p.309
[71] Carver, 2005, p.107

a well-preserved Viking ship, numerous grave-goods and a four-wheeled waggon; it was apparently the grave of a middle-aged woman, who may have been accompanied by a female slave.[72]

Barrows were regarded as highly significant monuments, and this applied equally to the Neolithic and Bronze Age structures which occur in England, where the geology allows.[73] Barrows were used as estate boundary markers, and probably often as the sites of fairs and markets.[74] Boundaries were significant in the Anglo-Saxon landscape and divided people as well as territories; people from beyond the boundary were not always entitled to legal protection unless they identified themselves and signalled their presence. Anglo-Saxon territorial boundaries often met at prehistoric monuments, suggesting that the territory had been divided by agreement among a group of competing claimants convened there for that purpose.

Boundary burials were also associated with dragons and hoarded wealth, and not unnaturally with the world of the dead. Ælfric railed against the practice of visiting burial mounds in order to learn about the future from the spirits dwelling there – spirits which could take on the form of the dead man to deceive the living:

> *Gyt farað wiccan to wega gelæton and to hæþenum byrgelsum mid heora gedwimore and clipiað to ðam deofle, and he cymð hym to on þæs mannes gelicnysse þe þær lið bebyrged swylce he of deaðe arise, ac heo ne mæg þæt don þæt se deada arise þurh hire drycræft.*

> Witches still travel to where roads meet and to heathen graves with their illusory skill and call out to the devil and he comes to them in the guise of the person who lies buried there, as if he would arise from the dead – but she cannot really make it happen, that the dead man should arise through her wizardry.

The association of witchcraft with burial at a crossroads is interesting for it was traditionally reserved for those whose presence might defile holy ground if buried in a churchyard, such as heathens, witches and various classes of criminal. An example of an adult male was found at Broad Town (Wiltshire) in 2000: the head was to the southwest and there were no signs of a coffin or mound or any grave-goods and the abraded ceramic fragments in the fill were evidently already present in the soil when the grave was dug. The dating of the burial was established as in the range595 to 665 AD.[75]

---

[72] Parker Pearson, 1999, p.99

[73] Carver, 2005, p.486; Haughton & Powlesland, 1999, p.341

[74] Grinsell, 1991; Semple, 1998, p.116

[75] Clarke, 2004

Crossroads were frequently used as boundary markers for estates, parishes, hundreds and even shires; they were essentially liminal territory – neither in one area nor another – and so formed a kind of 'limbo' into which the soul of the dead man could be consigned, and from which it was believed it could not return. Likewise, burial mounds were frequently used as boundary markers, immovable objects which formed fixed points from which to lay out territory. That witchcraft (necromancy, in this case) should be enacted at a place with strong supernatural associations is surely indicative of a persistent regard for the mounds as repositories of power: the Christian homilist puts it down to the devil appearing in the dead man's guise to the witch in order to deceive her, but another explanation would be that burial mounds were the resting places of the ancestral dead. In some heathen traditions, as for example the Icelandic notions regarding *Helgafell*, the dead continued their existence on another plane within the mound, and in this sense the mounds were liminal territory between this world and the next.[76] It is worth noting that the practice of *utiseta* 'sitting out' in order to commune with one's ancestors, often took place on a gravemound in Scandinavian tradition.[77]

Scandinavian mythology makes much of the ability of certain characters to pass between the worlds, as when Óðinn is hanged and stabbed on the World Tree for nine nights – the tree acts as his 'terrible steed' (ON *yggdrasill*) on his journey to the land of the dead and back – or when Hermóðr rides to Hel's hall to try to win back Balder the Bright. In order to get in touch with a powerful dead kinsman, what could be more natural than to visit the grave? People even today sit by the grave of a loved one, yet there is no reason to think it is a purely modern reaction to stress or grief.

The Rus funeral witnessed by Ibn Fadlan on the Volga in ca. 922 AD involved a number of ritual acts prior to burning the dead man and his ship on a huge pyre, then constructing a mound over the remains and erecting a large birch post in the centre of the mound on which the name of the dead man was written.[78] The English burials show evidence of such rites: ship burial, cremation, mound burial, marking with a post.

---

[76] Aspeborg, 2005; Kaliff, 2007, p.177

[77] Wilson, 1992, p.170; Aspeborg, 2005, p.217. The Sutton Hoo barrow cemetery has been seen as an expression of links to Scandinavian culture in opposition to the encroaching Frankish-Christian world.

[78] Bauschatz, 1982, p.34ff; Parker Pearson, 1999, p.2-3

Ship Burial

Forms of ship- and boat-burial are of some antiquity among the Germanic folk and their neighbours. There are two main formats for the rite: either (i) the dead person was placed in or by a ship or boat, surrounded by personal possessions and animals, and the whole complex was covered with soil to form a mound; or (ii) the body and possessions were placed in a ship or boat which formed a pyre, the complex was burnt and a mound erected above the remains.[79] A third form is the 'symbolic' ship formed from large upright stones, erected in an elliptical shape which acts as a more permanent substitute for the perishable wooden original;[80] this custom has never been recognised in England.

There are over four hundred known boat- and ship-burials dating from the Later Roman Iron Age onwards in northern Europe. The earliest known example is the boat-burial at Wremen (Lower Saxony, Germany) from the 5th c, close to the famous Migration Period village of Feddersen Wierde.

Ship burial in England is a form of chamber burial in which the chamber was formed in part using the hull of a ship; burials of vehicles (e.g. chariots) are found in many early European cultures.[81] At Sutton Hoo, two different approaches were taken: in Mound 1, the chamber was built within the midships hold of the vessel from large timbers, while in Mound 2 the timber-lined chamber was dug into the earth and the ship's hull was used to roof it over. It is not known for certain which of these two mounds was built first, and therefore which was the first rite practiced there, although many commentators have assumed that the Mound 1 burial was the initial ritual act on this site.[82]

The ship and its contents were covered with a mound of earth. Given that the Sutton Hoo Mound 1 ship was around 90' long, the mound must have been colossal in size, even if the ship's hull was sunk below ground level and the stem- and stern-posts were not fully covered but allowed to protrude. Alternatively, these posts may have been de-mounted before the ship was hauled ashore, a tradition which was known among later North Sea sailors who did not want to arouse the hostility of the land-spirits by showing the fierce dragon-prows of their vessels.

---

[79] Major, 1924; Ellis Davidson, 1950; Allan, 2004; Gerds, 2007, p.153

[80] Sigvallius, 2005, p.159-63

[81] Bauschatz, 1982, p.37

[82] Halsall, 1995, p.7

An earlier ship burial took place, not far from Sutton Hoo at Snape (see below), of a vessel about half the size of the Mound 1 ship. In the same cemetery there were also smaller log-boats which had been converted to coffins.[83] Also in East Anglia, parts of boats were laid over graves at Caister-on-Sea in what may have been a more symbolic evocation of the same association of the dead with sea-faring.[84] Alternatively, we may see the association of the dead person with flowing water – as symbolised in the vessel itself – as a connection to the idea of running water as the passage of time.[85] As a ship is also a container, which impedes the flow of water, it may have been considered especially suitable as a symbol of the Otherworld where quotidian time does not exist.

Ship burial in particular was not a traditional rite in England (i.e. a continuation of familiar practice) but was rather an innovation, a break with the past and an experiment in negotiating symbolism and wealth, power and status. It was part of a new ideology in the process of formation. Significantly, ship burial was confined at this period to a small area of East Anglia and a small area of eastern Sweden, although it remained longer in use in Scandinavia than in England.[86] Ship burials of many sizes continue to be discovered in Norway and Sweden, while the disposal of actual vessels co-existed with symbolic settings of stones erected in the overall shape and profile of a ship.[87] Scandinavian traditional burials from the turn of the first millennium echoed rituals established in the Roman Iron Age, nearly a thousand years before; the English tradition was interrupted by the adoption of both the Christian religion and the mediaeval European notions of death.[88]

Ship burial in later Scandinavia could involve several variations: cremating the deceased and his or her ship; cremating ship and body and burying them together; burying them together unburnt; setting fire to the ship carrying the

---

[83] Ekengren, 2007, p.110 notes that tree-trunk coffins were associated with richer burials back into the Roman Iron Age in northern Europe; these may be a variant of the same idea.

[84] Meaney, 1964, p.19

[85] Bauschatz, 1982, p.33ff

[86] Carver, 1990; Carver, 2005, p.301-3; Franceschi, Jorn & Magnus, 2005b, p.31; Jennbert, 2007

[87] Kure, 2007, notes the symbolic association of the ship as the vehicle of passage to the Otherworld (Hel) with elliptical stone-settings, while three-pointed stone-settings appear to replicate the threefold roots of the World Tree (Hållans-Stenholm, 2007). In both cases the association is with passage from one world to the other.

[88] Jennbert, 2007, p.135; Pollington, forthcoming

deceased out to sea.[89] The archaeological evidence for the latter is lacking, of course, and indeed the practice is inferred only from literary sources, such as the tale of the funeral of Baldur and the account in *Gislasaga*.[90] The immediate purpose of ship burial has never been clarified: it may have been selected as a practical use of superannuated sea-going vessels as mortuary chambers or cremation pyres; or it may have been a purely socio-political statement of wealth and power; or it may have been an ideological statement of association with a particular religious cult (e.g. *Skíðblaðnir*); or even a symbolic means of transport to the Otherworld, restricted to the class of leaders with the wealth to own and use such a vehicle.[91]

Horse-burial was often part of the more lavish ship-burial rite in Scandinavia: indeed, later Scandinavian ship-burials contained the remains of many animals, horses, dogs, sheep, cattle and pigs being the most common, along with hunting birds – all domesticated rather than wild animals.[92] All these items – ships, horses, food animals, armour and weapons, feasting equipment, rich textiles – may be viewed in Jennbert's neat phrase as 'lifestyle metaphors', symbolic items demonstrationg the deceased person's place in the world of wealth and prestige, of *weorð* as it might be described in OE.

Probably the last great ship-burial in the north was the Danish leader buried in the mound at Ladby on Funen, some time around 950AD.[93] The mound had been plough-damaged but fortunately the disturbance had not reached the ship itself, which was found complete with its anchor. The ship had been inserted into a carefully prepared trench, positioned so that the prow and stern-posts were still visible above ground at the time of burial. As at Sutton Hoo Mound 1, the midships section of the ship formed a treasure-chamber, roofed over once the vessel was in place. A jumble of skeletal material around the outside of the ship proved to be the remains of eleven horses which had been slain for the funeral; a small iron axe was found which may have been used to despatch them. Some dogs were also included, although complete skeletons were difficult to discern. Among the grave-goods were riding gear and harnesses for the horses; a complex leash for a dog; many iron buckles and one of silver; a shieldboss; some arrowheads; an axe (but no sword); iron cooking vessels and some finer tableware, including a bronze dish of British manufacture. A small cemetery of about twelve graves surrounded the ship burial.

---

[89] Du Bois, 1999, p.71 ; Gerds, 2007, p.156

[90] Du Bois, 2007

[91] Gerds, 2007, p.156-7

[92] Jennbert, 2007

[93] Thorvildsen, 1975

Burial with a Horse

If ship burial symbolises the power of the dead person to travel between the worlds – which itself entails the ability to return to Middle Earth at some point – then no less does horse burial imply the possibility of travel for the dead person. As the dead man's mount is itself dead, it is transformed into a ghostly steed which can carry him anywhere he wishes on land, at sea or into the sky – just as Óðinn's horse *Sleipnir* was able to do.[94] As with Sleipnir, the steed could take its rider down to the gates of Hel if need be.

The horse was an economically important animal among the Anglo-Saxons, and was probably venerated: this is implied by the fact that heathen priests were allegedly denied the use of male horses, a transgression of the outward display of their male gender paralleled by the taboo on their use of weapons. Horse-heads are a common form of decoration on Anglo-Saxon cruciform brooches, especially among the earlier examples: later ones transform the design so that the eyes become roundels and the nostrils spirals.[95]

Another instance of horse-symbolism is the Scandinavian *niðstöng* or scorn-stake, which survived in English rural tradition (see p.226). The horse's head - real or carved - may have empowered the magic in the stake and made it active.[96]

There is a distinction to be drawn between the 'agricultural' animals (sheep, pigs, cattle) which are represented in graves as cuts of meat, and the 'pastoralist' animals such as horses and dogs, which are present as whole beasts.[97] There is an association in England as on the Continent, between the finds of horse burials and adult males with military equipment: the horse-and-rider burial is essentially a warrior-status burial (even if not all those who claimed this token status were actually warriors).

There are thirty-two whole or partial horse burials known in England, of which a few – for examples, Springfield Lyons (Essex) and Snape (Suffolk) - consist of only the head. There are a further eleven examples of bridles or riding tack not actually associated with horse-remains. The presence of horse bones in cremations is also common in some areas, such as East Anglia. The distribution of the finds is concentrated on the eastern seaboard, with

---

[94] Loumand, 2007; Pollington, forthcoming

[95] Pollington, forthcoming

[96] Loumand, 2007, p.153, cites an Icelandic parallel whereby a horse was buried with its head cut off and placed in the grave between its thighs: the phallus thus acted as the stake. The combination of sexual (phallus) and intellectual (head) power would give the stake a forceful magical effect.

[97] Fern, 2007, p.92

extensions into the East Midlands and to the north of the Thames Valley. The westernmost examples are multiple horses at Fairford (Gloucestershire) and an unusual cremation at Roundway Down (Wltshire) in the barrow burial. The examples at Saltwood (Kent) are also isolated, although a horse's head was found at Sarre in north-east Kent.

Fern divides the burials into two main types: Group A burials have the horse and rider in a single, large grave, both having their heads in the same position relative to their bodies. The horses are saddled and bridled and apparently ready to set off. These burials are typically early, from the first half of the 6th c. Group B burials feature a separate grave-cut for the man and his mount, and the bridle is either in the human grave or, if in the animal's, it is not in place for riding. This group belongs to the later 6th c. or to the 7th.

The purpose of horse burial appears to be associated as much with expression of identity and status as the enactment of myth, and in this respect it is perhaps pertinent to recall that the earliest Anglian leaders of whom we know anything more than the name were called *Hengest* 'stallion' and *Horsa* (derived from *hors* 'horse').

Bed Burials

Bed-burials in England are a 7th c. phenomenon, an enhanced version of chamber burial in which the deceased is laid on a bed, which is often only identifiable by the iron frame and fittings in England, although Scandinavian and Continental examples in a better state of preservation are known.[98] The arrangement of the body on a couch or table is a feature of chamber burials at least as far back as the Hallstatt culture, with several notable examples from Central Europe, such as the chieftain's grave at Hochdorf (Germany).[99]

It is notable that Ibn Fadlan's account in the 10th c. mentions that the Rus chieftain's body was laid on a couch, within a tent built on the deck of his ship, and that beer, fruit, meat and musical instruments were laid about him; it appears that his favourite pastimes in the hall were being made available to him in the afterlife.

Certain examples of bed burial in England are few, and perhaps surprisingly the majority appear to be of females; for example, all three possible examples at Shudy Camps (on the Cambridgeshire – Essex border) were probably female. The known English bed-burials are mostly of females.

---

[98] Lethbridge, 1936; Speake, 1989; Ramqvist, 1990; Carver, 2005, p.293-4
[99] Ellis Davidson, 1988, p.41; Parker Pearson, 1999, p.79

The woman buried in Sutton Hoo Mound 14 may have been laid on a bed within her burial chamber. The male royal burial at Prittlewell may also have been laid on a bed in his chamber, although this is not certain: it may have been a specially-made bier or other platform.

The English bed-burials are mostly in the Anglian cultural area and are mostly of females. Incontestable examples in England are few, mainly because the metal fittings of the bed are easily confused with those of a coffin, and it is often only the special fittings for the headboard which point conclusively to the presence of a bed, although mineralised fabric within the iron corrosion products is also a valuable visual clue. The likely presence of iron-bound wooden chests in high-status burials cannot be excluded in some cases.

Iron fittings attached to wood include splice-plates, which are iron plates used to join lengths of wood to each other side-by-side. They are normally attached to both pieces of wood with rivets or nails, presumable carefully peened to avoid sharp edges. The bedding itself was supported on a framework of wood and leather, perhaps a form of suspended strapping which would be more comfortable to sleep on than wooden planks. However, the Oseberg bed apparently had wooden slats to support the mattress. The headboard supports were metal brackets which attached the headboard to the frame of the bed, sloping away at a shallow angle. Some are decorative, such as the twisted examples from Shudy Camps, Swallowcliffe Down and Edix Hill. Occasional additional features include metal side-rails, as at Swallowcliffe Down and metal pins as at Saltburn.[100]

The fittings suggest that the beds were all quite small, being about 2'6" (75cm) wide and 6' (1.9m) long, and therefore not intended for use by more than one person at a time. However, in no English case has the footboard been found, so length is only determined by the extent to which the iron fittings can be traced.

Are these beds really beds? It is possible that the burial beds are not examples of domestic furniture at all, but were made solely for the burial, along with the burial chamber itself, and the rather awkward angle of the headboard in some cases may support this. If the bed was made for the funeral rites, then the headboard may have been designed to show off the deceased in her finery.

---

[100] Malim & Hines, 1998; Williams, 2006a, p.31; Sherlock & Simmons, 2008.

4. Heathen Burials

Low, Barrow, Howe and Harrow

Burial mounds, large or small, invoved considerable effort to construct and were not built on a whim: these were permanent sites with long-term intended use. Apart from housing the significant dead, what purpose could barrows serve?

Carver has suggested that East Anglian barrows were raised in defiance of the predatory advances of the Christian – Kentish culture of the island's wealthiest kingdom. In this reading, barrows are 'flagships of the unconverted', a gesture of denial of authority against both Roman church and Frankish governance.[101] There is a sense in which the barrow-building tradition mirrors the contemporary church-building imperative: both were appeals to supernatural powers to intercede on behalf of their followers, expressed in large-scale construction works. (The evidence of the Danish King Harald Bluetooth, who had his parents' remains dug out of their barrow at Jellinge and re-interred in his new church after he converted to Christianity, implies that the structural parallels between barrow-burial and church-burial were obvious in such societies during the period of conversion.)[102] This rather reinforces the argument for ancestor-worship as a key part of Anglo-Saxon religious experience. If Norse evidence can be adduced, the dead leader in his prominent barrow must have become an ancestor or land-spirit.[103] These supernatural beings were connected to the elves in some manner and were involved with the protection and well-being of the family and of the community. There is thus something of the air of the 'temple' or 'holy site' about the barrow.

Grinsell has studied the charter evidence relating to the West Saxon kingdom (confined to Berkshire, Dorset, Gloucestershire, Hampshire, Wight, south Oxfordshire, Somerset and Wiltshire) relating to barrows. As a naming principle, the Saxons used the word *beorh* 'high place, mound' for pre-existing prehistoric barrows, and *hlæw* (Anglian *hlaw*) for their own burials; *beorh* could also be used of a natural hill. For secondary burials, there does not seem to have been any specific preference, nor did they distinguish long- from round-barrows with separate words.

---

[101] Carver, 2002, p.140 This argument may also apply less forcefully to the Scandinavian barrow tradition, but is not relevant in relation to the Slavic material.

[102] Ellis Davidson, 1950, p.175

[103] Kershaw, 2000, p.26-30; Augustyn, 2002, p.26-30

While no English edicts seem to regard the practice as especially pernicious, it is notable that Continental authorities were anxious to stamp out the custom of barrow-burial among Christians. A late 8th c. text, *Capitulatio de Partibus Saxoniae* is a ban issued by Charlemagne on burial near or in a barrow in respect of the Saxon regions, while a 10th c. text, *Decreta Synodorum Bavaricarum* extends punishment to those who bury their dead *ad tumulos quod dicimus more gentilium hougir* "in mounds, which we call in the native manner *hougir* (howes)".[104]

Beorh is another 'tumulus' word, based on a PIE root **bhrgh-* meaning 'high' which also gives rise to 'borough' and '(ice)berg' as well as folk-names such as *Brigantes* and *Burgundiones*.[105] There are more than twenty examples of OE names based on *ruh beorh* meaning 'rough mound' implying an untended monument, but only one 'rough low' (at Chetwode-Hillesdon, Buckinghamshire) which points to a tradition of communities maintaining their own burials.

The Anglo-Saxon charter evidence is often very helpful in researching local burial sites, since barrows played a greater part as local landmarks than they do today. When parishes and estates were laid out in the 7th c., barrows were frequently cited as the points from which boundaries extended.[106]

There are occasional examples of barrows named for the person believed to be interred there, such as *Cwichelmes low* at Ardley (Oxfordshire), another *Cwichelmes low* at Scutchamer Knob (Oxfordshire), *Chellenberghe* or 'Ceola's Barrow' at Piddletrenthide (Dorset) and Taplow or 'Tappa's Low' (Berkshire). Many have since been re-named, so that *Pegan beorh* 'Pega's barrow' (Dorset) is now called *Wor Barrow*. Pre-Christian burials often occur in the charters as *æt þæm hæþenan byrgelse* 'at the heathen burial' without further qualification.

Another term, *howe*, is sometimes encountered. It is usually derived from ON *haugr* which properly refers to a sacred spot marked by a pile of stones, but by extension it can refer to a burial beneath such a cairn. The OE term *hearg* or *hearh* survives as the word 'harrow' and refers to a sacred place in the landscape, a focus for tradition.

As an aside we have the Norse tale concerning the Norwegian king Óláfr Tryggvason who was staying a farmstead called Ögvaldsnes when he was visited by an old man with one eye wearing a low-brimmed hat, bearing a gift

---

[104] Pedersen, 2007, p.351-2

[105] Mallory & Adams, 2006, p.292

[106] Speake, 1989, p.120-2

of beef for the feast.[107] The stranger began to tell the king about the history of the region and the heathen King Ögvald who had ruled there, who was always accompanied by his cow, Síbilja, whose lowing struck fear into the king's enemies. Óláfr was fascinated by the old man's tales and stayed up late listening to them, whereby he nearly overslept and missed his morning Christian prayers. Realising that the old man had tried to lure him into a trap, the king threw out the beef and had the mound broken open and there they found the bones of an old man and a cow, which the Christian exhumed in order to purge the district of its heathen past.

The part barrows played in the ancestor-cult is hard to appreciate fully but their importance is quite evident. The grave need not be viewed as a static 'container' for the remains of the dead, but may instead be part of ongoing processes of ritual and social renewal.[108] Graves and barrows share some features with altars and should be seen as part of the monumental architecture of their creators. Since barrows held a physical remainder of the dead, they were viewed as 'altars to the ancestors' and this is especially true of the barrows which held founder-burials: in such cases the spirit of the deceased went on to be a protective *genius* for the locality and those who honoured it.

The role of the barrow as tangible evidence for myth should not be undervalued. Mythic tales – that is, tales expressing poetic truths about the nature and order of the world – are used in a secondary semiotic system to create and maintain social structure and orderliness; this is never more important than when the social structure is under attack, be it from within or without.[109] With each new rehearsal of the tale of Tæppa, for example, recounted periodically at the site of his grave-mound the participants in the rituals and their audience were effectively re-affirming their conscious will to belong to the group of which he was the founder or ancestral chief. The borders of their social group were renewed by the inclusion of the participants as well as the exclusion of those not deemed appropriate to take part.

---

[107] Larrington, 2006, p.150

[108] Kaliff, 2007, p.79-80, 89 Roman barrows sometimes had holes into which offerings to the dead could be inserted, just as the god Freyr's barrow was said to have had 'windows' for the same purpose (see Appendix 1). The physical presence of the mortal remains could tempt the soul to remain in Middle-earth, whereas cremation liberated it promptly for the jouney to the Otherworld.

[109] Lincoln, 1989

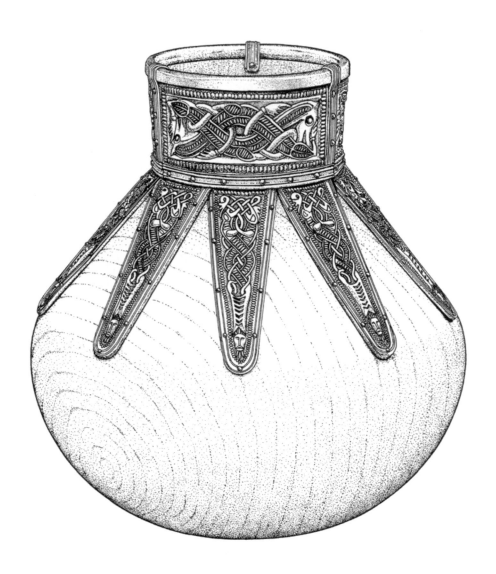

Wooden 'bottle' or serving vessel with gilded copper-alloy mounts.
From Sutton Hoo, Mound 1 (drawing by Lindsay Kerr)

Hoarded Gold

The *Exeter Book*, a miscellany of OE poetry, has a section usually called *Maxims II* – sententious statements concerning the way of the world and the appropriate behaviour of people in it. It says (line 26-7) *draca sceal on hlawe* 'a dragon shall be in a barrow', meaning that it is customary and right for a dragon to be in a burial mound. Why should this be? It would be easier to understand the statement if it referred to *lic* 'a corpse' or *mære þeoden* 'an illustrious leader'. Why would it be expected that a *draca* – a dragon, a firedrake – should inhabit the house of the dead? The answer lies in the next half-line, and the whole statement reads: *draca sceal on hlawe / frod frætwum wlanc* 'a dragon shall be in a barrow, old and proud with treasures'.[110]

Dragons in Germanic myth were associated closely with treasure and with burial mounds, and also with fire – as for example, when Finn asks his men at the opening of *Finnsburh*:[111]

> *..hornas byrnað næfre."*
> *Hleoþrode ða heaðo-geong cyning:*
> *"Ne ðis ne dagað eastan, ne her draca ne fleogað,*
> *ne her ðisse healle hornas ne byrnað...*
>
> *Finnesburh*, l.1-5

> ...the gables never burn.
> Then called out the battle-young king
> "It is not dawning in the east, nor does a dragon fly here
> nor are this hall's gables burning here..."

The dragon is associated here with two other gleaming signs in the sky: a blazing thatch and the rising sun.

---

[110] Irwin, 1982. A parallel tradition exists in India where anthills are revered as entrances to the underworld, and where it is believed a fire-breathing serpent resides guarding a hoard of treasure.

[111] Ellis Davidson, 1950, p.182

To delve into a barrow in search of the pot of gold which tradition insisted rested there was to risk arousing the dragon within, and to endanger the community.[112] This is clear in the tale of the 'Last Survivor' in *Beowulf* (l.2230-70) where the sole survivor of a defeated people reflects on the fate of his companions and their fine property:

> *Hyne se fær begeat*
> *sincfæt geseah. Þær wæs swylcra fela*
> *in ðm eorðhuse ærgestreona*
> *swa hy on geardagum gumena nathwylc*
> *eormenlafe æþelan cynnes*
> *þanchycgende þær gehydde*
> *deore maðmas. Ealle hie deað fornam*
> *ærran mælum, ond se an ða gen*
> *leoda duguðe, se ðær lengest hwearf,*
> *weard winegeomor, wende þæs ylcan,*
> *þæt he lytel fæc longgestreona*
> *brucan moste. Beorh eallgearo*
> *wunode on wonge wæteryðum neah,*
> *niwe be næsse, nearocræftum fæst.*
> *Þær on innan bær eorlgestreona*
> *hringa hyrde hordwyrðne dæl,*
> *fættan goldes, fea worda cwæð:*
> *"Heald þu nu, hruse, nu hæleð ne moston,*
> *eorla æhte! Hwæt, hyt ær on ðe*
> *gode begeaton. Guðdeað fornam,*
> *feorhbealo frecne, fyra gehwylcne*
> *leoda minra, þara ðe þis lif ofgeaf,*
> *gesawon seledream. Ic nah hwa sweord wege*
> *oððe feormie fæted wæge,*
> *dryncfæt deore; duguð ellor sceoc.*

---

[112] Ellis Davidson, 1950; Rauer 2000, shows that in Germanic tradition barrow-dwelling dragons were usually content to sleep on a bed of gold and were not considered dangerous unless provoked. The motif of a threatening dragon, attacking man and beast and laying waste the countryside, is drawn from Christian stories, usually culminating in a saint expelling the dragon with holy words of exorcism; rarely do saints physically fight dragons, with the main exceptions being George and Michael. The *Beowulf* tale seems to combine elements of both ideas: the king attacks the dragon due to its destructive raiding, but in the encounter he seems more concerned with winning the hoard for his people than with destroying the beast. Here the poet shows again his mastery of both Germanic and Christian traditions in his spinning of two separate strands of story into a single narrative.

Sceal se hearda helm hyrsted golde
fætum befeallen; feormynd swefað,
þa ðe beadogriman bywan sceoldon,
ge swylce seo herepad, sio æt hilde gebad
ofer borda gebræc bite irena,
brosnað æfter beorne. Ne mæg byrnan hring
æfter wigfruman wide feran,
hæleðum be healfe. Næs hearpan wyn,
gomen gleobeames, ne god hafoc
geond sæl swingeð, ne se swifta mearh
burhstede beateð. Bealocwealm hafað
fela feorhcynna forð onsended!"
Swa giomormod giohðo mænde
an æfter eallum, unbliðe hwearf
dæges ond nihtes, oððæt deaðes wylm
hran æt heortan.

…Danger befell him
he saw the jewelled treasure. There were many of such things
- ancient acquisitions - in the earth-dwelling
just as in olden days one of the warriors -
the great remnant of a noble kindred -
in mournful mood hid there
the precious treasures. Death took them all away
in former times, and then the only one
of the people's warband who stayed there longest -
a keeper sad for his friends - expected the same,
that for a short space the old treasures
he should enjoy. Fully ready the barrow
stood on the plain near the sea's waves,
new-built on the headland, safe in its skilful closure.
He bore inside the lordly treasure,
the keeper of the hoard-worthy part of the rings,
of golden vessels - he said a few words:
"Earth, hold thou now that heroes no longer can
the possessions of lords. Lo, before on thee
good men obtained it; war-death took them -
the greedy life-bane - each of the men
of my people, those who gave up this life,
they saw hall-joys. I have none who may wield a sword

or clean a sheathed vessel,[113]
a dear drinking-cup; the troop went elsewhere.
The hard helm adorned with gold
shall be shorn of its plates; the polishers sleep –
those who should make ready the battle-mask;
likewise the war-coat, which in strife awaited
the bite of iron over the breaking of shields
wastes away with the warrior; nor can the mailcoat's ring
follow widely after the war-maker,
at the side of the hero. There is no joy of the harp,
no game of the glee-beam, nor does a good hawk
swoop across a hall, nor does the swift steed
tread the courtyard. Baleful killing has
sent forth many of the race of men."
Thus in sorrowful mood he bemoaned his young companions,
alone out of them all, he sadly endured
by day and night until death's surge
touched at his heart.

The dragon who later inhabited the barrow took charge of the ancient treasure:

> ... *oððæt an ongan*
> *deorcum nihtum draca ricsian,*
> *se ðe on heaum hofe hord beweotode,*
> *stanbeorh steapne; stig under læg,*
> *eldum uncuð. Þær on innan giong*
> *niða nathwylc, se ðe neh gefeng*
> *hæðnum horde ....*

Beowulf, l.2210-6

> ...until a certain one began
> to rule on dark nights – a dragon,
> who warded the hoard in the high hall,
> the steep stone-mound; a path lay beneath it,
> unknown to men. Inside there went
> a certain wrongdoer who by chance took
> from the heathen hoard ...

---

[113] The *fæted wæge* is a cup or vessel with some form of outer casing. It is tempting to see in this terminology a reference to the sheet-metal plates decorated with embossed designs and plated in gold or silver, such as were found at Sutton Hoo, Taplow, Prittlewell and elsewhere.

The thief (*niða nathwylc*) who stole a cup from the hoard, after the dragon had taken possession of the mound and its contents, roused the *wyrm* to anger, and set in train a series of events which resulted in the death of the king and the destruction of the Geatish polity. The poem is quite clear that the dragon took possession of the barrow after the last survivor had died, but the evidence of the Norse Fafnir story rather suggests that it was the last survivor himself who became a dragon in the original tale.[114]

As an aside, we may note that the *stanbeorh* 'stone-hill' of the text is not necessarily a purpose-built barrow and may be a natural cave; a spring issues from its entrance, which supports this idea, but it is clearly conceived as a dwelling (*hof*) and a path leads to it. It is perhaps incorrect to try to tie the poetic image closely to physical reality and the poet may have had in mind a cleft in a hill without wishing to specify exactly what its origin might be.[115]

Welch has suggested that the phenomenon of grave-robbing, which was common in east Kent but rare elsewhere in Anglo-Saxon England, may represent an attempt by the family of the deceased to retrieve their valuables.[116] Having made a public show of sacrifice of material goods in the barrow, it might be tempting to quietly re-open the grave and rescue valuable items. While this this an appealing idea, it would suggest that the mourners had little respect for their ancestral dead - in which case the costly funeral would have been a mere piece of window-dressing. It is also unclear why this practice should have been confined to east Kent, unless this is due to Merovingian Frankish influence, since the practice of looting graves was common among them.

Treasure of any kind taken from a barrow was regarded as potentially cursed, and the wretched thief who stole the cup to compensate his master is not shown as malicious or malevolent, merely desperate; nevertheless, his selfish and thoughtless act brought disaster to his folk, but this was due to the nature of hoarded wealth.[117] This theme is not unique to Anglo-Saxon tradition: the Icelandic tale of Grettir also includes an incident where the

---

[114] Ellis Davidson, 1950, p.181 Fafnir only became a dragon once he had taken over a great treasure, and he then retired to a barrow to guard it. Already by 858 AD, the story was known of a Frankish bishop who dreamt that the tomb of Charles Martel was opened and a dragon rose up out of it. Probably the underlying notion is of a subterranean dragon guarding buried wealth, with overtones of the creature Níðhoggr in the *Völuspá* who inhabits the lowest and coldest regions of Hel.

[115] Rauer, 2000, p.140

[116] Welch, 2007, p.222-3

[117] Orchard, 1995, p.145-6

hero delves into a burial mound in search of treasures, and takes all he finds back to the house of Þorfinnr where he spreads out the treasures and his gaze falls upon a splendid knife. This weapon he uses in several fights, and it is the last thing Grettir gives up in his final fight with a *draugr*, a walking-dead. While Grettir certainly did win his weapon from the Otherworld, the dead claimed him in the end.

The *draca* represents the selfish, retentive side of heroic life, the inclination towards acquisition of wealth and its retention. Instead of sharing his gold as a good king should do, the dragon insists on keeping what he has. This is a rather negative image of the purpose of placing treasure in a burial mound, implying that the goods taken out of circulation are beyond the reach of men, or as the *Beowulf* poet says (l.3168) of the hoard Beowulf won for his people, that it was *eldum swa unnyt swa hyt æror wæs* 'as useless to men as it was before'.

Hollow Hills

The English folklore tradition of the 'hollow hill', where a king or famous person lies sleeping, is one possible remnant of the tradition of mound burial. Another is the 'fairy hills' where it was believed that cunning men could hear the music of the Otherworld at certain times of day, or enter into the realm of the "Good Folk".

Some of these hollow hills were believed to be the repositories of great treasure, and Harte cites several examples of such lore:[118] for example "in 1621 two speculators turned up in Dorchester, 'to dig in a hill at Upway … for some treasure that lies hidden underground', but three days' labour turned up 'nothing but a few bones'."

The folklore motif of the mound as a burial chamber is commonly found throughout Europe, and aroused considerable interest among early antiquaries who thought that such tales might represent distant, garbled memories of the building and use of the mounds as repositories for the souls of the ancestral dead. The story motif is applied randomly to genuine barrows, to disused defensive earthworks and to natural features, which undermines somewhat the reliability of local tradition. In fact, very few of the 'hollow hill' or 'fairy hill' legends are actually attached to genuine tumuli and we must suspect that the concept of the 'hollow hill' gained currency at some point (perhaps in the later mediaeval period) and was then transferred by the storytellers to whatever suitable local feature presented itself. Furthermore, some of these 'local' traditions appear first in the pamphlets of 17th c. writers who simply collected

---

[118] Harte 1997 citing Grinsell 1959

quaint folktales from all kinds of sources, included printed books, and recorded them as if they were local traditional knowledge.

Few mounds in the British Isles can ever have been large enough for a man to enter easily, as often happens in stories where a traveller is attracted by a light and finds in the side of the mound an open door through which he passes. Maes Howe on Orkney is probably the only such tomb to have been open in mediaeval times, as we know from the 12th c. Norse runic graffiti inside, which was large enough to accommodate more than one or two travellers. One of the runic texts records that the barrow had been robbed of its great treasure previously by one Hákon.

Weapons, vessels and other metalwork could be credited with supernatural origins if taken from a barrow: when the *Beowulf* poet describes the removal of the defeated dragon's treasure, he ascribes its making to giants:[119]

> *Ða ic on hlæwe gefrægn hord reafian,*
> *eald enta geweorc ...*
>
> *Beowulf* l.2773–4

Then I heard of the robbing from the barrow of the hoard,
the old works of giants ...

A Norse tale of barrow-entry is known in English as *The Waking of Angantyr*; it is found in the Icelandic *Hervarar Saga*. The story concerns Hervor, a determined shield-maiden, who visits her father's barrow in order to communicate with his ghost and secure possession of the sword *Tyrfing*. Her father is very reluctant to fulfil her wish since the sword bears a curse and he foresees that possession of it will bring doom to her family, but she insists and states her intention to destroy herself in the flames which surround the barrow rather than relent. Angantyr hands her the sword rather than see his daughter perish, but cautions her against using the weapon.

In the mediaeval poem *Sir Gawain and the Green Knight*, which seems to have a strongly legendary (not to say 'mythical') background, the eponymous hero is on his way to meet his challenger at the appointed spot, the Green Chapel, but he cannot find any such place:

---

[119] Pollington, 2000, p.485-6. It might be thought that the 'work of giants' refers rather to the chamber than to the treasure: giants are associated wirh large engineering projects, while treasure is more often the work of dwarves or Welund. However, the grammar here shows that *geweorc* is acc.sing. and in apposition to *hord*, not to *hlawe* which is dat. sing.

save a lyttel on a launde, a law as it were,
A balw berw bi a bonke the brymme bysyde

Hit hade a hole on the end and on ayther syde,
And overgrowen with gresse in glodes aywhere;
And al was holw inwith, nobot an olde cave

'but a little further on the heath there was a low, as it might be
a bare barrow by a bank beside the brook

It had a hole at the end and on either side,
and it was overgrown with grass in clumps everywhere;
and all was hollow inside, it was no more than an old cave'.

Sir Gawain and the Green Knight, l.2171—2182

All the features are here which indicate a tumulus, as which the poet clearly intended it to be construed when he called it a '*law*' that is to say a 'low' (OE *hlæw*). The notion of a grassy knoll pitted with holes alerted the audience to the presence of an entrance to the supernatural realm. Here we may recall the fate of St Guthlac, who made his dwelling in the cave in such a mound and was attacked by the spirits of the place, who screamed at him in Welsh.[120]

Perhaps an Icelandic parallel might bring a new light to the problem. The holy mountain of *Helgafell* was regarded as an entrance to the Otherworld, a sacred place which men turned to in adversity. It was believed that when the men of the district died, they would enter the hill and carry on a form of afterlife within. In *Eyrbyggja Saga* a shepherd sees the mountainside standing open like an open door and the ancestors all within enjoying a feast.[121]

In Scandinavia, the barrow was a place on which kings and chieftains would sit in order to gain insight and inspiration, as well as being the site for gatherings, for investitures and for formal announcements.[122] Barrows such as those at Old Uppsala had a flattened top which could act as a platform for public display. Seers would sometimes sleep on the top of the mound in order to have prophetic dreams, and the implication appears to be that the barrow's occupant would come to the sleeping man and communicate with him through dreams.

---

[120] Ellis Davidson, 1950, p.176-7 ; Shook, 1960

[121] Ellis Davidson, 1988, p.13-4

[122] Ellis Davidson, 1988, p.19, 131

Snorri Sturluson relates in *Ynglingasaga* that the god Freyr was so beloved of the Swedes that when he died they did not want to discontinue worship of him, so they kept him in a barrow and provided windows into it so that men could continue to make offerings, which the god accepted, and he would send helpful dreams and omens to his followers.[123] (See Appendix 1.) From this deception, the practice of mound burial was adopted and the tradition of cremation was broken.

It is difficult to resist the idea that barrow-burial was above all a celebration of a single and unusual life, and that the erection of a permanent and visible monument was only worthwhile because the occupant was held to be in some way still present – perhaps still accessible – in the mound.[124]

---

[123] Ellis Davidson, 1988, p.33, 116

[124] Meaney, 1964, p.18-9

Taplow Burial Chamber
see information page 170

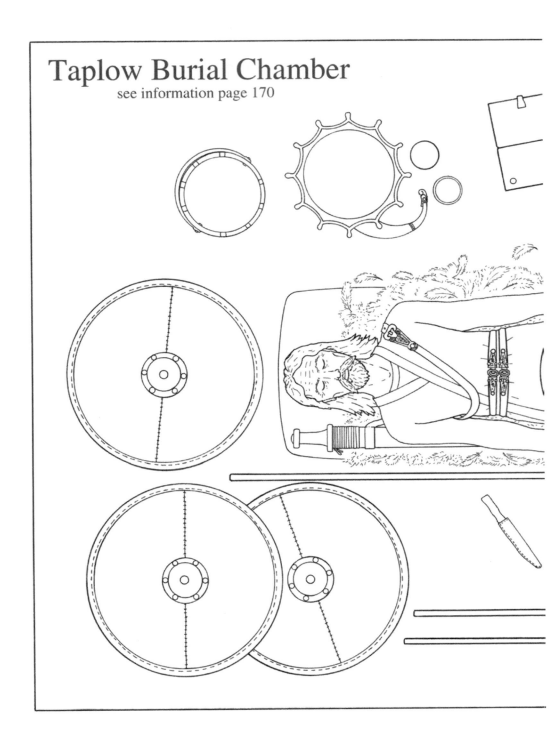

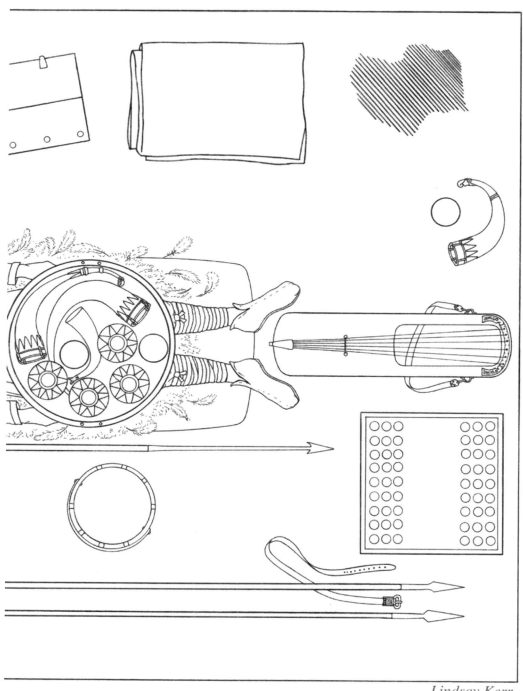

Lindsay Kerr

Bronze Coptic bowl from the burial mound at Taplow

5. Decline

*The Saxons did not value human life as highly as their
predecessors, and made little fuss of burial except of their
chieftains. Most of the men were buried with iron knives, and
most of the women with beautiful and sometimes costly disc-
brooches. The Saxon chief Taeppa was buried in his hlaew or
barrow at Taplow with a plentiful supply of glass drinking
horns and a large bucket which may have contained the wine.
If he arrived at the netherworld sober it was a wonder.*

Grinsell, *The Ancient Burial-Mounds of England*

Grinsell's slightly jaundiced view of Anglo-Saxon funerary practice was
probably unremarkable when he wrote in 1936 but we have learnt a lot since
his day about the burials of chiefs and followers, high-born ladies and low-
born maids.[125]

The Theatre of Death

The purpose of such pronounced monuments as solitary barrows in high
places was partly commemorative for the dead man or woman within, but no
less was it a statement of wealth, power and authority for the kindred who
were able to use the permanence and bulk of the barrow as a means of
staking claims to legitimacy for their rule. The funerary customs were an
idealised presentation of the social structure, and the implicit message was
that the leading kindred was authorised to retain power through such displays
of confidence and claims to permanence.[126]

The grouping of high-status sites along busy waterways, which allowed them
to be seen from afar, can be no accident, e.g. Taplow (Buckinghamshire) and
Orsett (Essex) above the Thames, Broomfield and Prittlewell in Essex on the
rivers Crouch and Thames, and the Suffolk sites at Snape, Sutton Hoo and
Bloodmoor Hill.[127] Evidently a permanent and highly visible presence in the
landscape, and in the traditions of the people who saw the mound, was the

---

[125] Grinsell, 1936, p.36-7

[126] Parker Pearson, 1999, p.23, 75

[127] Bruce-Mitford, 1974, 1978, Ch.V; Hedges & Buckley, 1985; Halsall, 1995, p.32-3;
Newman, 1996; Filmer-Sankey & Pestell, 2001; Carver, 2005, p.283-4; Dickens,
Mortimer & Tipper, 2006..

desired effect. This tradition was remembered in the poem *Beowulf* where the dying king asks that his burial should be well-known and visible:

> *...Cwico wæs þa gena,*
> *wis ond gewittig; worn eall gespræc*
> *gomol on gehðo ond eowic gretan het,*
> *bæd þæt ge geworhton æfter wines dædum*
> *in bælstede beorh þone hean,*
> *micelne ond mærne, swa he manna wæs*
> *wigend weorðfullost wide geond eorðan,*
> *þenden he burhwelan brucan moste.*
>
> Beowulf, l.3094-100

....He was then alive
wise and aware – he spoke much
being old in cares – and sent greetings to you,
bade that for your friend's deeds you should make
a high barrow in the balefire's place,
a great and famed one, for he was among men
widely across the earth the most honourable of warriors
while he was able to enjoy the stronghold's wealth.

> *Geworhton ða Wedra leode*
> *hleo on hoe, se wæs heah ond brad,*
> *wæglidendum wide gesyne,*
>
> Beowulf, l.3156-8

Then the Weders' nobles made
a barrow on a spur of land, it was high and broad,
widely seen by seafarers

Most barrows appear to have been special burials within established cemeteries, and in some cases they are the foundation grave for the cemetery which spreads out from the base of the mound. Solitary barrows in high places are a feature of only certain regions: parts of England and Bavaria, for example.[128]

Single person graves, whether of inhumation or cremation, were essentially individual statements and served to divorce the occupant from his community and his kindred. In a sense, this rite of separation may lie behind the OE word

---

128 Effros, 2003, p.199; Carver, 2000, p.134

hel meaning 'hell', originally 'grave, place where one is hidden'.[129] It was not a place of punishment by torture for past wrongdoing, in the manner of the Christian concept, but rather a cold, dark room where one could not take part in the ongoing life of the kindred. To some Anglo-Saxons, the dank and cheerless burial chamber up on the lonely hill may have seemed the last place they would want to spend eternity.

The impetus to divorce the leading families from the communities they led, which gave rise to these high-status burials in the later 6th c., did not recede but did change direction with the arrival of Christianity.[130] From the early 7th c. it became possible for the wealthy to show off their distinction by endowing a church and by being buried inside it. This was not a new idea, since the Merovingian royal family had been burying its illustrious dead in the cellar of the cathedral of St. Denis since the 5th c. at least.[131] What was new was the idea that this facility could now be available to Anglo-Saxon rulers and their kin.

At Sutton Hoo and a few other sites, we see a new order being established and rooting itself firmly in the landscape; based on Scandinavian rather than Frankish models, it was seeking, as Carver puts it, to "achieve kingship without Christianity, enacting an extravagant series of Scandinavian-style burials in order to oppose the imperialism of the Christian Franks, proclaiming the rhetoric of independence and individual enterprise in a 'theatre of death'."[132]

Church Burial

Chamber burial was apparently not prohibited for Christians, and high-status persons were buried under this rite down to the middle of the 7th c. in England, at least two generations after the coming of the new faith and during the process of conversion. The burial at Swallowcliffe Down may be from the late 7th c., by which time Christianity had been adopted by all Anglo-Saxon kingdoms and the process of missionary work among the Continental Frisians and Saxons had begun.

However, with the arrival of Christian ecclesiastical authority came the erection of churches, and the Frankish custom of burying the illustrious dead within or beneath the church's walls. This custom eventually superseded the chamber burial tradition, because it tied the families of high-status to the church and it marked a clear distinction between the high-born and the rest of society. As

---

[129] Augustyn, 2002, p.28-30

[130] Carver, 2002, p.132-3

[131] Fleury & France-Lanord, 1998

[132] van der Noort, 1993; Carver, 2002, p.133

Anglo-Saxon society became more successful and rigidly stratified, the old idea of chamber burial became less attractive to those with access to wealth. It is hardly to be doubted that the ecclesiastical establishment promoted the idea of building a church to be buried in: this policy could only bring the new faith to the countryside and increase its support.

Burials near barrows continued throughout the 7th c. and in some places into the 8th so that a review of dating evidence from known sites might provide many more examples.[133] Around 900 AD there was a brief revival in the practice of barrow-burial in northern and eastern England, and it is tempting to link this resurgence to the influence of Scandinavian settlers. The graves were accompanied inhumations, and the grave-goods were all masculine gendered – mainly weapons, but some items connected with production and commerce.[134] Indeed, when church and churchyard burial were re-imposed, a new class of monument appeared: the churchyard cross with overt masculine symbolism, usually a carving of a warrior or a hunting scene.

A Landscape of Terror

In the Middle Saxon Period, the ideas surrounding appropriate burial rites were changing. This must have been influenced by the change in religious climate, although that may not be the entire explanation.[135] Certainly, Christian ideas concerning the rejection of amulets and the like were not adopted for many years, perhaps centuries, and it is notable that early monastic cemeteries often contain graves with inclusions such as pillowstones. While the church did not forbid the provision of grave-goods, neither did it approve of reverence for the dead – other than the approved, saintly dead whose relics contained considerable beneficial power.

The *OE Herbarium*, MS. V has an entry for a plant called 'lithewort':[136]

> *Ðeos wyrt þe man ostriago & oðrum naman lyðwyrt nemneð bið cenned abutan byrgenne & on beorgum & on wagum þæra husa þe wið duna standað*

> This plant which one calls 'ostriago' and by another name 'lithewort' is produced around a burial mound and in mountains and on the walls of houses that stand across the downs.

---

[133] Hadley, 2004, p.306

[134] Hadley, 2004, p.314

[135] Geake, 1992, p.89; Semple, 1998

[136] Pollington, 2000, p.137

The plant has not been successfully identified, but possibilities are dwarf elder, wayfaring tree or goat's rue. The text implies that the plant is 'produced' (*cenned*, usually 'born') around barrows, without human agency or cultivation, perhaps pointing to a self-sown, prolific or stubborn genus. A similar description is given for mugwort, and *lyðwyrt* may be a by-name for that plant.

In Christian times, the sites of heathen graves gained a new importance as unconsecrated ground. Barrows were designated as *cwealmstowa*, places of legal execution, and there are many examples of Middle Saxon burials around and between such mounds; presumably the punishment extended to the afterlife where the soul would be attacked by the mound's inhabitant.[137] This was the fate which befell St. Guthlac when he built his hermit's retreat in the side of a burial mound: he was beset by harmful spirits.[138] A passage from Ælfric includes the following admonition concerning witches and burial mounds:[139]

In this connection it is pertinent to recall the entry from the *Lacnunga* manuscript, usually viewed as an example of a verse charm of pre-Christian origin:[140]

135. Hlude wæron hy la hlude ða hy ofer þone hlæw ridan / wæran anmode ða hy ofer land ridan. / Scyld ðu ðe nu þu ðysne nið genesan mote / Ut lytel spere gif her inne sie. / Stod under linde under leohtum scylde / þær ða mihtigan wif hyra mægen beræddon / & hy gyllende garas sændan / ic him oðerne eft wille sændan / fleogende flanae forane togeanes. / Ut lytel spere gif hit herinne sy. / Sæt smið sloh seax / lytel iserna wund swiðe / Ut lytel spsre gif herinne sy. / Syx smiðas sætan wælspera worhtan / Ut ut spere, næs in spere. / Gif herinne sy isenes dæl / hægtessan geweorc hit sceal gemyltan / guf ðu wære on fell scoten, oððe wære on flæsc scoten / oððe wære on blod scoten [oððe wære on ban scoten][141] */ oððe wære on lið scoten næfre ne sy ðin lif atæsed / gif hit wære esa gescot, oððe hit wære ylfa gescot / oððe hit wære hægtessan gescot nu ic wille ðin helpan: / þis ðe to boter esa gescotes, ðis ðe to bote ylfa gescotes / ðis ðe to bote hægtessan gescotes, ic ðin wille helpan. / Fleah þær on fyrgenholt, fyrst ne hæfde / hal westu nu, helpe ðin drihten. / Nim þonne þæt seax, ado on wætan.*

---

[137] Grinsell, 1991, p.51 "Heathen burials" were sometimes cited in charter bounds as the points from which estates could be measured; Geake, 1992, p.88-9; Semple, 1998; Carver, 2002, p.133; Carver, 2005, ch.9 details the 8th to 11th c. burials around the mounds at Sutton Hoo.

[138] Ellis Davidson, 1950, p.176-7; Williams, 2006a, p.204-7

[139] Pollington, 2000, p.53

[140] Text and translation from Pollington, 2000; see also Price, 2003, p.353-4; Hall, 2007, p.2

[141] This phrase is not in the original text and was supplied by Jacob Grimm to complete both the verse line and the formula; it is a merism of a standard kind in magical charms.

135 "Loud were they, lo! loud as they rode over the barrow / they were determined as they rode over the land. / Shield yourself now, so you may escape this attack. / Out, little spear, if it be in here. / [I] stood under linden, under a light shield / where the mighty women declared their might / and yelling they sent spears. / Back to them I wish to send another / a flying dart in opposition. / Out little spear, if it be in here. / A smith sat, hammered a knife / a small weapon, a serious wound. / Out, little spear, if it be in here. / Six smiths sat, wrought slaughter-spears. / Out, spear, be not in, spear. / If there be in here a piece of iron, / the work of witches, it must melt away. / If you were shot in the skin, or you were shot in the flesh / or were shot in the blood, [or were shot in the bone] / or were shot in the limb, may your life never be threatened, / if it were the gods'142 shot, or it were the elves' shot, / or it were the witches' shot, I will now help you. / This as a cure to you for the gods' shot, this as a cure to you for the elves' shot, / this as a cure to you for the witches' shot, I wish to help you. / There it fled to the mountain [wood, no rest] did have. / Whole be you [now], may the Lord help you." Then take [out] the knife, put it into the liquid.

Semple also adduces the Franks Casket text here, where "Here Hos sits on the mound of sorrow" and the accompanying image of a winged creature with a long neck perched on top of a shallow semicircle.[143] This is discussed in Appendix 4.

---

[142] The OE *esa* is presumed to be the genitive plural of the element *os* found in personal names (e.g. *Oshere* on the Coppergate helmet) and in the *OE Rune Poem*. The word *os* is generally held to signify a pre-Christian god (from Germanic **ansuz*). While the phonological correspondence is not exact, the balance of probabilities favours this identification in a context where witches (*hægtessan*) and elves (*ylfe*) are also invoked. The similarity between this charm's use of flesh, blood, bone and the *Second Mersburg Charm* is not coincidental.

[143] Semple, 1998, p.122

6. Later History

"I was born in lands now ruled by the Huns. I do not even know who tills the soil that holds my father's bones, and no one knows where those of my grandfather lie. But when my time comes, my grandsons will pour out the offerings on my howe. That is how a land is claimed, by giving it our blood and our bones!"

Diana L. Paxson, *The Lord of Horses*

At a certain point at the end of the 6th c. the long-recognised but never common practice of mound and chamber burial was adopted as the preferred funerary rite of the Germanic élite across northern and western Europe. The phenomenon was not confined to rich leaders and warriors, but could include important, valued or dominant females. Evidently a network of political contacts and alliances was at work, creating the conditions which would spark off interest in this highly theatrical form of interment. It spread to Scandinavia, or perhaps its adoption in Europe encouraged revival of an existing custom there. However that may be, the Scandinavian promotion of the chamber burial proved decisive for its later history.

The level of internal conformity among these burials is remarkable, even down to certain specifics such as weapon- and vessel-types. Links between the Sutton Hoo and Prittlewell cemeteries are evidenced by the presence of spears of Swanton's groups D2 and E3 in both Mound 1 and the East Saxon warrior burials excavated in 1923. Furthermore, details such as the presence of an iron pedestal lamp and a baptismal spoon in each of the chamber burials (Mound 1 and Prittlewell) also suggest that a common tradition was being followed. Indeed, Prittlewell and Taplow are the closest matches in overall wealth and in grave-goods to the Mound 1 discovery.

As table next page shows, there was a clear if never encyclopaedic ideal grave assemblage for males and females to which the various actual examples approximate, to varying degrees. For example, the presence of a gold belt buckle seems to have been desirable (Mound 1, Mound 17, Prittlewell, Taplow) and gold items were generally important in the display. Presumably, the mourners wanted to show off access to gold and if the middle-income mourners had a suitable item, they were inclined to use it.

	S Hoo Mound 1	S Hoo Mound 2 (robbed)	S Hoo Mound 5 (robbed)	S Hoo Mound 17	Taplow	Prittlewell	Broomfield	Snape	Saltwood (3 barrows)	Lowbury Hill	Benty Grange	Asthall	Caenby (robbed)	Cuddesdon (robbed)	S Hoo Mound 14 (robbed)	Bloodmoor Hill	Shudy Camps (29)	Swallowcliffe Down
Gender	m	m	m	m	m	m	m	m	m	m	m	m?			f	f?	f?	f
Chamber Burial	X	X			X	X	X	X	X					?	X			X
Personal Adornment																		
gold belt buckle	X			X	X	X												
gold coins	X					X				X							X	
other gold items	X	X			X	X	X	X									X	X
other garment fittings										X					X		X	
comb	X			X						X								X
Style II decoration	X	X		X	X	X	X				X	X			X			X
Feasting																		
feasting vessels	X	X			X	X	X		X	X	X	X						X
drinking horns	X	X			X	X	X				?							
metal-rimmed cups	X	X			X	X	X				X	X			X			
squat blue glass jars		X			X	X	X	?						X				
glass claw beaker					X			X										
Coptic bronze vessels	X				X	X			X			X			X			
suspension chain	X						?				X							
Entertainment																		
harp	X				X	X								?				
gaming pieces	X				X	X			X			X						
Military																		
sword & other weapons	X	X		X	X	X	X	X	X	X					X			
helmet	X										X		?					
Grave																		
iron lamp	X					X	X			X								
ceramics	X					X	X				X							
textiles	X	X			X	X	X	X			X							X
adjacent burials	X	X		X		X		X	?	X				X		X	X	?
horse harness		X							X									

Characteristics of Princely Burials in 6th & 7th century England

It is perhaps significant that so few actual chamber burials have been found in Kent, which was certainly the wealthiest Anglo-Saxon kingdom for a large part of the 6th c. and into the early 7th. The techniques of barrow construction were evidently understood, as there are many examples of small barrows over single graves in the kingdom. If restricted access to the materials needed for the burial and the lack of technical knowledge were not the cause of this scarcity – and we must presume that they were not – then the reason for the rarity of this type of burial must lie elsewhere. It is probably in the realms of ideology and religion that the answer will be found. The Kentish model was, from the early 6th c. onwards, always Frankish – the Kentish court was tied to the Merovingian Frankish royal family through marriage and through enmeshed cross-Channel trade links upon which the kingdom's wealth was founded. The Franks had certainly known and practised chamber burial in the 5th c., but it does appear that this form of interment was superseded by church (i.e. intramural) and churchyard burial by the 6th c. If so, then the reaction of the court at Canterbury would have been to follow suit, since Kent's wealth depended on the favour of the Merovingian court. In Kent, therefore, chamber burial may not have been widely adopted as an élite funerary rite, and the small numbers of examples known may be due to early abandonment of the practice before it could become established.

Obvious Targets

> The tendency of Anglo-Saxon barrows to be eroded to the point of invisibility is well illustrated by the fate of the boat-barrow at Snape in Suffolk ... and the smaller barrows at Finglesham in Kent ... while their normal lack of ditches could render them invisible to aerial photography. So at almost any time during rescue excavation ... a royal burial might just turn up.
>
> Sonia Chadwick Hawkes, *The Early Saxon Period*

How true these words would prove when, in the course of rescue excavations prior to road-widening to the north of Southend-on-Sea, the most spectacular find of the twenty-first century so far was made – the Prittlewell chamber grave. The point is well made though: Anglo-Saxon mounds generally have no large stone components which would show up using remote-sensing equipment, no large ring-ditch which might show up as a parch-mark, no lasting footprint in the landscape at all beyond the mound of earth.

Barrows were once a familiar sight in the English countryside, and seem to have attracted grave-robbers and treasure-hunters from early times: indeed, the Anglo-Saxon re-use of Bronze Age monuments could itself be construed as an attempt to despoil the original burial and to capture the power and significance of those landscape features. The plundering of the mounds at sites such as Sutton Hoo is very regrettable due to the vast amount of information which could have been extracted by careful excavation in modern times.[144] Aside from the deliberate damage done by mound-diggers and treasure-hunters, many have been destroyed or damaged by modern agricultural techniques.

Thomas Bateman, the Victorian antiquary, is known to have opened scores of gravemounds in his career, perhaps as many as 200, and assisted with as many again. While we may deplore his cavalier attitude to the subject, we do at least have his records to assist us, in the form of his book *Ten Years' Diggings in Celtic and Saxon Grave-hills* published in 1861, and we may take some small solace from the fact that many – perhaps most – of the mounds that Bateman dug had already been opened. Therefore his terse records can at least demonstrate whether a mound was intact or not when he decided to dig it. Bateman's attention was focussed mainly on the mounds of the Peak District. He did not work alone but seems to have been accompanied by friends, including fellow antiquary Charles Roach Smith and Reverend Stephen Isaacson; it was the latter who assisted on the 1845 digging season in which 37 barrows were opened in Derbyshire and North Staffordshire.

The quest for buried treasure was strong, long before tales of pirates' gold were common: the mediaeval Icelandic saga of Grettir the Strong relates how the hero opened an ancestral mound to retrieve a famous sword for his own use. Such treasures were not always benevolent, however: the motif of wealth which brings with it a powerful curse lies behind the story of Regin and Fafnir and Sigurðr Fafnisbani, and leads to the Wagnerian *Ring of the Nibelungs* operatic cycle. Treasure from the earth might be feared as much as it was coveted. If so, then the finder may have wished to be rid of it. It is possible that a lavish gold disc-brooch found in Woodbridge (Suffolk, near Sutton Hoo) may have originally belonged in one of the Sutton Hoo barrows, nearly all of which were robbed: it is of the standard Kentish type, but has mushroom-shaped cloisons which are not usually found outside East Anglia, and they tie the item to the royal workshop which furnished the Sutton Hoo barrows.[145] The brooch is in a

---

[144] Carver, 2005; the copious information retrieved from the undisturbed burials in Mound 17 should be contrasted with that from the robbed mounds.

[145] Bruce-Mitford, 1974, p.262-6 Other examples of this type have been found in Kent, and demonstrate the ties which bound East Anglia and Kent together in the late 6th c. There was a barrow burial in Woodbridge itself, although next to nothing is known of it, and its contents – a male buried with a spear – do not suggest the kind of wealth associated with such a treasure (p.159).

sorry state, having had the stones gouged out of the settings and the front plate removed from the rear. It was found by a ploughman who began breaking it up in preparation for melting down, but the circumstances of its finding are not recorded. Could it have been taken from one of the mounds, then hidden again for fear of its deadly power? The history of the Sutton Hoo site is littered with pillaging forays by treasure-hunters, gentlemen antiquaries, naval engineers and opportunistic modern thieves. That so much material survived their attention is little short of miraculous.

Some Investigators

Fausset, Douglas and Roach Smith

Bryan Faussett was born in 1720 at Heppington (Kent).[146] As a child, he narrowly escaped death when the family's pet monkey threw him on the fire. He graduated from Oxford in 1745 and became a Fellow of All Souls College; he was interested in Latin literature, ancient history, antiquities and anatomy – then a novel subject which was just becoming acceptable for study. It may have been the fascination with anatomy which spurred Faussett to take up the investigation of graves. This anatomical knowledge enabled him to describe the position of bodies within graves with great accuracy, and to assign age and sex to skeletons on the basis of dimensions and wear. He was ordained in 1746 and married in 1748; in 1750 his father died, allowing him to return to Kent to care for his widowed mother, and so to inherit the whole family estate on her death in 1761. He had few clerical duties and ample leisure time in which to indulge his interests, although he lacked congenial neighbours with whom to share his passion and consequently corresponded at length with like-minded persons in London.

In 1759, he was visiting Ash (Kent) when he noticed that sand extraction had partially destroyed some graves, which he proceeded to investigate; initially, he had not shown any interest until the local miller's servant had pointed out to him that a small projection from the quarry side, which he had taken for a root, was in fact the end of a spearhead. The servant and his mate opened the grave in front of Faussett, but in so doing managed to destroy most of the contents; this revelation set him on the path to devising better and less destructive means of opening graves so that the contents could be examined. This chance discovery was to provide him with a life-long interest in the practice of excavation, as well as a large quantity of artefacts from the largely unregarded graves and barrows of the local area.

---

[146] Laing & Laing, 1979; Hawkes, 1990; Rhodes, 1990

Faussett's son, Henry, had accompanied his father on many digs and had disinterred the famous Kingston brooch. Henry was to prove very helpful in preparing neat, detailed illustrations for Faussett's work, the *Inventorium Sepulchrale*, which provided a full catalogue of the objects he discovered, including their original resting places. Henry subsequently entered the legal profession, but maintained links with the nascent study of archaeology through his friendship with Captain James Douglas, who in 1793 (after Faussett's death) published the monumental work *Nenia Britannica*, a catalogue of finds which also recorded details of the graves and mounds from which they had been taken. Douglas's work was an important step forward, in that the author took pains to establish a reliable system of description and cataloguing the finds, so that new examples could be related to existing ones; it also established the principle of working from objects of known provenance and date to those for which these data were unknown – establishing relative chronologies and typologies, in effect.

James Douglass was born in January 1753 in Mayfair, London;[147] his father, John, was the innkeeper of the *Hercules Pillars* in Hyde Park. The young James was put to work in the booming cotton trade in Manchester but was not successful in this enterprise. He later travelled throughout Europe due to his interest in classics, geology and 'antiquity' – what would later become the field of archaeology. He had a keen military mind and was an expert in tactics and field fortifications, and accepted a commission in the Austrian army. He later became an early member of the Corps of Royal Engineers and took up a post at Chatham (Kent) where he was able to develop his antiquarian leanings in the company of men such as Faussett.

Douglas worked partly from his own observations and partly from the collections of other antiquaries; although he was anxious to gain access to Faussett's collection, Henry was reluctant to allow this and would not make his father's notebooks available. Douglas had become interested in techniques of excavation through his work as a naval engineer at Chatham, which had involved the destruction of many Anglo-Saxon graves; he collected as much information as possible about the grave and its content, and noted it all down. Douglas was one of the first antiquaries to recognise that the artefacts were Kentish and not Roman in origin; this idea was not widely accepted in his own time, as antiquarians generally consulted classical works for their historical narratives and were loath to assign any items of splendid workmanship to uncouth barbarians. Faussett did not live long enough to discover that the

---

[147] Jessup, 1975

magnificent finds he had made were not, as he believed, Roman, but rather were the products of Anglo-Saxon workmanship.

Faussett's will, drawn up in 1769, provided that all his sermons should be destroyed, and that his collection of antiquities should be preserved intact in the hope that generations to come might profit from studying it. He died in 1776 and was buried in the church at Nackington (Kent) where his body still lies beneath an inscribed memorial stone.

Faussett was important not only for the work he did in opening Kentish barrows and recording their contents: he was himself a collector of antiquities and the Fausett Collection – his artefacts and papers – was recognised on his death as an important asset for the understanding of the early past in England. However, rivalries among scholars and the need for patronage were to play a decisive part in the collection's history. The Faussett Collection was offered to the British Museum, but the sum of money requested was considered too large by the trustees – and the Museum's priorities were not directed towards British antiquities in any case; the board of trustees comprised mostly persons who had been appointed due to holding some other high office (the Speaker of the House of Commons, Archbishop of Canterbury, First Lord of the Admiralty, amongst others) and none had any interest in the day-to-day affairs of the Museum, which were therefore effectively run by a small clique of wealthy socialites whose main interest was collecting Greek antiquities. A generous benefactor, Joseph Mayer, offered to buy the collection outright, pay for its publication and present it to the Museum. The plan came to nothing due to the antipathy between Edward Hawkins of the British Museum and Charles Roach Smith, who had been appointed to the task of publication; Hawkins refused to allow Smith access to the documents, and this arrogance impelled Mayer to withdraw his offer. Mayer subsequently bought most of the Collection, apart from the coins and seals which were sold separately at auction. The Museum's handling of the affair was clumsy and high-handed, and dissuaded other collectors from offering it their materials. The Faussett Collection finally came to rest in Mayer's home city of Liverpool in 1867.

Bateman

Thomas Bateman was born in Rowsley (Derbyshire) in 1821, the son of a clergyman and amateur antiquary; his mother had died before his first birthday. Having inherited a fine library from his father, Bateman cultivated contacts in the worlds of historical investigation. He developed a friendship with Charles Roach Smith, and began his excavations with William Parker, who became his bailiff and eventually his brother-in-law. (Bateman had a long-term love affair with a Bakewell girl, Mary Mason, the wife of a boatman; Bateman's grandfather, on whom he was financially dependant, strongly disapproved and the relationship ended in 1847; the marriage to Parker's sister safeguarded his financial position and the future of his research projects.)

With Roach Smith's encouragement, Bateman was one of the early members of the new society founded for the study of antiquity, the British Archaeological Association. He took part in a demonstration of the appropriate methods of opening a barrow and conserving its contents at Canterbury in 1844 and on his return to Derbyshire set about opening every tumulus he could identify in the Peak District. He amassed a splendid collection of archaeological and geological finds from these activities and had a fine private museum in his purpose-built mansion, Lomberdale House, near Middleton (Yorkshire). The peak of his barrow-digging took place in 1845, accompanied by Rev. Stephen Isaacson. The pair were able to travel the northern counties to be on hand when antiquities were unearthed in the construction of the railways. Subsequently, Bateman appointed intermediaries to carry out the excavations and to report their findings to him along with any significant remains: Samuel Carrington in north Staffordshire and James Ruddock in the Vale of Pickering were two such agents.

In his later years, Bateman's interest in history declined, perhaps because he had exhausted all the obvious targets in his area. He endowed a small religious foundation and settled down to the task of running his estates and the care of his five children. His health, which had never been robust, also began to fail. He died in his bed in August 1861 at the age of 39.

On his death, the collection was split up for sale and Sheffield Musuem acquired the archaeological material, where it formed the nucleus of the city's collection. Among the more important finds thus acquired was the Benty Grange helmet.

Lethbridge

Thomas Charles Lethbridge was born in 1901 into a well-to-do West Country family with its fair share of churchmen, lawyers and even an eccentric explorer who set off to find the source of the Nile. Lethbridge went to Cambridge University to study classics, but his imagination was fired by archaeology and landscape history, especially by the more romantic stories of local folklore, by maritime exploration and mythology. Eventually, he became Keeper of Anglo-Saxon Antiquities at Cambridge Archaeological Museum, although his substantial private income allowed him to roam widely in developing his other interests. He published many serious academic papers and site reports, including that for the important Anglo-Saxon site of

Shudy Camps (Cambridge). He also wrote several books about seafaring, and about his own marine journeys, including a trip to Iceland and several voyages into the Arctic regions.

At some point, his creative and artistic leanings superseded his academic training. He suggested, in his book *Merlin's Island* (1948), that pre-Roman British explorers had visited not only Ireland and Atlantic Europe but also Iceland, Greenland and North America, and that the documented Viking seafarers had followed in the wake of the British pioneers. He backed this claim up with attempts to find parallels in the culture of Iron Age Britain and the Inuit of Greenland. *Herdsmen and Hermits* (1950) continued this theme, but drew in another subject which would fire his imagination: witchcraft. *Boats and Boatmen* (1952) developed the theme of superstitions among those who regularly journey on the sea, including launching ceremonies and the appeasement of hostile gods. In 1954, *The Painted Men* was published, dealing with the perennial problems of the Picts; it was the last conventional history book from his pen. In *Gogmagog – the Buried Gods* (1957), Lethbridge was on a road less travelled: chalk hill figures in the Cambridgeshire countryside, which he linked to tales of an ancient cult known to history as the witches' coven; these ideas paralleled those of his contemporary, Margaret Murray, although there is no evidence that the pair collaborated in any way. After his retirement in 1961 he wrote a number of books on unorthodox aspects of archaeological research, including dowsing, paranormal research, psychic questing, extra-sensory perception and legends of divine beings who stepped in to tweak humanity's course down the evolutionary path. Lethbridge died in 1971, but a final book on dowsing, *The Power of the Pendulum*, was compiled from his unfinished draft and field-notes.

Bruce-Mitford and Brown

The name of Rupert Bruce Mitford is forever linked with the Sutton Hoo treasures although he did not discover them. He was born in 1914 in Streatham, London. His father was a geographer and writer, and Rupert qualified for a scholarship to Hertford College, Oxford, studying history from 1933; he subsequently took up a temporary post at the Ashmolean Museum, Oxford as Assistant Keeper working with Robin Flower, under whom he was studying for an art degree. In 1938, he transferred to the British Museum, abandoning his further degree to become Assistant Keeper of the Department of British and Medieval Antiquities, headed by Thomas Kendrick, a noted Anglo-Saxonist who had done much to bring the Museum's growing mediaeval collections to public attention. In 1939 Bruce Mitford carried out the excavation of a deserted village at Seacourt (Oxfordshire), allegedly the first mediaeval excavation in Britain to employ the current standards of archaeological method. He served in the Signals during World War II, and on his return to civilian began conservation and publication of the Sutton Hoo objects. Bruce-Mitford oversaw conservation of the objects and organized their display beginning in 1947. He published a brief book on the subject *The Sutton Hoo Ship-Burial: a Provisional Guide* the same year and began to compile the complete catalogue of finds. Four volumes were planned, dealing with the ship and grave (vol.1); the arms, regalia and armour (vol.2); the harp, feasting equipment and small finds (vol.3); a summary setting the ship and its contents into its appropriate context (vol.4). The last volume was never published, but the first three began to appear between 1975 and 1983.

He retired from the British Museum in 1977 and took up a teaching post as Slade Professor of Fine Art at Cambridge and professorial Fellow of Emmanuel College for the year 1978–9. He was married three times, but was not financially independent in his latter years and sold many of his books. His retirement was spent researching a long-term project *A Corpus of Late Celtic Hanging Bowls, AD 400–800*, which was published posthumously. He had a long history of heart problems and succumbed to an attack in 1994.

The first excavator of Sutton Hoo was a local archaeologist by the name of Basil Brown. Brown is sometimes described as an 'amateur' but this epithet belies his true status: he was one of the first persons in England to earn his living solely by excavation of archaeological sites. He was already over 50 years old when he undertook the commission at Sutton Hoo from the landowner, Mrs. Edith Pretty, working always under the supervision of the Ipswich Museum. Once the significance of Brown's discovery – a 90' long ship remaining vestigially as a stain in the sandy soil – was made known, a team of experts from London descended on the site and Brown had to pick his way carefully between the local authorities and the British Museum team led by Charles Phillips, who had a low regard for Brown and the Suffolk team. This arrogant attitude was unwarranted, for Brown was a gifted excavator, an astronomer and was proficient in several languages. He died in 1977.

Barrows Today

The treatment of Anglo-Saxon barrows has not generally been respectful and many today appear rather forlorn. As Anglo-Saxon period tumuli rarely have any quantities of large stones in their construction, they are not so easily identifiable as Neolithic long barrows, but the physical qualities which allowed them to sink into the background landscape as nondescript humps also encouraged 20th c. farmers to plough them flat, regarding them as impediments to the tractor. There are apocryphal stories of farmers, horrified at the prospect of having a feature on their land designated as a scheduled monument, deliberately destroying the site before investigation could take place.

Few Anglo-Saxon barrows are still impressive to look at, or at least not in the way that they were intended to be. The Taplow mound, for example, was subject to 'aesthetic improvement' when the grounds of Taplow Court were landscaped, and the barrow was made more regularly conical than it must once have been. Some of the Sutton Hoo barrows were still visible in 1939, which meant two things: first, that they could be identified on the ground for excavation, and second, that they could be used for the training of tank drivers in taking advantage of the cover afforded by a hull-down position on uneven terrain.

The Prittlewell barrow was probably not prominent even when the rail- and road-links were put in place in the late 1800s. By the mid-20th c. no trace of surface structure was to be seen on the site, which had been landscaped and planted with decorative shrubs as a cosmetic roadside feature. At the time of writing, the barrow's location is marked by a temporary encampment of travellers and road protestors who are seeking to impede the road-widening scheme; it was the precautionary excavation prior to carrying out this work which first revealed the chamber.

Barrows do not need to have been inconveniently sited to have suffered destruction. Harrison remarked of the barrow at Uncleby (Yorkshire):[148]

> *At the time of its examination, the barrow, which had an overall diameter of 28.65m and a height of only 0.60m, was, essentially, a residual feature within the landscape; it had been very much reduced and spread by ploughing in the years following enclosure, in the late 18th century, when the area underwent a transformation from open sheepwalk to arable cultivation. Today (1994) through continued ploughing, the site has almost completely disappeared from view as an upstanding field monument.*

---

[148] Harrison, 1997, p.1

Of the larger barrows mentioned in this book, the following are visible and accessible:

Tumulus	Location	Notes
Asthall (photo. p. 99)	Between Burford and Witney, Oxfordshire, beside A40	Close to the roundabout junction with the B4047 Minster Lovell road
Leafield	Leafield, Wiltshire, between Witney and Burford	In a privately-owned field behind the village, the highest point in the area
Scutchamer Knob	Near Wantage, Berkshire (signposted from the Ridgeway)	In woodland, down a path off the Ridgeway at East Hendred; sadly ruined by the ill-conceived excavation and the attention of modern trials bikes, partygoers and vandals.
Sutton Hoo (photo. p. 102)	North of Woodbridge, Suffolk (signposted from the A12)	In a country park overlooking the River Deben; a modern visitor centre operated by the National Trust offers excellent opportunities for interpretation and discovery. Changing exhibits; open all year round.
Taplow (photo. p.103)	Near Maidenhead, Berkshire	In the grounds of Taplow Court, a retreat for a Buddhist foundation; limited visitor facilities are accessible from April to October. Public access is from the main road, without entering the grounds of Taplow Court.

Many other barrows survive as barely-recognisable lumps in the landscape and go unregarded by locals and visitors alike.

Burials of the Rich & Famous

As the following outline list and the accompanying map shows, the majority of barrow burials were sited along the eastern seaboard and in view of major rivers draining into the North Sea. This fact alone should indicate that the need for chamber burial was felt by long-established Germanic communities who were in the process of transforming themselves from local chiefdoms, built around the personalities and loyalties of a handful of leading men, into kingdoms with a permanent territory, bureaucracy and tax-gathering apparatus, religion and ceremonial tradition.

The principal exception to this pattern is in the north, in Deira and Bernicia, as Lucy remarked:[149]

> *Isolated burials in prehistoric barrows are known from Wiltshire and the Peak District, but only in East Yorkshire are whole cemeteries regularly found focused on them.*

Nearly 40% of East Yorkshire Anglo-Saxon cemeteries are sited with regard to an adjacent earthwork, whether a Bronze Age round barrow, a linear earthwork (Bronze or Iron Age) or an Iron Age square barrow cemetery.

The grouping in the following site-listing is based around the old Heptarchy model of Anglo-Saxon political geography, but the Thames Valley is treated as a separate group because it later formed part of Wessex but, at the time in question, its cultural affinities are with the south Midlands and the Anglian cultural zone. Kent and Sussex are treated as a unity, because, although they have separate political identities, they share very similar mound-burial traditions; Kent west of the Medway shares its material culture with the Sussex, Surrey and southern Essex zones, rather than with east Kent, at least down to the later 6th c. Likewise, I have included the Surrey - Middlesex - London area under Essex because of the historical links among these zones, although it could be argued that the East Saxons were later greatly influenced by the Frankish-dominated kingdom of Kent by the late 6th c., as was the area of Taplow, and therefore the Taplow barrow should fall within the Essex rather than the Thames Valley zone. Given that such burials were traditionally sited on the *borders* of political units, deciding on which side of the border they fall is always problematic.

---

[149] Lucy, 2000, p.13

References are given throughout to Meaney's classic work (1964). Where the corresponding entry in O'Brien's work is marked as either 'certain' or 'possible' for presence of a barrow, the relevant reference has been included. Barrows from areas outside Anglo-Saxon England have not been included (e.g. Shetland, Fife, Clwyd).

See page 104 for notes on photographs

1. Adam's Grave

2. Asthall

3. Kingsplay Hill

4. Beggarbog

5. Roseberry

6. Plumberow

7. Roundway Down

8. Sutton Hoo Mound 2

102

9. Yatesbury

10. Taplow

Notes on photographs

1   Adam's Grave (Wiltshire) is the landscape feature on the skyline. Although not a West Saxon construction, it was the focus of attention in the heathen Anglo-Saxon period. Named *Wodnesbeorg* 'Woden's Barrow', it dominates the area known as *Wodnes denu* 'Woden's valley' and the linear earthwork feature *Wodnes dic* [Woden's ditch', the *Wansdyke*. (The name was changed to a more acceptably Chrisian 'Adam's Grave' later.) The Anglo-Saxons re-mythologised the British landscape, claiming places of special power for their own gods and heroes, as for example Wayland's Smithy and Horseborough. The feature in the foreground is a Bronze Age barrow.

2   Asthall Barrow (Oxfordshire). The circular barrow sits beside the A40, one of the major east-west routes of southern Britain. It was about 12' (3.8m) high at the time of its excavation, and is about half that height today. The perimeter of the barrow is reinforced with dry-stone walling, visible on the right where the surrounding vegetation has been cleared.

3   Kingspaly Hill, Kingsplay Down (Wiltshire). The barrow is located on the very summit of the ridge and can be seen as a darker, flat feature against the creamy colour of the background field, to the right of the crop of yellow rape on the hilltop. The barrow is located in a commanding position on a spur of land with a sheer drop on three sides and at its original height it would have been visible from most places in the valley below.

4   Beggarbog Barrow (Northumberland). The barrow is opposite the modern car park for Housesteads Roman fort on Hadrian's Wall. The effect of the 1830 excavation was to drive a V-shaped trench through the centre, leaving the barrow reduced in height and looking sadly deflated.

5   Roseberry Topping. A natural feature in West Yorkshire, Roseberry Topping was known as *Óðins bjarg* 'Odin's hill' during the Norse occupation of the area and it was the focus of local cult activities, much as Adam's Grave was for the West Saxons. It has been customary to climb the hill for the views offered from the summit since at least the 18th century.

6   Plumberow Mount (Essex). The barrow contained an Anglo-Saxon inhumation, although it is believed to have been built as a Roman signalling station for the Saxon Shore defences. The railing has recently been added to prevent further damage from cyclists.

7   Roundway Down (Wiltshire). The barrow sits on the skyline above the village of Bishop Cannings.

8   Sutton Hoo (Suffolk) Mound 2. This was the first barrow on the site tackled by Basil Brown in his 1938 excavations. The barrow originally held a ship and treasure chamber, probably every bit as splendid as the more famous Mound 1, but sadly robbed long before Brown's day. The monument was restored to its original height after the 1990s excavations under Martin Carver and now forms part of the National Trust's exhibition on the site.

9   Yatesbury (Wiltshire). Two barrows stand barely visible in a field behind the modern hamlet, deliberately reduced to mere bumps to facilitate modern agriculture.

10   Taplow (Berkshire). The mound stands beside the church and next to Taplow Court, seen in the background here. The original profile of the barrow was not restored after the Victorian excavations which also removed the ancient yew tree which once grew on its summit.

A Unique pendant from a royal female gravemound at Saltburn (Yorkshire), perhaps that of Queen Æþelburh the wife of King Edwin of Northumbria. The fine garnet cloisonné and gold setting are characteristic of the finest Kentish or East Anglian output of the early 7th century.   Reproduction:D. Roper.

Kent & Sussex

Sussex has many examples of Neolithic and later tumuli, especially on the Downs, but few are known to have any Anglo-Saxon content. However, as Meaney noted in 1964, there are many barrows in Sussex which are poorly furnished and have yielded no dating material beyond an occasional knife or spearhead, and, on the basis that poorly furnished graves are typical of the 5th rather than the 6th or 7th c., from this it is possible to argue that barrow-building in England began among the South Saxons.[150] However, it might be more accurate to say that the people of Sussex and West Kent shared a common tradition of barrow-building, and that the rise of the East Kentish court in power and importance in the late 6th c. encouraged the spread of the custom throughout lowland Britain.[151] This suggestion does rather underplay the role that barrow-burial enjoyed in Continental Germanic Europe and in Scandinavia.

The barrows of Susex, in common with much of Kent, Surrey and the Isle of Wight, regularly occur in clusters rather than singly, as is usual elsewhere in the country – another regional peculiarity. However, it should be noted that the barrows of Sussex are rarely the imposing monuments met with elsewhere and there are no known chamber burials from this region; many of the graves marked with a surrounding ditch are very poorly provided with grave-goods. Also, since the 1960s, many more cemeteries are known in the south-east and along the rivers draining into the North Sea, and ring- ditch marks surrounding single graves are no longer such a rarity as was once supposed. Sussex had many examples of grave-mound groups, especially in the area of Brighton and Lewes.[152] It must be assumed that many more such clusters have been lost or destroyed by later ploughing and building work.

In common with Sussex, Kentish barrows are unusual in that there are few very high-status burials, and the richest burials are often beneath middle-range barrows: the smallest and the largest tend to be less opulent, and indeed some prominent barrows yield very sparse grave-goods.[153]

---

[150] Meaney, 1964, p.19

[151] Welch, 2007, p.190

[152] Grinsell, 1936, p.29; Welch, 1971

[153] Meaney, 1964, p.18-9 It may be that the erection of a large barrow was itself a sufficient statement of importance that lavish grave-goods were not necessary. We also have to bear in mind that the present size of the monuments is often greatly reduced from the original.

The name of Bryan Faussett features large in the records of Kent as this early barrow-digger made many finds in the county in the late 1700s. As with Bateman in the Midlands, while we may regret his zeal for opening tumuli, we do at least possess some records of what he found and where he found it.

Saltwood

The three cemeteries uncovered at Saltwood near the coastal town of Hythe, in the construction of the Continental high-speed rail link, are very interesting. The eastern one was apparently centred on a Bronze Age barrow.[154] The excavated cemetery contained 101 human inhumations and a single horse burial, but the edges of the site extended further beyond the excavated area. One of the Anglo-Saxon graves was placed close to the centre of the existing barrow, and it contained a fine array of 7th c. material including two shields, a sword, an angon, a Coptic bowl, horse harness and 45 gaming pieces of antler; the horse burial may have been associated with this grave, although it was 4.5m (15') to the east. Many of the grave-goods are typical of chamber burials but the grave appeared to have been cut into the mound without provision of a chamber, and Welch has further proposed that they do not qualify as 'princely' burials due to the limited range of grave-goods.[155]

However, on the edge of the Bronze Age barrow, to the south of the first major grave, a penannular ditch 19m (65') in diameter suggested that an Anglo-Saxon period barrow had been raised, and this structure contained an inhumation in a wooden coffin. Again, weapons such as shield, sword and angon were present, as well as a Coptic bowl, a bucket and a horse harness. To the south of this grave was another rich burial, but without evidence for a surrounding ditch. Weapons, a bucket and a bronze Coptic bowl were found here. The three important graves were situated equidistantly and in line, and each contained a similar assemblage. Multiple shields were present in all three graves, as well as a sword and angon. It may be that these burials are to be considered as founders' graves.[156] A rich female burial was found nearby, and there were at least twenty more burials beneath shallow mounds on the site.

Other Kentish Barrows

Kent has no other certain example of 7th c. chamber burial, which is surprising given the evident wealth of the kingdom in Anglo-Saxon times

---

[154] CAT, 1999; Cook, 2004, p.68; Welch, 2007, p.227

[155] Welch, 2007, p.230

[156] Ellis Davidson, 1950, p.174 The Scandinavian term *oðalshaugr* is used to refer to a barrow which gives the heirs of the person interred rights to the surrounding territory.

and its proximity to, and close links with, the lands of both the Franks and the East Saxons, who both certainly practised this form of burial rite. Also, there are many rich graves which were apparently not covered by a mound, while some poor ones were: cemeteries such as Crundale and Faversham revealed a quantity of rich metalwork, but there is no indication that there were visible signs of graves on the surface. Finglesham was the site of a large and rich inhumation cemetery of heathen Anglo-Saxon date. Meaney does not note any barrows in the records of the various excavations.[157]

It may be that the early antiquarian fashion for barrow-digging destroyed the evidence in this area. This, in conjunction with the fact that accurate records of the excavations were not kept, and finds belonging to a single collector were sometimes jumbled together regardless of provenance, makes for a difficult time in assessing the Kentish material.[158]

Neolithic structures, such as *Kit's Coty House*, were early identified by antiquaries as the graves of fallen British warriors, but none of these structures appears to have held any Anglo-Saxon period burials. The 'Kit' of the monument's title was associated with the name *Catigern*, an alleged relative of Vortigern the *superbus tyrannus* 'proud despot' of the Britons in the 5th c.

The *ASC* MS A, s.a. 455 mentions how Horsa was slain in battle:

> *Her Hengest 7 Horsa fuhton wiþ Wyrtgeorne þam cyninge, in þære stowe þe is gecueden Agælesþrep, 7 his broþur Horsan man ofslog; 7 æfter þam Hengest feng to rice 7 Æsc his sunu.*

> Here (in this year) Hengest and Horsa fought against Vortigern the king in that place which is called Agælesþrep and his brother Horsa was killed, and after that Hengest succeeded to the kingdom and Æsc his son.

The site *Agælesþrep* would now be known as 'Aylesthorpe'. There is a later tradition that a mound was erected over Horsa's grave. This has sometimes been identified with the spot called *Hawsborrow* or *Horseborough* overlooking Folkestone harbour (but which may rather have been a natural chalkland knoll). The mound was destroyed (whether by human agency, coastal erosion or internal collapse is not recorded) and legend says it was found to contain a

---

[157] Meaney, 1964, p.119-20; O'Brien, 1999, ref.686. Finglesham presumably reflects OE *fengles ham* 'settlement of the prince'.

[158] Meaney, 1964, p.116 The material from Crundale, for example, was collected by Durden, who also owned the Sarre material and seems not to have recorded which items came from which cemetery.

quantity of treasure. An alternative legend has Horsa buried beneath the *White Horse Stone*, a lone sarsen now located in Westfield Wood (Kent). The stone may perhaps be the last remnant of an unrecorded Neolithic chamber structure. (There is another 'Horsa's barrow' or *Horsan hlaw* at Orslow (Staffordshire).)

Alfriston At Alfriston (Sussex), the presence of barrows in the locality was common knowledge.[159] In 1763 a local magnate had one of them opened; the contents included a full skeleton, iron knives and 'spikes' (presumably spearheads) as well as charcoal, animal bones and an item of 'yellow metal' (brass?). A cremation burial was found in the centre of the mound, indicating secondary Anglo-Saxon inhumation in a Bronze Age tumulus.

Ash The Gilton, Ash (Kent), cemetery contained several very rich graves but no traces of any mounds.[160] The graves were dug into a sandy soil and it is possible that any original elevated structures had been destroyed in the construction of a mill nearby. Publication of the dig was in Douglas's 1793 book, *Hydrotaphia*.

Barfreston see Sibertswold

Barham An early case of barrow-digging is recorded at Barham (Kent) from the reign of King Henry VIII, in which a cremation urn was found containing objects of corroded iron and some large bones. The mention of iron objects implies an Anglo-Saxon rather than any earlier form of burial.[161] On Barham Downs several ploughed-out barrows of probable Anglo-Saxon date were visible from the air in the early 1940s. Many finds of inhumations have been made in the area, but if these were from barrows which had been levelled by industrial or agricultural activity, this fact was not recorded.

Bay Hill see St. Margaret's at Cliffe

Beakesbourne At Beakesbourne (Kent), in 1773, Fausset excavated 46 skeletons buried in tumuli, situated on a high part of the downs on either side of the road to Ileden.[162] Some of the barrows were large and prominently sited, and they were grouped into two or three clusters.

---

[159] Meaney, 1964, p.246-7

[160] Meaney, 1964, p.121-2

[161] Meaney, 1964, p.108; O'Brien, 1999, ref.1114

[162] Meaney, 1964, p.108-9; O'Brien, 1999, ref.667, 712

Two barrows each contained two burials, and there were two skeletons in a seated position. Coffins were found in twenty-five graves, of which all but two had been burnt.[163] Grave-goods were recovered from twenty of the graves. Another Anglo-Saxon cemetery was discovered in the construction of Beakesbourne aerodrome in 1914, but no barrows were recorded at this site.

Beddingham Hill see **Firle**

Beeding An isolated grave at Beeding Hill (Sussex) contained a male skeleton with a knife.[164] It is possible that it was previously covered by a barrow, since ploughed out. It was excavated in 1874.

Bishopsbourne In 1771, Faussett opened nine barrows at Bishopsbourne (Kent) which stood beside the Roman road.[165] There were ten sets of human remains, but little in the way of grave-goods: two knives, a pin, and three pots. Faussett recorded his opinion that 500 yards to the northwest, about 100 more mounds were visible on Hanging Hill, and that still more had been ploughed out even in his day. Several barrows were opened by Lord Conyngham in the 1840s, with sparse results. Wartime intensive agriculture destroyed the visible evidence for the remainder. At Bourne Park, Bishopsbourne, two barrows were dug in 1844, both containing stave-buckets of the Anglo-Saxon type. One of the barrows had been robbed previously.[166]

Borstal At Borstal, near Rochester (Kent), there was an "overgrown earthen mound some 10 feet in height and between 30 and 35 feet in diameter at its base. It has been known to map-makers for some long time, and has been variously described by them as a tumulus, a castle, and a fort."[167] By the mound was a large stone which marked the boundary of the City of Rochester. The fact that the mound had no obvious features and that it stood on the territorial limits of the city suggests that it may have been an Anglo-Saxon barrow.

Bourne Park see **Bishopsbourne**

Bow Hill see **West Stoke**

---

[163] It is possible that the timber had been scorched or charred, a traditional method of delaying decomposition in wood.

[164] Meaney, 1964, p.247; O'Brien, 1999, ref.240

[165] Meaney, 1964, p.110

[166] Ellis Davidson, 1950; Cook, 2004, p.62

[167] Jessup, 1942, p.71

Breach Down Early diggings at Breach Down (Kent) by Mantell in about 1809 were unrecorded, but recovered finds include some buckles, beads and a Roman coin used as a pendant.[168] In 1841, Lord Conyngham recorded 113 barrows in the area and dug 59 of them, a total of 64 graves, of which 38 were furnished with grave-goods, five richly so. In 1843 several smaller mounds were opened, yielding small grave-goods such as beads, coins, buckles, pins and rings. The inaugural excavation of the first Congress of the BAA opened eight more barrows, also yielding a few more finds. One barrow yielded some high-status female grave-goods: a curious item is a 4.3" long hair-pin of bronze with a cross pattée head and ring-and-dot decoration on the upper, flat portion of the shaft.[169] This may indicate that the burial was of mid-7th c. date when Christianity was already the dominant tradition for the aristocracy. By the 1940s, only 45 barrows were still visible, and the largest of them had been partially destroyed by graverobbers.

Brighton In 1837 a male skeleton was discovered beneath a barrow at Kemp Town, Brighton (Sussex). Grave-goods included a sword, spearhead, a boar's tusk, some bone pins, and part of a horse.[170]

Broadstairs Preparations for a private roadway at Valletta House, Dumpton Park, Broadstairs (Kent) in 1910 revealed an Anglo-Saxon cemetery, despite the surface showing no evidence of disturbance.[171] A quantity of high-status grave-goods was recovered from the gravefield of over 100 burials. The following year, a large bare patch was noticed on the lawn and further investigation revealed two concentric trenches, one 46' (14m) in diameter and 4' (1.25m) wide inside another 70' (21m) in diameter. Although there were Anglo-Saxon graves associated with them, it is not clear whether this was a genuine barrow or a prehistoric feature. A further possible Anglo-Saxon barrow was found in the area of St. Peter's Tip.[172] Excavations at Bradstow School in the same area in 2006 revealed a large Bronze Age barrow which had been disturbed; if there had been any related Anglo-Saxon activity, it could not be detected.

---

[168] Meaney, 1964, p.111; O'Brien, 1999, ref.672

[169] Meaney, 1964, p.111; Jessup, 1974, p.51; Speake, 1989, p.124

[170] Meaney, 1964, p.251; O'Brien, 1999, ref.151

[171] Parsons, 1929; Meaney, 1964, p.112; O'Brien, 1999, ref.675

[172] O'Brien, 1999, ref.1133; Welch, 2007, p.228

Burpham see **Peppering**

Chartham Workmen found a skeleton while widening a road at Chartham Down (Kent) in 1729, and further investigation took place the following year.[173] There were between 80 and 100 barrows visible on the top of the hill, of which twenty were dug; only six were recorded, of which two were rich female inhumations with bracteate pendants and other 7th c. accoutrements. The others contained little material, but some rather upmarket buckles and some spearheads suggest Anglo-Saxon dates for the group. Faussett was moved to dig 53 of the mounds between 1764 and 1773; most of the barrows were of the medium size-range, and they were furnished and unfurnished in about even proportions. The only weapon was an angon-head, and there was no jewellery; knives, beads and plain iron buckles were the most frequently found items. The cross design was found on several objects; in itself, this proves nothing about the religious affiliation of the owners (crosses are among the commonest designs on heathen funerary urns) but in Final Phase contexts the symbolism may indeed represent Christian influence. By 1856, all traces of the barrows had been ploughed out.

Chatham In constructing the military fortifications for Chatham (Kent) in 1756, the soldiers who were constructing the 'Chatham Lines' found many bones and fragments of iron.[174] When repairs were made in 1779, spearheads and other items were disturbed as the earthwork crossed several small tumuli visible in the area. Between 1779 and 1782, excavations of the barrows took place and records were kept of seven of them, all accompanied inhumations. Brooches, an ivory purse-ring, beads, a glass bangle, belt-studs, a perforated spoon and some Roman items were among the grave-goods described.

Cherry Garden Hill see **Folkestone**

Clapham Two round barrows at *Harrow Hill*, New Barn Down, Clapham (Kent), were excavated in 1933, near the Bronze Age enclosure.[175] One was flat-topped and had been robbed, but the construction of the grave in the chalk subsoil makes it likely that it was Anglo-Saxon. The second was difficult to discern apart from its ring-ditch. It held a grave similar to its neighbour, containing a male skeleton with a *seax* by his

---

[173] Meaney, 1964, p.114; O'Brien, 1999, ref.678

[174] Meaney, 1964, p.114-5; O'Brien, 1999, ref.180

[175] Meaney, 1964, p.252; O'Brien, 1999, ref.155

right side and a small piece of iron by the skull (perhaps the remainder of a spearhead?). There are six other barrows of similar construction in the area. The ground on which the barrows are located is called *Harrow Hill*, a presumed derivative of OE *hearh* as with *Mount Harry* at Hamsey.

Compton A cemetery at Compton (Sussex) was excavated in the early 1980s; among its one hundred and thirty two graves was evidence for a number of barrows.[176]

Coombe One plausible – if now unverifiable – example of a chamber grave is the barrow at Coombe, Woodnesborough (Kent), which was dug before 1855.[177] The mound was about 20 yards (19m) in diameter and the grave lay 6' (2m) beneath the top. A copper bowl with short legs and handles was found (a Coptic bowl?), containing some burnt human bones, of which part of the jaw was identifiable. The grave also held two swords and an iron spearhead, some glass and amber beads, and part of an ornament bearing garnets and coloured glass (perhaps a belt-fitting, if not a brooch); a glass cup may also have been present in the grave. One of the swords appeared to have been wrapped in a cloth, and a cloth covering was placed over the bowl.[178] The grave pit lay 6' below a clay spread of about 60' (18m) in diameter, which contained the metal bowl holding cremated human remains.[179] It has been suggested that the clay was actually the product of a collapsing barrow, with soil filtering through the timber structure as it disintegrated. Cremations are unusual in barrows – though far from unknown – and are usually associated with the period up to the late 6th c., after which the rite appears to have declined rapidly. Some of the items are presently housed in Saffron Walden museum (Essex), including several small objects which were not reported from the excavation.

Coombs On the Sussex Downs at a site called Coombs, Dixon opened a mound some time before 1849; it contained an iron *seax* of Anglo-Saxon date.[180] The barrow is quite large and may be a primary Anglo-Saxon construction.

---

[176] O'Brien, 1999, ref.1150

[177] Meaney, 1964, p.115; O'Brien, 1999, ref.679; Welch, 2007, p.230

[178] It may be that the remains of cloth on the scabbard were from linen tapes, which were regularly used to bind the outside of 7th c. swords as at Sutton Hoo Mound 1. (Mortimer, forthcoming)

[179] Ellis Davidson, 1950; Dickinson & Speake, 1992, p.116, 119

[180] Meaney, 1964, p.248

Deal The cemetery at Mill Hill, Deal (Kent) is an unusual example of a graveyard spanning the pre-Roman, Roman and Anglo-Saxon periods.[181] Its situation on a prominent hill may have encouraged its use by several different cultural groups over the centuries. Investigations were carried in 1901, 1908, 1933, 1939, 1986-9. Although no surface remains of barrows were visible, Parfitt and Brugmann surmised that eleven burials in Plot A were so regularly spaced that it was likely that barrows had been erected over them, and likewise two burials in Plot B, with a probable further isolated example at the edge of the excavated zone. Several graves were surrounded by ring-ditches which probably represent the trenches for low mounds.

Ditchling Welch suggested that some barrows at Ditchling Beacon, near Lewes (Sussex) may be of Anglo-Saxon origin but no investigation has ever been published.

Dumpton Park see **Broadstairs**

Eastry Excavations at Eastry (Kent) in the mid-1960s revealed a small cemetery in which indications of barrows were present.[182]

Falmer The presence of barrows at Falmer and Stanmer Park, near Brighton (Sussex) is well-known. Welch suggested that they may be of Anglo-Saxon date.[183]

Firle The area around Firle (Sussex) shows a lot of evidence for barrow-burial in the Anglo-Saxon period. The highest point in the area is here and the region must have been chosen as a burial ground for this reason. Akerman noted that the prehistoric barrows tend to be sited on the highest point while Anglo-Saxon ones are more often sited on the brow of the Downs (i.e. on the skyline as viewed from the valley) and are usually not far from settlements with Anglo-Saxon names.[184] Beddingham Hill on the South Downs has three tumuli – again sited on the skyline - above the villages of Beddingham and West Firle, near Lewes.[185] The cemetery contained 5th c. material, in common with many others in this part of Sussex. The mounds yielded human remains, frequently accompanied by just an iron *seax*. One prominent mound was opened some time before 1824 and was found to contain

[181] Meaney, 1964, p.117; Parfitt & Brugmann, 1997; O'Brien, 1999, ref.682

[182] O'Brien, 1999, ref.1158

[183] O'Brien, 1999

[184] Meaney, 1964, p.248

[185] Meaney, 1964, p.247; Welch, 1978; O'Brien, 1999, ref.239

three bronze disc brooches and a belt buckle; there are several examples of buckles and brooches from this site in the British Museum. Also above Firle, there was a cluster of barrows opened by Coles Child in 1843.[186] Each contained a human skeleton but no grave-goods, although there were rust stains on the chalk in one grave of an adult male, 6'4" tall with a large sword-cut in the skull. Akerman excavated some barrows on the Downs between Firle and Litlington in 1849. Each contained a skeleton, but apart from two knives there were no grave-goods.

Folkestone In 1848 Roach Smith investigated a barrow on top of a hill west of the earthwork known as *Caesar's Camp* on Cherry Garden Hill, Folkestone (Kent).[187] He discovered some human remains and a jug of 6th c. Merovingian Frankish type. It is presumed to have been a secondary inhumation in an existing landmark.

Freedown In 1945 excavation of a barrow at Freedown (Kent) revealed the inhumation of a middle-aged man.[188] There are two Bronze Age tumuli nearby, but the burial was dated to the heathen Anglo-Saxon period, possibly a secondary inhumation in a third Bronze Age barrow.

Gilton see **Ash**

Glynde At Glynde (Sussex) on Sexton Down, several barrows were opened in 1819.[189] Those on the northern edge had iron knives buried with them and their graves were surrounded by large flints. Two spearheads appeared in antiquities publications, which, from the description, appear to belong to this group of barrows.

Greenwich In 1714 a park-keeper dug into barrows in Greenwich Park (Kent) and extracted several valuable items.[190] In 1784 around fifty of the barrows in the cluster were opened by Douglas who remarked on the preservation of hair and cloth. Artefacts included a shieldboss, spearheads and a *seax*. More were destroyed in the construction of a reservoir on the site.

---

[186] Meaney, 1964, p.248; O'Brien, 1999, ref.243

[187] Meaney, 1964, p.120

[188] Meaney, 1964, p.121

[189] Meaney, 1964, p.254; O'Brien, 1999, ref.163 On re-opening one of the barrows in 1916, two pennies were found in the grave, both dated to 1805, deliberately left by the 19th c. diggers.

[190] Meaney, 1964, p.122; O'Brien, 1999, ref.187

Hamsey Around 1800 some barrows on the Sussex Downs in the vicinity of Offham Chalk Pit were opened by a Mr. Shrapnall.[191] The first contained a skeleton, perhaps female but unaccompanied. The second held part of a skeleton, also believed to be female. The third had already been disturbed and contained jumbled bones, with several skulls. The fourth contained a skeleton wrapped in a tinder-like black substance (perhaps the remains of a decayed wooden coffin?). The fifth one opened was larger and had some satellite burials; they all contained human skeletons and they were covered with a large flint stone. These barrows were identified by Grinsell with a cluster at Hamsey (Kent). These were all sited near a local hill called *Mount Harry*, the name of which has been associated with the OE *hearh* 'harrow, heathen place of worship'.

Harting There are barrows and other earthworks near Harting Beacon (Sussex). Most famous is the Iron Age hillfort of Cissbury Rings. Anglo-Saxon material is believed to have been retrieved from some of them.

Hollingbourne At Hollingbourne, Whiteheath (Kent), a tumulus was disturbed in the construction of the road from Maidstone to Ashford in 1819.[192] There were two Bronze Age barrows with secondary Anglo-Saxon burials, including cremation urns and shieldboss, beads and a spearhead.

Iford There were at least two barrows at Iford (Sussex) of presumed Anglo-Saxon date, one on Front Hill and the other on Pickers Hill.[193] The data were collected by Welch, who suggested further Sussex barrows at Rottingdean (two examples at Saltdean), Falmer, Stanmer Park, Ditchling Beacon and Harting Beacon.[194]

Kemp Town see **Brighton**

Kingston Down (see p. 16) Workmen digging on Kingston Down (Kent) in 1749 disturbed a number of hill-top barrows.[195] The burials contained two or three human skeletons, one with a spear and other weapons. Further work in the area over the next few years revealed more burials and assorted grave-goods including glass beads, some iron weapons and glass vessels. Faussett stepped in and, in two excavation

---

[191] Meaney, 1964, p.249; O'Brien, 1999, ref.1039

[192] Meaney, 1964, p.124

[193] O'Brien, 1999, ref.2229,2230

[194] O'Brien, 1999, ref.2231-4, 2237, 2245

[195] Meaney, 1964, p.125-6; O'Brien, 1999, ref.693

seasons between 1767 and 1773, he opened 263 mounds and 45 associated flat graves. More than two hundred of the burials had identifiable grave-goods, but most of these were simple iron knives. There were only eleven rich graves, of which three were exceptional. The cemetery seems to have been in use into the 7th c., and some of the graves were apparently Christian in character; one female bore two small silver crosses. For all the exploratory zeal which Faussett showed, we have remarkably little information concerning the finds and not even a map to locate the mounds and graves. One barrow, which Faussett missed, was dug in 1850 and was found to contain a wealthy female burial with beads, brooches, shears, a chatelaine and so on. Evison tried to evaluate the site in1959 using sondages, and discovered three further flat graves, all poorly furnished.

Lewes In Lewes (Sussex), knowledge of the difference in local barrow construction between Anglo-Saxon and prehistoric types was available by 1824: the Anglo-Saxon ones were generally smaller.[196] All were rounded, with a shallow ditch at the base and a circular cavity in the centre at the top. Some Anglo-Saxon barrows had been opened and the contents removed for examination. Grave-goods included iron swords, shieldbosses and spearheads from presumed male graves, while female and juvenile ones often held beads of glass, amber or amethyst, brooches with garnet inlay, pendants and buckles. Coins were also sometimes found, especially those of the later Roman Emperors.

Litlington see **Firle**

Lyminge Workmen building a mushroom shed at Lyminge (Kent) in 1953 found eight graves; further excavations revealed fifty-five more.[197] There was no surface indication of their presence, but excavation showed that one had been covered with a mound of chalk. Several other graves were surrounded by a gully, which may have been a form of ring-ditch. An Anglo-Saxon date was assumed.

Margate An Anglo-Saxon inhumation cemetery was discovered at Margate (Kent) in 1863 when the top of a hill was lowered.[198] Although there was no indication of gravemounds still in existence, the hill-top location would be typical for barrow burials in this area. The finds included ceramics, a buckle, a knife and a spearhead.

---

[196] Meaney, 1964, p.251-2; O'Brien, 1999, ref.2226, 2227, 2228 (St. Ann)
[197] Meaney, 1964, p.126; O'Brien, 1999, ref.199
[198] Meaney, 1964, p.128

Mill Hill see **Deal**

Minster-in-Thanet In 1841, a large jewelled brooch was found at Minster on the Isle of Thanet (Kent) by a labourer digging in the chalk, along with a bronze vessel.[199] The spot was known locally as the site of many burial mounds and a stone sarcophagus had allegedly been discovered nearby some years before. Loose Anglo-Saxon beads have also been found in the vicinity.

New Barn Down see **Clapham**

Ozengel see **Ramsgate**

Patching Near Patching (Sussex) excavations were carried out by Pull between 1922 and 1929, examining the local flint mines and the associated burial mounds at a site called *Blackpatch*.[200] All were of Bronze Age date, but three contained secondary inhumations. Barrow 2 held an adult male without a head. Barrow 10 was a large mound, 32' in diameter and 3' high, containing an adult male with severe damage to his left leg. Barrow 12 was found to contain three Anglo-Saxon period burials, one of which was headless. The high incidence of detectable physical trauma among these skeletons may argue for the presence of military leaders at this site, although the lack of grave-goods is therefore all the more unusual.

Peppering Near a pond at Peppering (Sussex) a barrow was opened in 1893.[201] There is some disagreement about the number of skeletons found, which may have been as many as thirteen; there was apparently a small number (perhaps four) of articulated skeletons and a heap of human bones, probably disturbed by rabbiters. Grave-goods were absent but a piece of Roman Samian ware was found in the earth, and some unidentifiable pieces of iron. A primary Anglo-Saxon barrow is suspected for the site. In the same area round Burpham and the same year, at Perry Hill one of four barrows was destroyed in the construction of a dewpond. It had contained an adult female skeleton. The barrow to the west was opened and found to contain an elderly male skeleton accompanied by a *seax* and with a bronze pin on his chest. The third held the skeleton of a young man, said to be 6'2" tall and with a sword-cut to the left side of his skull. The fourth barrow contained the skeleton of an old female with an armlet and a bead.

---

[199] Meaney, 1964, p.128-9; O'Brien, 1999, ref.699

[200] Meaney, 1964, p.247; O'Brien, 1999, ref.241

[201] Meaney, 1964, p.253; O'Brien, 1999, ref.158, 159

There were traces of human bone in the soil between the mounds, as well as fragments of Bronze Age and Romano-British pottery.

Plumstead Clusters of grave-mounds are not uncommon in Kent and many were visible when the early antiquaries set about opening as many as possible.[202] Plumstead Common and Winns Common (Kent) have a number of Bronze Age mounds, allegedly seven in all, but much reduced in height. There is no surviving evidence of their re-use for burial in Anglo-Saxon times.

Polhill At Polhill (Kent) in 1880 two skeletons and a spearhead were unearthed near the churchyard in an earthen bank.[203] Thirteen more came to light in 1956 in the chalk during road-widening.

Ramsgate At Ozengel, Ramsgate (Kent), an Anglo-Saxon cemetery was discovered in 1845-50 during construction of the railway.[204] The place overlooked the sea and had previously held prominent mounds which had been ploughed flat. More than a hundred burials were destroyed before the local antiquary was able to record them. A range of male and female grave-goods was recovered including weapons, brooches, pins, beads and ceramics. Some of the pieces were of fine workmanship, such as a keystone garnet brooch. The presence of silver *sceatta* coins indicates that the cemetery lasted into the 7th c. at least.

Richborough A barrow at Richborough (Kent) was dug in the 18th c. and the notes record the discovery of two elegant *fibulæ* and some beads of 'British' type, subsequently identified as Anglo-Saxon by Smith.[205]

Ringlemere A field at Ringlemere, near Sandwich (Kent), yielded a spectacular detector find in 2001 in the form of a beautiful Bronze Age golden cup (similar to the Rillaton cup from Bodmin Moor, Cornwall) which had been damaged by modern ploughing.[206] Investigation by Canterbury Archaeological Trust in 2003 revealed a complex story on the site: a Bronze Age burial mound which had been re-used in the early Anglo-Saxon period (ca 500 AD) for the burial of a high-status female with a glass-bead necklace, as well as the focus for a cemetery containing both cremation urns (dated 450-550 AD) and inhumations of the same

---

[202] Grinsell, 1936, p.29

[203] Meaney, 1964, p.132; O'Brien, 1999, ref.704

[204] Meaney, 1964, p.131; O'Brien, 1999, ref.1208

[205] Meaney, 1964, p.133; O'Brien, 1999, ref.866

[206] References include Current Archaeology, 216, p.4-5 and www.canterburytrust.co.uk/ringleme.html

period. The mound was calculated to have stood to a height of 5 metres (16') originally, making it a large barrow for the area, and strangely a *Grubenhaus* had been cut into the surface around 600 AD.

Rodmell In 1931, a barrowfield was identified at Rodmell (Sussex).[207] It contained twenty-three mounds, between 4 and 6 yards (3.5 and 5.5m) in diameter and up to 4' (1.25m) in height. Some have hollows in the centre, a feature often found on Anglo-Saxon period barrows.

Rottingdean A group of about thirty small barrows stood on *The Bostle* near Rottingdean (Sussex) which was investigated in 1939.[208] Two of the barrows were large, and some of the smaller ones were surrounded by still-visible ditches. The records are poor but seemingly human remains were discovered in at least six barrows in the western group, without grave-goods apart from a bronze knife. A later, more detailed excavation was undertaken in 1949 of one of the smaller barrows. It contained human remains but only the leg bones were in situ, suggesting that the grave had been opened previously and any associated grave-goods removed; this is likely to have been the case with the other mounds, opened previously. An Anglo-Saxon date was suggested, but on little evidence.

Sexton Down see **Glynde**

Shoreham Near Old Shoreham (Sussex) stands the mound called *Thundersbarrow*, near the earthworks on Thundersbarrow Hill.[209] Reports of Saxon urns recovered from the digging out of the mound in construction of a pond appear to have been misleading since all the remains recorded seem to be Roman. However, the name *Thundersbarrow* may well record the site of a heathen place of worship.

Sibertswold Faussett dug a number of graves at Sibertswold (Kent) in 1772-3; allegedly there were 168 of them in the 'lower burial ground', mostly beneath barrows.[210] Some of them were multiple burials beneath a single mound. Not all were richly furnished, some having just a knife, and there was no correlation between the size of the present barrow and the quantity or quality of the contents. The 'upper burial ground', some 40 yards away, yielded another thirteen graves. These barrows had been

---

[207] Meaney, 1964, p.253; O'Brien, 1999, ref.1068

[208] Meaney, 1964, p.253-4; O'Brien, 1999, ref.1067. Another barrow at Rottingdean is recorded at 2231.

[209] Meaney, 1964, p.256

[210] Meaney, 1964, p.136-7; O'Brien, 1999, ref.714

levelled in order to take the soil as a dressing for the fields. The cemetery continued into the neighbouring parish of Barfreston, where the barrows were arranged inside a formation bounded by steep slopes on three sides and a deep trench on the fourth. There were about twenty eight graves within the Barfreston parish portion.

South Downs Some time before 1895 Collyer excavated six barrows on the South Downs overlooking the River Arun in Sussex.[211] They were each about 25' (14m) in diameter and covered graves cut into the chalk subsoil. All had been disturbed previously but were assigned an Anglo-Saxon date.

South Heighton At Manor Farm, South Heighton (Sussex) an isolated grave was investigated in 1923.[212] It contained part of a human skeleton accompanied by a sword and shieldboss. The grave stood on a prominent hill crest and was probably originally covered by a mound.

St. Margaret's at Cliffe At Bay Hill, St. Margaret's at Cliffe (Kent), stands *Bay Hill Round Barrow*, a Bronze Age tumulus from which later (presumed Anglo-Saxon) remains were excavated in 1920 when the site was partially cleared for the construction of a tennis court.[213]

St. Peter's Tip see **Broadstairs**

Stanmer Mantel took a gold ear-ring from a barrow near Stanmer Park (Sussex) in 1846.[214] In 1956 a tree which had blown down in the park was being cleared, and human remains were found beneath the roots which may have been the same burial, but there were no associated finds.

Stodmarsh In 1847, a mound of sand on the brow of a hill near Stodmarsh Court (Kent) was being removed by a labourer when he discovered a grave within.[215] The human remains were no longer extant, but the grave-goods indicate the double burial of a man and a woman: spearheads, shieldbosses, bronze bowls, two square-headed brooches, a brooch set with garnets, a gilt-bronze belt buckle, a gilt pierced spoon and some belt fittings. A second barrow nearby was opened by Akerman in 1854; this had been surmounted by an old elder tree the

---

[211] Meaney, 1964, p.255; O'Brien, 1999, ref.2223

[212] Meaney, 1964, p.250; O'Brien, 1999, ref.248

[213] Meaney, 1964, p.135; Grinsell, 1992; O'Brien, 1999, ref.709

[214] Meaney, 1964, p.255; O'Brien, 1999, ref.2234

[215] Meaney, 1964, p.137; O'Brien, 1999, ref.716

roots of which had seemingly destroyed the contents. A third barrow nearby was thought to be empty, but in 1907 a sword and shieldboss were found on the site.

Stowting An inhumation cemetery of Anglo-Saxon date was discovered at Stowting (Kent) some time 'many years' before 1844, when skeletons with iron weapons were found in a field where Roman coins were also discovered, known locally as the site of many barrows.[216] More graves were revealed when a road was constructed. There were several finds of weapons and keystone-garnet brooches, but many of the graves were poorly furnished.

Sullington In 1868 a group of about a dozen Anglo-Saxon graves was opened on Sullington Hill (Sussex), grouped around a Bronze Age round barrow.[217] Two Anglo-Saxon cremations were found in a barrow nearby.

Temple Ewell At Temple Ewell (Kent), several barrows stood beside the London Road; these were excavated in the early 18th c. and found to contain bodies accompanied by iron swords and spearheads.[218] Three tumuli on the site were investigated in 1880.

West Stoke The Reverend Henry Smith decided to open a cluster of barrows at West Stoke, Bow Hill (Sussex) in about 1870.[219] One of the larger mounds contained platforms of flints but no human remains; the second held a scatter of ashes, covered with chalk and brown earth, but no urn. Several of the smaller mounds contained cremation urns, one with fragments of iron and a bone comb of Anglo-Saxon date. Several pits between the mounds were investigated and found to contain flints which had been subjected to fire – perhaps the site of the cremation ceremonies.

Whiteheath see **Hollingbourne**

Winns Common see **Plumstead**

Wolverton A Bronze Age barrow and associated Anglo-Saxon cemetery were discovered during excavations at Chilton Farm, Wolverton near Dover in 2007.[220] One of the graves (no.5) contained a quantity of rivets which may indicate a boat-burial, one of very few such burials known from Anglo-Saxon contexts.

---

[216] Meaney, 1964, p.137-8

[217] Meaney, 1964, p.255-6; O'Brien, 1999, ref.165

[218] Meaney, 1964, p.139

[219] Meaney, 1964, p.255; O'Brien, 1999, ref.601

[220] Burrows, Richardson & Hamilton, forthcoming

Woodnesborough see **Coombe**

Wye A roadside barrow was opened in 1858 at Wye (Kent).[221] It was found to contain a male skeleton with a shieldboss, sword, drinking vessel and some other objects. A group of barrows on the hilltop had been disturbed and robbed, but one was found to contain a male with a spearhead and seax. Many other valuable objects from this site were collected by Durden, and later acquired by the British Museum, but it is impossible now to identify which items came from Wye and which from the high-status cemetery at Sarre. All the graves at Wye were within a short distance of each other and must have constituted a single barrow-cluster. Also within the district of Wye, but at some distance along the chalk ridge, a barrow was discovered in 1939; it had been disturbed, perhaps by Faussett in 1757-9, and was empty but consistent with an Anglo-Saxon structure.

---

[221] Meaney, 1964, p.142; O'Brien, 1999, ref.722, 861

Paul Mortimer with some of his replica Sutton Hoo war-gear.

Essex and the Lower Thames

The archaeology of Essex in the 6th and 7th c. has much in common with west Kent, Surrey[222] and Sussex. While chamber burials are not unknown – Broomfield, Prittlewell and probably Clacton – it is perfectly possible that there were others, swallowed up in the sprawl of London as it encroached on the surrounding rural areas.

Broomfield

Workmen excavating a gravel pit at Clobb's Row, Broomfield, near Chelmsford (Essex) in 1888 found a collection of iron objects at a depth of about 7' (2.2m) below the present ground surface. The presence of a small gold pyramid set with garnets prompted full excavation by Sir Hercules Read, which took place in 1894.[223] The grave had been partially destroyed and the internal chamber was irregularly shaped, about 8' (2.5m) long, its walls covered in charred remains of wood, and the backfill contained worked flints and Roman tile. From this a post-Roman date was inferred. There was no sign of a barrow on the surface.

The grave-goods included a fragmentary circular bronze bowl with two drop handles, containing the tip of a drinking horn; various textile remains, some woollen and others linen; fragments of another drinking horn; two squat blue glass jars; two lathe-turned beechwood cups with gilt-bronze rims; two stave-built wooden vessels of 10" deep and 12" diameter (25cm x 31cm) with iron fittings, sunk into the earth at floor level; a hemispherical iron container on a four-footed pedestal, later identified as a lamp; an iron cauldron; weapons including a sword, spearhead and shield boss; a broken wheel-thrown ceramic pot. There were other remains of wood and iron bars in the chamber which may have formed a coffin. The bowl and textiles lay on a wooden structure, made of birchwood stakes placed close together.

The sword was broken in two but on its blade were the mineralised remains of the wooden sheath. The hilt had completely vanished – a not uncommon feature on swords of this period, found also at Sutton Hoo Mound 17, probably due to its having been made up from antler, bone, leather and wooden components. The upper part of the sheath was bound with strips of finely woven linen tape, another feature of 7th c. swords paralleled at Sutton Hoo Mound 1 and elsewhere.

---

[222] Poulton, 1987; Welch, 2007

[223] Read, 1894; Smith, 1923, p.45, 63; Ellis Davidson, 1950; Meaney, 1964, p.85; Speake, 1980, p.38-9; Jones, 1980, p.89-90; Wilson, 1992, p.129; O'Brien, 1999, ref.43; Cook, 2004, p.52-3

Read noted that no bones were traceable in the burial, but there was a quantity of charcoal and from this he reasoned that the body had been placed in a stout, iron-bound wooden coffin and then burnt where it lay. However, given the parallel examples of 'vanishing' bodies at contemporary mounds, it may be that the charred items were from a graveside meal and the human remains had thoroughly decomposed in the soil. However, a cremated body within a chamber does have a parallel at the Asthall barrow.

The presence of the sword and other weapons and the rare vessels implies a high-status male burial, and nothing in the other grave-goods contradicts this impression.

Prittlewell

The Prittlewell chamber burial, unearthed in the winter of 2003-4, was almost miraculously preserved in an urban environment which had seen huge construction works in the immediate vicinity over the last two centuries. The mound had been raised on a ridge or bank above the Prittle brook, and may have been visible from both the River Thames and the River Crouch at the time of completion. The barrow was comparatively small at 33' (10m) in diameter, but the chamber within was among the largest ever found in Europe: 13' x 13' (4mx4m) and 5' (1.5m) deep.

Both a modern road and a railway line with sidings had been constructed within a few yards of the chamber, and in the development and extension of the latter a cemetery of accompanied and unaccompanied inhumations had been found in successive phases; the 1923 excavations had been handled by archaeologists rather than railway navigators, and further work in 1930 had revealed more details of the site.[224] There were 16 certain and 11 possible inhumations identified in the 1923 excavations, and the 1930 finds were some way distant from this. Occasional occupation evidence is also known from the immediate area, such as an SFB with evidence for glass, pottery and bone.[225] The full extent of the cemetery is still not determined, and other high-status burials may await discovery.

The commonest spearhead types among the known graves on the site are Swanton's C2 and C3, which range from the 5th to 7th c., and those of Swanton's E series which are of 6th and 7th c. in date; none of the other weapons were closely datable, but the shield bosses were of types usually assigned to the 6th c.

---

[224] Meaney, 1964, p.87; Jones, 1980, p.94; Tyler, 1988; Baker, 2006, p.122

[225] Wymer & Brown, 1995, p.181

One of the graves apparently had both a sword and a large seax, a high-status weapon combination known from the later 6th c. The five swords were all pattern-welded and radiographs demonstrated that the blades were made in double-thickness, i.e. two layers of twisted wire placed back-to-back. The high-status jewellery included two pendants of probable Kentish manufacture, and two Saxon saucer brooches of late 6th or early 7th c. date.

The high-quality swords found in these burials suggested that a wealthy group had been using the cemetery; and in the few detected female graves were some very costly pieces of gold-and-garnet jewellery. It is notable that nearby a stone-built church had been erected in the mid-600s, a rarity for this area at that time, part of which remains in the fabric of the present St. Mary's church until today.[226]

The chamber probably owes its remarkable state of preservation to the gradual decomposition of the roof timbers, which allowed the cavity to fill slowly with sand; this meant that the grave-goods were held in position within the chamber, but the acidic nature of the soil destroyed any trace of the body and a large part of the organic remains.

Among the identifiable finds were a Coptic bronze vessel; a gold belt buckle; an iron-framed folding stool; squat blue-glass jars; a harp; gaming pieces; gold coins; an iron lamp; a sickle;[227] feasting gear such as horns, glass cups and wooden vessels from which to serve drink. The king wore a battle-coat, a wrap-over garment associated with high-status males of the later 6th and early 7th c. depicted on the helmet plates from Sutton Hoo Mound 1; the remains of the gold brocade lapels were still in the mound although the textile had perished.

The most curious inclusion in the chamber was a pair of small, gold foil crosses placed on the dead king's upper body; this tradition was common among high-status males of the *Langobardi* (the Lombards of Italy and the *Alemanni* of southern Germany. The coins were Merovingian tremisses from France, and can only be dated in the range 570 to 670 AD. Some of the material shows strong links with the Merovingians, which was probably due to the close association of the East Saxon royal house, the *Sleddingas*, with the court of the kings of Kent, themselves firm allies and marital kinsmen of the Merovingian royalty.

---

[226] Potter, 2001

[227] Nordin, 2005. Högby grave 87 (Gotland, Sweden) is a 2nd c. burial also containing a sickle; it is a female cairn burial.

There has been considerable speculation as to the likely identity of the man in the mound, and the possible dates for the burial. Indications are that the funeral rites must have taken place within a decade either side of Sutton Hoo Mound 1, which is conventionally dated to ca. 625 AD. There are several East Saxon royal candidates from this period, but perhaps most telling pieces of evidence are (i) the fact that the personal items are rather plain (no Style II decoration), (ii) the presence of a baptismal spoon and (iii) the inclusion of the gold foil crosses: these facts, taken together, suggest a Christian burial, albeit conducted with considerable display of excess, for the benefit of a mainly heathen or recently-converted people. It is tempting to nominate King Sæberht on this basis, since this king was the first one of the East Saxons to accept baptism in 604 AD, and on his death in ca.616 his three sons repudiated the church and expelled the bishop from London. It might be expected that the sons would have honoured their father with a traditional form of burial, while allowing his personal possessions to be included, despite their Christian iconographic content. However, this king may have been associated with – and commemorated in the name of - the town of Sawbridgeworth, now on the Essex-Hertfordshire border but well within the original East Saxon kingdom. The town's name was *Sabrixteworde* in Domesday i.e. *Sæberhtes worþig*, 'Sæberht's land by the river'. The fact that the town was associated with a man of this name does not necessarily mean either that King Sæberht was buried there, nor that this Sæberht was the same man as the king of the same name. Sæberht's wife, a Kentish royal lady named Ricola, may have had an estate in the west of the kingdom at the place now called Rickling, OE *Ricolingas* 'people associated with Ricola'.

If this grave did not contain Sæberht, which are the other contenders? The next known Christian East Saxon king, Sigeberht, was baptized in 653 AD which would probably be too late for the assemblage of grave-goods in the Prittlewell tomb, although there are occasional examples of mid-7th c. chamber graves such as the one at Swallowcliffe Down (Wiltshire).

Other Lower ThamesBarrows

Intensive agricultural activity in southern Essex has levelled many prehistoric earthworks, some of which would certainly have held Saxon secondary inhumations.[228] Essex was fortunate in having many Iron Age tumuli erected by the Belgic tribe occupying the territory, the *Trinovantes*, affording ample opportunities for East Saxon re-use of still imposing monuments. The Lexden tumulus near Colchester is an example of an Iron Age mound which

---

[228] Tyler, 1996, p.114

survives into modern times; while there is evidence for early Saxon occupation of the town, no barrow burials – primary or secondary – have yet been discovered.

Roman period barrows are also found here, such as the still impressive example on *Barrow Hill* on Mersea Island, which contained a cremation in a glass vessel. The *Bartlow Hills*, on the Essex-Cambridgeshire border, comprised seven barrows which were allegedly the largest burial mounds in Europe. Four of the barrows were destroyed in the construction of the railway and two others were subsequently damaged. The single survivor is 45' high, second only to Silbury Hill in height as an artificial mound in England. They are dated to the Roman period, but presumably draw on Belgic tradition.[229]

Saxon period tumuli also had an effect on the subsequent landscape use. For example, at Orsett the early mediaeval field boundaries appear to respect some of the Anglo-Saxon graves, which implies that the covering mound was still large enough to be both visible and recognisable as a boundary marker when the fields were laid out.[230]

Addington At Addington (Surrey) a barrowfield on the Common was shown to a visitor in 1728; broken pieces of cremation urns were found in one of the mounds.[231] There were about twenty-five barrows, of which the largest was nearly 40' (12m) in diameter. The land was known as *Thunderhill* or *Thunderfield Common*, which might imply that the site was associated with *Þunor* originally. The barrows are no longer visible, but were detectable still when some trees were cut down during the First World War.

Alresford Three ring-ditches were identified at Broomfield Plantation Quarry near Alresford (Essex) with Roman pottery in the backfill, implying a post-Roman date.[232] Superficially they are similar to the ring-ditches at Orsett.

Banstead Downs see **Reigate**

---

[229] Grinsell, 1936, p.28-9

[230] Jones, 1980, p.91

[231] Meaney, 1964, p.237

[232] Bedwin, 1986; Baker, 2006, p.125

Chelmsford Traces of a ring-ditch suitable for creating a mound were found in the cemetery at Springfield Lyons, Chelmsford (Essex).[233] The cemetery comprised about two hundred and fifty burials, evenly distributed between cremations and inhumations.

Clacton A probably important barrow was sited at Great Clacton (Essex) but the opening of it was undertaken in conjunction with its destruction; the only find known to have been conserved is a glass drinking vessel which was displayed in 1847.[234] The barrow is said to have contained broken tiles. The importance of the barrow would lie in its situation overlooking the seaways – as at Prittlewell and Sutton Hoo – and in the use of (Roman?) tile in its construction; both these factors imply a kingly burial of the early 7th c. It may be that the barrow had already been robbed before the 1840s destruction.

Coulsdon Barrows stood on the open land called Farthingdown, near Coulsdon (Surrey).[235] As early as around 1760, an antiquary journeyed down from London, opened one of the mounds and took away the contents. In 1871, sixteen of the remaining barrows were opened by Flower, all of which contained inhumations; the barrows were grouped into 'northern' and 'southern' groups, the latter higher on the down. The grave-goods of one male burial included a sword, a tall shieldboss (sugarloaf?), a bucket, a belt-buckle. Other items from the graves were another bucket, a wooden drinking vessel with a bronze rim, two silver pins, a small gold pendant, two iron knives, a spearhead, an iron buckle and some beads. On the western edge of the southern group, cable-laying in 1931 uncovered a skeleton accompanied by a spearhead and knife; there was no visible mound above this burial. Further investigation in 1948 revealed more flat graves respecting the barrows. In 1950, four barrows opened in the 1871 dig were re-investigated: one still contained a small child's burial with a small iron knife, which the Victorians had missed. The largest mound was also partially excavated, and the skull of a child wearing a fur cap was discovered, as well as a bag with iron and bronze fittings.

---

[233] O'Brien, 1999, ref.1221

[234] Meaney, 1964, p.86; Jones, 1980, p.90; O'Brien, 1999, ref.16, 850; Baker, 2006, p.119-20

[235] Meaney, 1964, p.240-1; O'Brien, 1999, ref.230

Effingham Barrows were discovered during construction of the turnpike road at Effingham (Surrey) in 1758; there were four or five separate skeletons but no records of any associated finds.[236] It is probable that these barrows were the meeting point for Effingham Hundred, and therefore they may be of Anglo-Saxon date.

Ewell In 1807 Ewell Downs (Surrey) were being enclosed for cultivation.[237] One parcel of land was the site of some mounds (apparently the remnant of a larger barrowfield) and in the process of levelling one of them, the owner, Thomas Calverley, discovered human bones and weapons. Showing remarkable restraint for a man of his time, Calverley had the remains re-interred and left the barrow standing.

Farthingdown see **Coulsdon**

Hackbridge The village of Hackbridge (Surrey) is the site of a Roman villa; in investigating that structure, an Anglo-Saxon cemetery was revealed nearby. One burial was in an elevated position, although the excavator, Addy, considered it unlikely that it was a man-made tumulus. However, Brock maintained that the present surface was due to the levelling of two Anglo-Saxon barrows.[238]

Harlow Harlow (Essex) is named from the *herehlæw* or 'army barrow', the meeting point where the troops should assemble in the event of a military campaign. The barrow in question is a Bronze Age structure and probably was only used as a gathering point, rather than for a burial.[239]

Hockley An existing, perhaps Roman, mound at *Plumberow Mount*, Hockley (Essex) included a probable secondary inhumation of Anglo-Saxon date, according to the dating evidence of some sherds of pottery. The mount was dug in 1913 by the local field archaeology club, and it was conjectured to have been used in Roman times as a signalling station for the Saxon Shore on the basis of the finding of a single coin of Domitian and a jet bead, and the burial to have been placed in the mound much later. A huge wooden post had stood near the centre of the tumulus. This barrow would be the closest neighbour to the Prittlewell mound, and occupies a commanding position over the

---

[236] Meaney, 1964, p.239

[237] Meaney, 1964, p.240

[238] Meaney, 1964, p.237-8; O'Brien, 1999, ref.224

[239] Ellis Davidson, 1950, p.175

Crouch valley.[240] It has been enclosed by a modern railing to prevent further erosion, already identified as a problem in the 1970s. 'Plumberow' is OE *plumbeorg* 'plum-tree barrow'.[241] (see page 101)

Kelvedon At Kelvedon (Essex) a large inhumation cemetery was discovered and subsequently investigated in 1899.[242] The graves were sited on land later used for gravel extraction, and no mounds were visible but the plot was named *Barrow Field* in 1758, and adjoining fields were known as *Barrow Hills*. It seems probable that a series of low mounds had been levelled in the process of adapting the site for industrial purposes.

Orsett Excavations at Orsett (Essex) in 1975 revealed the ring-ditches of two Anglo-Saxon period barrows and several surrounding graves.[243] A further three ring-ditches were found in a separate gravefield to the south.

Rainham At Gerpins Farm, Rainham (Essex) Anglo-Saxon furnished graves were uncovered during gravel extraction, in association with a flattened mound.[244] Grave-goods included swords, spearheads and brooches, implying both male and female burials on the site. Remarkable glass drinking horns were among the more unusual finds, as these were always a rarity and very few have been found in England. Baker estimates between ten and twenty burials were involved, but it is likely others were destroyed without record.

Redbourne An early account of barrow-digging is recorded in Roger of Wendover's *Chronicle*, s.a. 1178: the story goes that St. Alban appeared to a man and told him that some mounds called the *'Hills of the Banners'* contained the mortal remains of St. Amphibalus.[245] The name of the site was ascribed to the fact that assemblies were held there annually as part of a solemn procession to St.Alban's shrine. Upon investigation by the monks, the mounds were found to contain several skeletons which the pious took for the bones of the blessed saint and

---

[240] Meaney, 1964, p.87; Jones, 1980, p.92; Baker, 2006, p.114 The name of the nearby settlement, Hockley, is associated with the OE personal name *Hoc* (which appears in *Beowulf*), in its weak variant *Hocca - Hoccan leah* would be 'Hoc's clearing'.

[241] Reaney, 1969, p.187

[242] Meaney, 1964, p.86; Jones, 1980, p.90; Baker, 2006, p.117

[243] Jones, 1980, p.91; Hedges & Buckley, 1985; O'Brien, 1999, ref.1116; Baker, 2006, p.120-1

[244] Baker, 2006, p.120

[245] Meaney, 1964, p.104

his companions; his identity was confirmed by the fact that St. Amphibalus had met a grisly end for his faith, and the skeleton had two knives – one in the skull and the other in the chest. It seems likely enough that the remains discovered were those of an Anglo-Saxon male with a *seax* at his side and a spearhead by his head. An inhumation cemetery at Redbourne (Hetfordshire) has been suggested as a possible location.

Reigate   At *Gally Hills*, Reigate (Surrey) there is a series of four small mounds, at least two of which are believed to be Anglo-Saxon barrows, sited on the crest of Banstead Downs.[246] They are 13m in diameter by 50cm high and 8m by 70cm high respectively, with surrounding ring-ditches. One of the barrows was excavated in 1972 and found to contain a supine human skeleton accompanied by a spearhead, seax, shield boss and bronze hanging bowl, all typical late 6th or early 7th c. grave-goods. The mounds had been used for public executions in the 16th c., and there were secondary inhumations believed to be the remains of hanged criminals. The name *Gally Hills* derives from the gallows sited there.

Rivenhall   At Rivenhall (Essex) an Anglo-Saxon cemetery was found in association with a late Roman villa.[247] It is possible that one or more graves was surmounted by a burial mound.

Royston   At Therfield Heath, near Royston (Hertfordshire), a Neolithic long barrow is still visible; it had several secondary inhumations at one end, all of Anglo-Saxon date, one with a spearhead.[248] It was dug in 1845 and 1858. It is uncommon – but not unknown - for Anglo-Saxon burials to have been made in long rather than round barrows. There are ten (probably Bronze Age) round barrows in the area, known as the *Five Hills*.

Shepperton   In about 1750 a stone bridge was under construction at Shepperton (Middlesex) on the north bank of the Thames, where a series of barrows was visible near Walton Bridge.[249] The foreman of the labourers opened several of the barrows and retrieved a shieldboss, some spearheads and ceramic vessels. By 1793 the barrows had been

---

[246] English Heritage's Record Of Scheduled Monuments, National Monument No: 23010; O'Brien, 1999, ref.1113

[247] O'Brien, 1999, ref.1212

[248] Meaney, 1964, p.105; Tyler, 1996, p.114

[249] Meaney, 1964, p.168; O'Brien, 1999, ref.170

levelled. A cremation urn was unearthed on Walton Bridge Green in 1867, and two others were later found close by but many had been destroyed previously.

Shoeburyness At Shoeburyness (Essex) some graves were found before 1903 which may have been of Anglo-Saxon date. In two cases, the bodies were arranged radially with the feet pointing inwards as if they had been covered by a circular mound; however, the headland was the site of a fortified Viking camp in 893 AD and the graves may relate to this period in the site's history.[250]

Springfield Lyons see Chelmsford

Sturmer A barrow at Sturmer (Essex) overlooking the River Stour is in a typical Anglo-Saxon location, but is rather large at 48m diameter for an Anglo-Saxon mound. (I have not been able to trace any reports of excavation on the site.)

Therfield Heath see Royston

Walton Bridge Green see Shepperton

Wendens Ambo A rise known as *Mutlow Hill* at Wendens Ambo (Essex) was dug by workmen in 1847, who found some inhumation burials containing spearheads and a shieldboss as well as unidentified fragments of iron.[251] The name *Mutlow* is from OE *gemot hlæw* 'burial mound for meetings' and implies that a barrow once stood over the graves.

Whitmoor Common see Worplesden

Worplesden In 1877, Pitt-Rivers opened some Bronze Age barrows at Whitmoor Common, near Worplesden (Surrey); nearby stood a group of six mounds which on investigation yielded burnt bones, an iron knife and other items.[252] These barrows were identified by Grinsell with some indeterminate humps on the Common south of Poor Jack's Wood.

---

[250] Meaney, 1964, p.89; Jones, 1980, p.90

[251] Meaney, 1964, p.89; Jones, 1980, p.89

[252] Meaney, 1964, p.245; O'Brien, 1999, ref.530

East Anglia

For the purpose of this study, East Anglia is deemed to include Norfolk, Suffolk and Cambridgeshire, being the territory closest to the fens. However, some of the material from Cambridgeshire is more typical of the East Midlands. Despite the very obvious mounds at Sutton Hoo and elsewhere, East Anglia is not so well furnished with barrow burials due to the prevalence of cremation as the funerary rite for most of the heathen Anglo-Saxon period.

Bloodmoor Hill

The Bloodmoor Hill (Carlton Colville, Suffolk) barrow was opened in 1758, and some of the finds were described in Douglas's *Nenia Britannica* of 1793.[253] The items were then in the collection of a London lawyer, Mathew Duane, although it is unlikely that he actually dug the barrow himself. A gold coin and an onyx intaglio pendant caused much speculation among antiquaries at that time: contemporary accounts indicate that they were found hung about the neck of a skeleton within the barrow. A necklace of garnets, described as having come from the same barrow, was also in his collection.

An engraved crystal was found in the same area in the mid 1700s, and may have come from the barrow or one of its surrounding graves; it too ended up in Duane's collection. There are further reports concerning the site having yielded glass beads, amber beads, spearheads, horse bits and stirrups; this local tradition ascribed to a fierce battle fought on the spot, but it seems more likely that these finds were being recovered from the Anglo-Saxon gravefield surrounding the barrow.[254] More recently, metal detecting finds from the site have included a gold pendant, a copper alloy square-headed brooch and a fragment of a gold composite brooch set with glass and garnet cloisons, a style typical of the early 7th c. Usage of the site into the 8th c. is evidenced by coin finds.

The area now called *Bloodmoor Hill* was, at the time of the enclosures, called *Mootway Common* and was in use as rough pasturage, and it was subsequently known as *Blood Mill Hill*; a windmill once stood on top of the barrow, which was a not uncommon re-use of a convenient existing mound. The hill forms part of the parish boundary between Gisleham, Carlton Colville and Pakefield, and indeed the three parishes meet on the summit of the mound.

---

[253] Meaney, 1964, p.231; Newman, 1996; O'Brien, 1999, ref.735

[254] Grinsell, 1936, p.46 The ascription of barrows to graves for the many dead from a battle is quite common in country lore.

It is likely that the point from which the three parishes were set out was the barrow itself. This is supported by the fact that the meeting point for Mutford Hundred, in which all three parishes lie, may have been in this vicinity; the name *Mootway* is suggestive of the 'moot' (OE *gemot*) or regular local meeting. The lost coins would tie in with the use of the site as a local meeting place, which would have had the character of a market in later Anglo-Saxon times.

The Anglo-Saxon cemetery at Bloodmoor Hill was associated with a nearby early settlement of 39 sunken-featured buildings and at least 8 post-built houses, overlying a Romano-British field system. Within the settlement area were 26 inhumations, and 3 more about 50m to the east. The main cemetery was aligned in roughly parallel rows, similar to a Frankish *Reihengräberfeld* or 'row-grave cemetery'. The grave-goods in the cemetery appear to date from the Final Phase although the dating evidence from the settlement extended from the 6th to the 8th centuries. The settlement contained no obvious high-status buildings, from which it may be inferred that the occupant of the barrow was not a local resident.[255]

The barrow, surrounded by the cemetery, lies on the crest of the ridge, southwest of the settlement. The barrow belongs to the very end of this tradition and must be seen as late 7th or even early 8th c., possibly among the last such monuments ever raised. The presence of a necklace, pendant and coin strongly suggest a high-status 7th c. (royal?) female grave in the barrow on the site, which was the focus for later burials.

Coddenham

Excavations in the Shrubland Hall Quarry in 1999, prior to gravel extraction on the site, revealed an Anglo-Saxon cemetery and an Iron Age settlement. The cemetery contained two rather small chamber graves: one female on an iron-framed bed, and the other a male with a traditional set of weapons.[256]

The female grave was found to contain over 100 separate iron components which were thought to be the remains of a small wooden structure, possibly a coffin, until it was realized that there were fittings which held an angled headboard in place, and the two side-rails of the bed had been de-mounted before placement in the chamber alongside the bed's frame. This quantity of iron parts makes the Coddenham bed the most complex ever excavated in England, of a small group of such finds. Thin iron straps were used to re-

---

[255] Dickens, Mortimer & Tipper, 2006
[256] Watson, 2006

inforce and decorate the headboard, which was made up from two or three separate boards. The ironwork was applied in a pattern of two concentric circles with connecting strips and diamond-headed studs. It was not possible to deduce whether the wood had been carved or painted, although this does seem likely on such a splendid piece of furniture.

Textile remains were present in the corrosion products of the iron fittings, suggesting that bedding had been used to complete the display. The lady, who must have been of some importance, was laid out in garments but her jewellery was not displayed: it was put into a small leather or textile bag, placed on her chest. Her belt or girdle was probably in place, and from it hung a small pouch at her thigh. Her shoes were also in place on her feet and the tiny metal buckles and tags used to close them were present in the grave finds.

The chamber was not large and was constructed from horizontally-placed timber planks with a curved wooden cover or roof. The similarities of the Coddenham grave and grave-goods to the Saxon example at Prittlewell and the Frankish Arnegund burial in St Denis (France) suggest a date in the early years of the 7th c.[257]

Sadly the male burial had been damaged by quarrying so that only the lower part of the chamber remained, to a height of up to 2' (60cm). Two large iron mounts were present on the grave floor, which may have been part of the grave's structure. The deceased was buried with some quite high-status grave-goods – weapons and feasting gear - but there is room for suspicion that the items were made for the funeral. The spearhead was attached to a small sapling rather than a finished spearshaft, and the board of the shield was rather flimsy despite its silver studs and boss with a garnet mounted on the flange. However, the seax was of standard type and in a metal-bound sheath, and there was an iron-bound bucket, a copper-alloy bowl and possibly also a drinking horn in the grave. From these considerations, it appears that the desired effect was display value rather than practical use. The shield had probably been attached to the wall of the chamber, as at Prittlewell, and had fallen to the floor at some point before the gravel excavator destroyed the upper part of the grave. Significantly no sword was found, which may mean that the male was of freeman status but his family were of limited means and were able only to give him a token weapon set for his last presentation to the world. However, the destruction of part of the grave means that no firm conclusions based on lack of remaining grave-goods can be drawn.

---

[257] Halsall, 1995, p.33-4

Lakenheath

In 1997, archaeologists were called in to the USAAF base at Lakenheath (Suffolk) to conduct excavations prior to building work on the site.[258] A large Anglo-Saxon cemetery of about 473 burials was discovered, or possibly three originally separate graveyards which had spread out towards each other. Such a large number of burials of 5th to 7th c. date offered a good opportunity to study undisturbed Anglo-Saxon remains in context. Thirty-four graves were already known from previous building work in 1959, and the more recent finds were considered to be evidently related.

There was one highly unusual burial in the 1997 excavations: a man of about 35 years old, buried in a coffin, alongside his horse with a magnificent leather bridle decorated with gilt bronze fittings, the first such articles to have been found in England. The horse had stood about 17 hands high, making it more like a large pony than a modern horse. The 6th c. grave contained the remains of an adult male with a full set of weapons including shield, spear and sword, as well as a copper alloy buckle; his coffin lay against the south wall of the grave-cut, which was large enough to accommodate the horse with its back against the north wall, accompanied by a wooden vessel, perhaps containing its feed. The bridle included a snaffle-bit and was in position on the animal's head. A mound had covered both horse and rider, and the burials surrounding the mound were all those of pre-pubescent children.

The Lakenheath cemetery had been laid out to respect a pre-existing Bronze Age burial mound which must have been prominent enough in the 6th c. for the local Anglian population to want to adopt it.

Another early Anglo-Saxon horse and warrior burial was discovered in 1999, among 60 graves on another part of the site. The second horse and warrior burial lacked the ceremonial bridle, but was otherwise similar to the first in that it was also originally covered by a barrow and surrounded by a shallow ditch. The quality of bone preservation in the second grave was poor compared to the first, but *in situ* examination of the animal's remains suggested it was 8 or 9 years old at death, and stood about 13 hands high, and was probably of lighter build than the 1997 find.

While many male graves contained knives and spears, only the 'warrior' burials had both a sword and shield each. The burials together provided clear evidence of the early Anglian tradition of animal sacrifice at the grave of a dead leader or chieftain. The horses had apparently been first stunned with a blow to the forehead, then had their throats cut. The shedding of blood was

_____

[258] O'Brien, 1999, ref.16

a powerful symbolic act in heathen religion, and evoked an emotional response from the mourners in their time of grief. Comparison with the 7th century find in Sutton Hoo Mound 17 was immediately made, and indeed the first Lakenheath horse's furniture was of comparable status, although the possessions of their riders were of a different order.

The female graves on the site were not as spectacular as the horse-burials, but there were finds of some large great square-headed brooches which signify important females within their communities.

Shudy Camps

Shudy Camps (Cambridgeshire) is the site of a late Anglo-Saxon inhumation cemetery discovered in 1887 by workmen digging a ditch, and excavated in the 1930s by T.C. Lethbridge, an archaeologist who later went on to enjoy a colourful reputation as a proponent of dowsing and other unorthodox techniques.[259]

The cemetery consisted of 142 excavated graves, aligned with the head to the northwest or southwest, which Lethbridge thought might be due to use of a common cemetery by groups from different settlements or with different religious views, which would account for the variance in position of burial. Most of the graves were unremarkable, containing the usual assortment of tweezers, firesteels, knives, girdle-hangers, beads, buckles, spearheads and shears.

However, one burial stood out clearly from the rest: grave 29 had been laid in a carefully dug trench 7'6" (2,3m) long and 3'3" (1m) wide. The fragmentary remains of a human skeleton were found, much decayed but with recognisable elements of the skull and pelvis, which Lethbridge took to be indicative of a male. The only recorded grave-good was a small fragment of bronze pin, found at the throat, and about 1" (2.5cm) in length. The head rested 1'9" (54cm) from the northern end of the grave, and in this gap was found a rusted metal complex comprising eight lozenges, each pierced by two nails, with a twisted iron side piece at either end. Further metal fragments were found along the outline of the grave, at the sides and feet, and Lethbridge deduced that "the whole contraption, which is extremely difficult to describe, was used to join together the woodwork at the head of a primitive wooden bedstead."[260] The platform of the bed was not recognisable, and he surmised that it might have been "three planks or

---

[259] Lethbridge, 1936; Meaney, 1964, p.69; Speake, 1989, p.98-102

[260] Lethbridge, 1936, p.10

perhaps leather straps across the middle to hold the mattress. The mattress is thought to have been made of straw covered with coarse cloth, for traces of both these materials could be observed on the rust of the twisted iron side-pieces." Lethbridge was quite clear that the frame was not a coffin or bier, by which he must have meant a flat platform on which to rest the body.

The grave was not a chamber grave of the classic sort, but a larger than necessary trench had been dug into the underlying chalk to accommodate the wooden frame; presumably the chalk subsoil needed no reinforcement to stabilise it. As the burial belongs to the Final Phase, no large quantity of grave-goods was deposited or splendid public display of gifts was likely to have been enacted at the graveside. Despite Lethbridge's ascription of male gender (based on very fragmentary skeletal evidence), from the presence of the bed and the copper alloy pin, which might have secured a headrail, it seems safer to assume that this is another example of an Anglo-Saxon female bed-burial.

Grave no. 74 in the same cemetery was also unusual. Lethbridge commented on the very regular sides of the grave, which was 6'6" (2m) long and 2'4" (72cm) wide. Along the sides were four iron 'straps' with projecting nails. The skeleton was that of an adult female and "between the thighs were three iron fragments of uncertain character, and a small bronze buckle. A fragmentary iron pin lay beside the face."[261] Here we appear to have a possible bed-burial, although the meagre size of the grave-cut suggests that it was perhaps more likely a coffin with iron fittings.

In grave 24 Lethbridge noted that the young woman "had been buried in or on some form of wooden contraption of which iron plates remained. In a hollow beneath the skull were four straight plates looking like nothing so much as bar magnets."[262] The iron fittings were in pairs joined by rivets about 1" (2.5 cm) long; two were horizontally placed at the head, three down the left side and two down the right side. "It is uncertain whether they formed part of the binding of a coffin, bier or even a bedstead", remarked Lethbridge. He was unable to account for the iron strips beneath the head, but from comparison with other bed-burials it is clear that ironwork is often used to clamp the headboard planks together. The only grave-good was a glass bead in a gold mount.

Grave 74 was at the centre of a small cluster of graves in the northwest sector of the cemetery; the other graves respect it, as if it had been covered

---

[261] Lethbridge, 1936, p.21

[262] Lethbridge, 1936, p.8

with a small mound. Grave 29 was to the south of this group with three possible satellite graves (nos.49, 52 and 47). Grave 24 lay to the west of this cluster, on a slightly different alignment to the other burials in this part of the cemetery (both 74 and 24 were with the head to the west; 29 was with the head to the southwest) and without close neighbours.

Snape

In 1862 a mound at Snape was excavated and found to contain a ship burial, the first known in England.[263] In the same area a series of cremation burials was discovered, some of Bronze Age date but at least one was in a typically Anglian urn with swastika decoration. It appears that the relationship between mound, urns and ship is no longer recoverable: was the ship inserted into a pre-existing Bronze Age mound, or was the Anglian mound built over an existing Bronze Age urnfield? It is unlikely that the Anglian cremation could be later than the ship burial, since cremation was already diminishing as a funerary rite when ship burial was introduced in the second half of the 6th c. Originally five barrows had stood close together, by the road to Aldbrough.

The ship was 48' (14m) in length, 4' (1.3m) deep and 9'9" (3m) wide at the widest point amidships. It was clinker built in the Anglo-Saxon style and held together with rivets. Within were some fragments of spearheads, a fragment of blue glass, pieces of jasper, a bundle of red fibre (assumed at the time of excavation to be 'hair' but subsequently identified as the remains of a shaggy cloak), fragments of a glass claw beaker and a gold ring set with a Roman intaglio. The blue glass is now lost and has been assumed to be Roman, but given the repeated association of princely burials with squat blue glass jars it cannot be excluded that the blue glass once formed such a vessel. The claw beaker is of mid-6th c. date. The gold ring was probably of Continental manufacture, re-using an existing Roman stone, as it is similar to one from Krefeld-Gellep (Germany).[264] An intriguing find is a convex copper plate which may have formed part of a helmet.[265]

The Snape burial is within the princely grade, with its body container in the form of a ship, its glass claw beaker and its intaglio ring, which could be used to seal documents. It seems likely that the Snape cemetery was the first burial ground for the East Anglian royal family, who later transferred to the new site at Sutton Hoo and brought the ship-burial tradition with them.

---

[263] Ellis Davidson, 1950; Meaney, 1964, p.232; Filmer-Sankey, 1990; O'Brien, 1999, ref.738; Filmer-Sankey & Pestell, 2001; Williams, 2006, p.123-35

[264] Doppelfeld & Pirling, 1966

[265] Meaney, 1964, p.232

There were other watercraft discovered at Snape: in two of the neighbouring forty seven graves log-boats had been re-used as coffins, a rarity in Anglo-Saxon England.

Spong Hill

Spong Hill (Norfolk) is the largest Early Anglian cemetery discovered and excavated in England, with 2259 cremations and 57 inhumations. Two inhumations in the cemetery were chamber burials, inhumations 31 and 40, which were both within ring-ditches.[266]

Inhumation 31

The timber chamber was composed of vertical side-walls and horizontal planks on the floor, with flint packing around the sides of the chamber; the timbers had probably been pegged in place as there were no metal fittings in its construction. The chamber's roof survived only along the south edge, where the wood had rotted but was still identifiable. The chamber was empty of substantial finds (other than some fragments of bone and the spear ferrule) but some remains were scattered outside, in the fill of an intrusive pit. The grave-goods were: a narrow leaf-shaped spearhead, found outside the chamber, to the south of the pit; a corresponding iron ferrule, found on the south side of the chamber; an iron shield boss and grip with wood adhering, found on the western wall of the chamber; two bronze plaques in the shape of fish were probably fittings for the shield's board; a fragment of silvered bronze strip; some iron objects wrapped in textiles, of which at least one was probably a knife; an iron D-shaped buckle loop; a buckle with an oval loop and plate; parts of Roman pots; some fragments of Anglian, Roman and earlier pottery and associated small pieces of flint and chalk.

Also within the same ring-ditch was Inhumation 32, a coffin burial. There were no traceable human remains but some of the grave-goods survived: an iron spearhead; an iron buckle with a rectangular loop; an iron knife, with traces of the leather sheath still on the blade; a small fragment of bronze strip. Some Roman potsherds were found in the backfill. A cremation urn had been buried on the inner edge of the ditch in the southeast quadrant.

Inhumation 31 had been robbed, which supports the idea that it was a visible tumulus, since it was prominent enough to attract the attention of barrow-diggers.

---

[266] Meaney, 1964, p.173-5; Hills, 1977; Hills, Penn & Rickett, 1984; O'Brien, 1999, ref.121

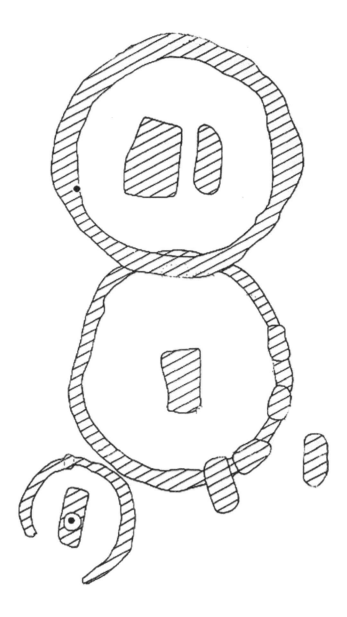

Spong Hill (Norfolk). A series of three barrows was sited on the eastern edge of the burial ground. The western (top) barrow contained two inhumations (shaded) and its ring-ditch overlay the adjacent barrow's edge which had four separate burials in the ditch itself. A smaller, incomplete ring-ditch to the south-east held another inhumation and a separate cremation, marked with a dot. A cremation was placed on the southern sector of the first barrow's ditch. (After Hills & Penn, 1981)

Inhumation 40

The ring-ditch around Inhumation 40 was cut by that for Inhumations 31 & 32 to the west, implying that this ditch was earlier.[267] Two other partial or penannular ring-ditches were close by: that around Inhumation 41 to the southeast and that around Inhumation 46 to the south of the intersection of the two chamber graves' ditches. There were further inhumations in the ring-ditch, numbers 42 (female with 2 pots, wrist-clasps, 2 small-long brooches), 43 (no human remains, with plain potsherds), 44 (female with 1 pot, rings, 2 annular brooches, knife and beads) and 47 (female with 1 pot).

There were no human remains in the chamber, and the roof was intact although it had subsided in the middle and there was evidence for the collapse of the timber frame at one end. If there had been a mound above the chamber, it had been removed long ago – perhaps in the construction of the neighbouring burial?

There was no evidence for a coffin, the finds apparently having been placed on the floor of the chamber. The grave-goods comprised: an iron spearhead and ferrule, found some distance apart, possibly due to the spear having been broken in the burial rites; a bronze-bound wooden bucket made from upright wooden staves; an iron shield boss and grip, with remains of the wooden board, leather covering and some textiles; an iron sword in its scabbard, with traces of the horn grip, and a gilt-bronze strip at the scabbard's mouth; three fragments of bronze strip, used to repair a wooden bowl; an amber bead found near the sword and probably an amuletic sword-bead; an iron strip, possibly part of the shield; a bronze buckle-plate. There were several pieces of broken pot and worked flint in the grave's backfill.

The chamber burial evidently contained a male with a splendid sword, a shield and a spear and the stave-bucket which is a feasting vessel. The sword was found to be pattern-welded with a chevron pattern, pointing upwards on one face and downwards on the other. The surrounding burials from the ring-ditch all appear to have been females, perhaps members of the male's family.

---

[267] Hills, 1977; Hills, Penn & Rickett, 1984

Sutton Hoo

The burials at Sutton Hoo were apparently divided between two cemetery- or burial-groups, of which the many graves covered by mounds are the most prominent. The mounds are in three main groups or axes on the crest of a ridge overlooking the River Deben (Suffolk). At least nineteen mounds were present on the site, and it is possible that others await discovery.[268] It is notable that no two mound burials appear to have been closely similar, which must surely suggest that the intention was to create a single event for each dead person; as well as using the available range of traditional burial rites, the East Angles adapted a variety of burial traditions from Anglo-Saxon England and southern Sweden in order to make a series of political and ideological statements. Clearly each burial was unique, and there was no attempt at repetition even when the same basic elements were used: e.g. both mounds 1 and 2 used a ship in the mound, but in mound 1 the chamber was built inside the ship, in mound 2 it was built beneath it. That said, the mounds were apparently all laid out similarly on the ground and therefore probably all looked quite similar when completed. If there were marker posts on the summits, these would presumably have been commemorative in nature in order to ensure accurate preservation of the names and traditions which these lavish burials commemorated.

The Sutton Hoo mound cemetery was established as a separate burial area from the pre-existing graveyard, and it may have been in use for only a century or so.[269] The ship-burials may have been among the last barrows on the site, although some of the nearby execution burials may have taken place at about the same time as the construction of the mounds; the majority of executions took place at the site of a gallows which stood here between the 8th and 11th c.

Mound 1

The ship burial in mound 1 at Sutton Hoo was a more lavish grave-gift than any ever bestowed on an Anglo-Saxon king.[270] The 90' (27m) long ship was not new when it was hauled to the top of the cliff above the River Deben, but it was still apparently seaworthy, and it was deposited in a trench 11' (3.5m)

---

[268]Meaney, 1964, p.233-5; Williams, 2006a, p.158-60; O'Brien, 1999, ref.42. A gap in the line formed by mounds 3, 10 and 11 may be the site of a lost or ploughed-out barrow.

[269] Wilson, 1992, p.170; Carver, 2002, p.133

[270] Ellis Davidson, 1950; Speake, 1980; Also Carver, 1990; 1992; 1992a; 1999; 2000; 2002; 2005.

below the contemporary ground surface. The sequence thereafter appears to have been as follows:[271]

- chamber built in the middle of the ship
- textiles used to decorate and line the chamber
- cauldrons placed along the eastern wall
- body placed in the chamber
- first object group placed by the body: pillow, shoes, hanging bowls, small bowl and cup
- second object group placed by the body: mailcoat (and flowers?)
- third object group placed by the body: leather garment, bowl, cap, ladle, wooden bottles, combs
- additional sets of objects placed around the body: helmet, gaming pieces, bell, spoons, bowls, spears, sword, bottles, drinking horns, large silver dish
- group of objects placed at the western wall: stack of spears, lyre, bucket, whetstone (sceptre), standard, shield
- final objects brought into the chamber: iron lamp, bucket, ceramic bottle

It is not clear whether the body was placed in a framed container, a full coffin, or was laid to rest on the wooden floor of the chamber.[272] Arguments for and against the coffin have been advanced and it must be said that no firm conclusion can be drawn. While the presence of a coffin would explain the arrangement of the helmet, gaming pieces, bell and so on – these could have been placed on the lid of the container – no evidence for the sides or supporting structure was found. Given that the burial was a splendid affair, it may be that the body was brought to the cemetery on a cart and that the flatbed of the vehicle was transferred to the grave. A wooden frame with few metal components cannot be ruled out, but nor is its presence a necessary conclusion from the excavation records.

The objects interred were mainly wrapped in textiles, and there were further piles of textiles on the floor and sides of the chamber; all were in shades of red and yellow, where colour could be determined, and this combination of hues echoes the magnificent garnet-and-gold jewellery and weapon-fittings, the buckle, purse and shoulder clasps. Indeed, as Williams noted, if the chamber

---

[271] Williams, 2006a, p.137-41

[272] Speake, 1989, p.110-2 discusses the coffin hypothesis and the possibility that they may have come from a bed-burial. There is insufficient evidence for any firm conclusion.

was lit by the flickering flame of the single iron lamp then the whole tableau would have appeared warm, wealthy and 'welcoming' in the rich, cosy tones displayed.[273] Indeed, the guttering light source might well have made the serpentine decorations of the buckle, helmet and other items appear to writhe.

Mound 17

The burial in Mound 17 at Sutton Hoo is one of the better understood grave-mounds in England due to the meticulous excavation by Martin Carver and his team.[274] The probable construction sequence has been admirably summarised by Williams as follows:[275]

- excavation of the first grave-cut
- grave-cut lined with moss and grass
- two spears placed in the bottom of the grave-cut
- a shield placed over the spears
- four vessels placed in the northern side of the grave (one iron-bound bucket, one cauldron with a ceramic pot inside, one bronze bowl containing meat in a bag)
- horse-trapping including saddle & harness placed at the foot of the grave
- a wooden tub laid over the harness
- the coffin lowered into the grave, possibly already containing the supine body of a young man with a sword, knife and purse on a belt mounted with a jewelled buckle
- an antler comb was placed in the side of the grave (or slipped off the coffin)
- the horse was sacrificed and buried in a second grave-cut
- the graves were covered and closed
- a mound was raised above the two grave-cuts

The coffin was a wooden dug-out, perhaps reminiscent of the dug-out log-boats used at Snape. It is notable that the spears and shield were outside the coffin and beneath it, which implies that the act of placing them in the grave was significant but they played no further part in the tableau, since they could not be seen once the coffin was put into position. Likewise, the horse furniture must have been intended to be included as ample room was left for it; perhaps the sacrifice of the horse was a symbolic act which was appropriate for the

---

[273] Williams, 2006, p.140

[274] Carver, 2005

[275] Williams, 2006, p.135-7

burial of a war-leader. It is likely that the dead man was displayed in his coffin before it was lowered into the grave-cut, and that his clothing and weapons were arranged around him at that time; it is not certain that the coffin was open when it entered the grave, and it was presumably closed before the comb was thrown or placed on the lid. It is not known whether the grave-cut for the horse burial was made at the same time as the one for the coffin or whether it was added afterwards. While it would have made sense to dig both pits at the same time, the closeness of the horse's pit might have interfered with the enactment of rites at the man's graveside.

Williams sees the sequence as enacting certain social roles in a planned order: the weapons evoke the military exploits of the young man; the horse furnishings likewise evoke both warfare and hunting; the coffin with the body bearing its sword-belt presents the idealised image of the dead person; the horse sacrifice is a religious rite as well as an appropriately lavish display of grief by the mourners; the filled graves and their joint mound effect a transformation into a 'fixed memory' which should be carried forward for the future of the community.

The Other Sutton Hoo Mounds

The following notes are based on the collaborative publication edited by Martin Carver.[276]

Mound 2   A ship burial including a wooden chamber in a trench excavated into
(see fig.8)   the soil surface. The chamber held weapons and feasting equipment.
A ship of about 80' (24m) was placed over the chamber, and a mound of up to 12' (4m) height was erected over it, made from the soil from the quarry ditch. This method of construction was used in the 8th c. mound at *Haithabu* (Hedeby, Denmark).[277]

The chamber was robbed of its portable treasures in the 16th c., the mound further damaged by ploughing and in 1860 a cartload of iron rivets taken from the ship was removed for reworking.

The modern excavations at Sutton Hoo were begun by Basil Brown with Mound 2, since it was evident that the mound had already been opened. The grave is believed to have been male, on the basis of the weapons. A small number of finds remained within the mound after the previous robbing, including:

some iron ship-rivets and other nails; drinking horn fragments

---

[276] Carver, 2005

[277] Carver, 2002, p.132

including a silver-gilt terminal, some mount fragments in silver-gilt foil and some cast gilt-bronze strip fragments; a gilt bronze roundel; a blue-glass squat jar; a gilt-bronze stud; a small silver buckle; a bronze ring; fragment of a sword blade; two iron knives; an iron blade; a sheath containing two iron blades; an iron ring attached to a rod; fragments of iron and wood; a blue faience bead; silver fittings for a wooden box; fragments of a silver bowl; silver and gilt-bronze cup fittings; a gilded copper alloy roundel and fragment of a gilt bronze fitting, both perhaps from a shield; fragments of a copper alloy cauldron and copper alloy bowl; a copper alloy pin and stud; a small piece of amber; remains of textiles and leather.

Mound 3   A cremated male placed on a wooden 'tray' or dug-out boat, with a horse. The mound had been robbed in the 16th c. The remaining grave-goods included:

a carved limestone plaque; a bronze ewer lid; bone fragments; a *francisca* head; a bone comb; remains of textiles.

Mound 4   A cremated male and female placed in a bronze bowl, as well as a horse. The mound had been robbed in the 16th c. The remaining grave-goods included some gaming pieces.

Mound 5   A cremation, which included some animal remains, deposited in a copper alloy container. The mound had been robbed at least twice, and little remained of the original contents. The burial is believed to have been male, based on the nature of the remaining fragments. The skull had received several blade injuries. The recovered items were:

a small piece of fused glass; fragments of a copper alloy bowl; silver mounts from a wooden cup; a pair of iron shears; an iron knife; twelve fragments of bone gaming pieces; two fragments of a bone comb; box fittings and an ivory box lid; a small silver collar; fragments of iron and organic material.

Mound 6   A cremation deposited in a bronze bowl, which had been covered with textile at the time of burial. The mound, which was probably for a male burial, had been robbed and the contents were consequently very sparse but included:

a copper alloy pin fragment; fragments of a bone comb; fragments of a bone box; fragments of gaming pieces; a bone wand. In the back-filled robber trench was a copper alloy sword pyramid, which may have come from this mound.

Mound 7   A cremation deposited in a thin copper alloy bowl, covered with textile at the time of burial and which had been robbed. Only a few fragmentary items were recovered, mostly from the backfill of the robber trench, including:

fragments of a copper alloy cauldron; fragment of an iron strip; a glass bead fragment; bone gaming pieces; fragments of a bone box; fragments of a copper alloy pin; the tip of an iron knife blade.

If the bead was from a 7th c. sword harness, then the grave might be male; otherwise, beads are usually associated with female burials. However, the bead was actually found in a rabbit hole on the edge of the mound and may have originated elsewhere.

Mound 8   Possibly robbed; not explored in modern times

Mound 9   Possibly robbed; not explored in modern times.

Mound 10   Possibly robbed; not explored in modern times.

Mound 11   Possibly robbed; not explored in modern times.
Site of a gun-pit in World War II.

Mound 12   Robbed in 19th c. not explored in modern times.

Mound 13   Robbed in 19th c. not explored in modern times.

Mound 14   An inhumation, robbed and destroyed, but with enough diagnostic fragments to indicate a high-status female burial. The remains included:

fragments of silver sheet, possibly from a bowl; silver fittings from a drinking cup; silver fittings from a purse; silver hinges from a box; silver wire and buckle loops; a silver loop-fastening; two copper alloy pins; a copper alloy and iron chatelaine, with suspension rings and a knife; iron nails; various fragments of wood, iron, quartz and organic material.

It is possible that the iron nails were from a bed-burial as they are too small to have been used for a ship or the timber chamber.

Mound 15   (not located)

Mound 16   (not located)

Mound 18   A cremation deposited in a copper alloy bowl, covered with textile at the time of burial, which had been robbed. All that remained apart from the bowl fragments was a fragment of bone comb and some organic material.

Mound 19 (no mound present)

Additional Burials of 7th c. Date

Burial 12   An inhumation, of which the mound had been levelled and the chamber robbed, containing a child's burial with a small spear- or arrow-head. The split socket is typical of Anglo-Saxon spearheads, and it may be that the find is a miniature weapon suitable for the burial of a noble child. The only other finds were a copper alloy pin and fragments of a small copper alloy buckle.

Burial 13   An inhumation, partially excavated. The finds were limited to part of an iron cauldron with textile covering and a curved piece of iron sheet. The cauldron appears to resemble the contemporary example from Broomfield (Essex).

Between Mounds 4 and 13 was found a garnet cloisonné gold cylindrical fitting; the cloisons are exceptionally well made and are comparable to the material in Mound 1. Its purpose is unknown, but a comparison with some of the sword harness fittings in Mound 1 is suggestive.

Burial 14   Cremation in a ceramic urn.

Burial 15   An inhumation, of which the mound had been levelled and the chamber robbed. The remaining grave-goods included a copper alloy buckle and counter-plate; a garnet and gold buckle and counter-plate; an iron knife and an iron nail. It is not possible to determine the gender of the deceased from these fragments, although the presence of two buckles is reminiscent of the two-belt costume of the Mound 1 burial.

Burial 16   An inhumation, of which the mound had been levelled and the chamber robbed. The burial was of a female, but there is little to indicate date or status in the remaining grave-goods, which included a glass bead; a copper alloy cylinder with fragments of wood and leather; an iron chatelaine; an iron knife; a copper alloy pin; fragments of a leather bag.

The possibility of other chamber mounds awaiting detection in the mound-field is unlikely, but it remains the case that research on adjacent land might reveal further 7th c. burials.

Other East Anglian Barrows

Barnham Heath At Barnham Heath (Suffolk) a Bronze Age barrow was investigated in 1914; a sword, seax, spearhead, shieldboss and grip were discovered, scattered in the fabric of the mound, and indicating an Anglo-Saxon secondary inhumation.[278]

Barrow see **Risby**

Bartlow On Linton Heath near Bartlow (Cambridgeshire) a mound was excavated in 1853, near the Linton-Horseheath road.[279] The mound had been deliberately reduced by ploughing and was barely visible even then. The mound contained 104 secondary burials of Anglo-Saxon date, accompanied by swords, brooches, Roman coins, buckets, a cone beaker and various urns. Some of the brooches bore enamelled decoration, which is generally rare in Anglo-Saxon contexts but there is some evidence for it having been re-introduced into East Anglia in the 6th or 7th c.

Bottisham At Allington Hill, Bottisham (Cambridgeshire) a barrow was excavated in 1876 following discoveries of Anglo-Saxon metalwork in the area.[280] The mound then stood just 2' (60 cm) high and the burial was dug 5' (150cm) into the chalk subsoil; a human skeleton with two gilt-bronze cloisonné mounts was found within. The decoration of the mounts is in Salin's Style II and the date is therefore likely to be late 6th or 7th c.

Brightwell see **Martlesham Heath**

Broome Heath The finding of three cremation urns on Broome Heath (Norfolk) in 1856 prompted a search of the area.[281] There had been many barrows erected on the heath between Broome and Ditchingham, but they had been systematically destroyed and the soil taken away. One such mound was excavated and a large human skeleton was found at a depth of 3' resting on a bed of gravel. The skull bore traces of reddish hair and a green stain, probably from a copper-alloy object which was not recovered. Other barrows were searched but only fragments of charcoal were found beneath them. In 1861 some objects from barrows on Broome Heath were exhibited, including an urn and a flint arrowhead.

---

[278] Meaney, 1964, p.224

[279] Meaney, 1964, p.67-8

[280] Meaney, 1964, p.60; O'Brien, 1999, ref.69

[281] Meaney, 1964, p.170; O'Brien, 1999, ref.726

Chatteris At Chatteris (Cambridgeshire) several skeletons were dug up in 1757 during gravel digging;[282] the site was described as a 'sort of tumulus' and it may once have been a barrow. A sword, spear, shieldboss, clawbeaker and a clay urn accompanied one skeleton.

Cherry Hinton At Cherry Hinton (Cambridgeshire) in 1949 eight or more Anglo-Saxon secondary burials were found in a Bronze Age barrow;[283] the grave-goods included an unusual hog-backed bone comb and a bronze-mounted crystal ball.

Chillesford In 1953 a barrow at Chillesford (Suffolk) was investigated and pronounced to be 'probably of Saxon date'.[284]

Earsham In about 1855 an Anglo-Saxon cremation urn was found in a mound at Earsham (Norfolk) and was exhibited in 1859, along with a horse's bit from another mound on the same site, near the church.[285] A complete urn and fragments of others were also found within the barrowfield. The ceramics were identified as Roman at the time, but have subsequently been assigned to the 6th c. Another urn of the same period was found in the grounds of Earsham Hall.

Edix Hill Hole Field (Cambridgeshire) is the site of one of the larger Anglo-Saxon inhumation cemeteries.[286] Excavation has proceeded at various times from 1858 to 1861 and 1989-91. In 1861 Wilkinson established that all the known graves were flat, but the quality of grave-goods was in line with those from middle-range barrows, e.g. swords, spearheads, shieldbosses, bronze brooches, glass and amber beads, hanging bowls and a bed-burial. The 1989 excavations found little direct evidence for barrows, but one feature (F121) was a layer of soil above three inhumations (graves 60,61,62) and there was likelihood of mounds above several other burials.

Fordham A series of three barrows were built beside the road between Freckenham and Chippenham, at Fordham (Cambridgeshire) in 1935;[287] skeletons with weapons were found as well as some other metalwork. Kentish type small square-headed brooches were among them.

---

[282] Meaney, 1964, p.63

[283] Meaney, 1964, p.63

[284] Meaney, 1964, p.226; O'Brien, 1999, ref.836

[285] Meaney, 1964, p.172

[286] Meaney, 1964, p.60-1; Malim & Hines, 1998, p.33; O'Brien, 1999, ref.88

[287] Meaney, 1964, p.63

Great Carbrooke At Great Carbrooke (Norfolk) a mound on a flat area called *The Battlefield* yielded some objects including a cruciform brooch in about 1844.[288] In 1856 from another mound, called *The Knight's Hill* was taken a necklace of amber and glass beads. However, the records of this area are considered doubtful and the locations may be unreliable.

Harford Farm In construction of a bypass round Norwich in 1989-91, excavations revealed an Anglo-Saxon cemetery at Harford Farm where a group of fifteen burials respected a prehistoric barrow.[289] The grave-goods were generally sparse, implying a late date for the burials which mainly contained just a belt-buckle and a knife each.

Icklingham Some time before 1888, Prigg recorded the finding of a cruciform brooch and some ceramic vessels at Mitchell's Hill, Icklingham (Suffolk).[290] A Bronze Age beaker was also recovered from the mound, implying that the Anglo-Saxon material must have come from a secondary inhumation. Several other finds attributed to the site were in the collection of Sir John Evans, including a great square-headed brooch set with garnets.

Ipswich A small Anglo-Saxon cemetery was found associated with a Bronze Age ring-ditch at Boss Hall, Sproughton Road, Ipswich (Suffolk) during ground clearance for a supermarket in 1989. Four cremation urns and nineteen inhumations were excavated. One of the inhumations was a large chamber grave, with the cremations as satellite burials. There was no trace of a mound or ditch, but any such traces would have been destroyed in the initial earthworking of the site.[291] An early Anglo-Saxon cemetery was found at Buttermaket, Ipswich (Suffolk) in 1988.[292] There were about seventy inhumations, with some evidence for barrows.

Ixworth A barrow at Stanton, Ixworth (Suffolk), excavated in 1856, contained the bed-burial of a high-status female wearing a garnet-and-gold pendant cross and a fine cloisonné applied disc brooch, both now in the Ashmolean Museum, Oxford.[293]

---

[288] Meaney, 1964, p.172; O'Brien, 1999, ref.844

[289] Penn, 2000

[290] Meaney, 1964, p.231

[291] O'Brien, 1999, ref.2116; *Med. Arch.* Vol. 34, 1990, p.211

[292] O'Brien, 1999, ref.2121

[293] Speake, 1989, p.124

Kettlestone see **Pensthorpe**

Langham In 1936 a Bronze Age mound on the parish boundary at Langham (Norfolk) was excavated.[294] Finds included an iron spearhead and shieldboss but no human remains.

Linton Heath see **Bartlow**

Martlesham Heath On the border of Brightwell and Martlesham Heath (Suffolk) three small mounds were excavated in 1921.[295] Two were of Bronze Age date but the third held a bronze vessel, covered with linen and taped, which contained the cremated remains of a larger (male?) adult; a smaller (female?) adult; the skull of a newborn baby; fragments of a fourth skull, probably foetal. Bones from cremated animals – an ox and a dog – were also in the bowl. Grave-goods included two bone combs with iron rivets; a decorated bone disc; a large ivory (purse?) ring; two glass beads; a clay object bearing decoration; fragments of pot; flint scrapers; some burnt wood.

Also on Martlesham Heath, a barrow was excavated in 1942, but it had probably been robbed previously as there was no discernable central burial.[296] Without datable remains there is no certain means of assigning the barrow to any period, but there were Bronze Age sherds and flints incorporated into the material from which it was made. Two deposits of cremated bones in the barrow had no accompanying objects. However, the mound did contain an interesting feature: a 'pan' of dark sand in the centre of the barrow (14" x 8") with a definite raised edge. This feature was also found in some of the Sutton Hoo mounds. It may have been used for the making of offering to the dead in the form of libations.

Mepal Fen A Bronze Age mound at Mepal Fen (Cambridgeshire) opened in 1859 contained an Anglo-Saxon secondary burial: a cremation in a large, plain urn.[297]

Mildenhall Three barrows stood on *Warren Hill*, near Mildenhall (Suffolk) near the road to Bury St. Edmunds.[298] In 1820 trenches were cut through each mound down to ground level but only pottery was

---

[294] Meaney, 1964, p.178

[295] Meaney, 1964, p.225; O'Brien, 1999, ref.730

[296] Meaney, 1964, p.225

[297] Meaney, 1964, p.68

[298] Meaney, 1964, p.236

recovered. The northern side of the central mound was disturbed during gravel extraction in 1866 and a Bronze Age burial was found, as well as a number of Anglo-Saxon graves; the sparse grave-goods were discarded by the labourers and only a handful of items could be recovered by Prigg, including a bronze toilet set and a Roman handle. Fenton managed to obtain four shieldbosses, two iron studs and four spearheads said to have come from this site. Between 1875 and 1877, Fenton went on to discover and record five Anglo-Saxon graves and another of a horse, found in pits on the hill. More Anglo-Saxon graves were unearthed in 1881 when a new road was constructed in the area. It seems likely that the barrows – probably Bronze Age in original construction – were the focus for Anglo-Saxon secondary inhumation and satellite burials.

Morning Thorpe An important cemetery at Morning Thorpe (Norfolk) excavated in the early 1970s held examples of barrow burial.[299] At least four graves were surrounded by ring-ditches, although some were disturbed, implying that mounds had been raised over them. One, grave 218, was an adult (perhaps elderly) male buried with an iron spearhead, iron sword, iron shieldboss and grip, a wooden bucket with iron fittings, a copper alloy buckle and counterplate, a knife with a horn handle, an organic mass with gold leaf adhering (perhaps a garment?) and a broken pot. A second grave-cut was within the ditch, but no grave was found within it. The sword was an early form with a cocked-hat pommel and herringbone pattern-welded blade. In all, these finds were rather rich for this cemetery and suggest that the occupant enjoyed considerable social standing.

Narborough In about 1600 Spelman wrote of a location called *'burg'* at Narborough (Norfolk) where human bones and weapons have been dug out.[300] It is possible that this was an Anglian barrow, although the site is near the end of the *Devil's Dyke* (an Anglian defensive earthwork) and the mound referred to may be the earth bank rather than a barrow.

Northwold Labourers working at Northwold (Norfolk) in 1838-41 were redistributing soil into a meadow from a low rise, and found beneath it a collection of earthenware, swords, spearheads, shieldbosses, brooches and glass and amber beads.[301] In about 1849, the remains of a circular shield were found in another mound at Northwold Mills.

---

[299] Green, Rogerson & White, 1987; O'Brien, 1999, ref.1192

[300] Meaney, 1964, p.179

[301] Meaney, 1964, p.179-80; O'Brien, 1999, ref.38

Probably further digs took place as objects said to have come from Northwold were exhibited in 1851 and 1852, although it is not certain that these were two separate sets of finds. It is not clear how many barrows there were, nor whether the Anglo-Saxon burials were primary or secondary.

Oxborough A small Anglo-Saxon cemetery at Oxborough (Norfolk) revealed seventeen inhumations, with some evidence for barrows.[302] Unfortunately, severe plough damage to the site made interpretation very difficult.

Pensthorpe A cremation cemetery was found at Kettlestone, Pensthorpe (Norfolk) covered by a series of mounds, visible across several fields.[303] The mounds were pitted with holes in which urns had been set. Ploughing had reduced the mounds to little more than slight elevations but it is said that the fields were scattered with pottery and bones. Tumuli were known to exist along the edges of Long Lane, Pensthorpe, a major droveway to Norwich. The earliest records date to 1826, consisting of a sketch of an urn with an enamelled brooch.

Poringland Heath Although the 1797 map shows no mounds on Poringland Heath (Norfolk), a manuscript in Norwich Museum refers to iron spearheads recovered from barrows there.[304]

Risby When the turnpike road was being laid out in 1777, part of the base of a mound between Barrow and Risby (Suffolk) was cut away to reveal some bones, and later a human skull.[305] Repairs to the road in 1784 caused labourers to damage more of the mound, whereby they discovered a cremation urn in the centre and a full skeleton. Remains of ash and a large timber post were also unearthed. In 1813 two spearheads were recovered from a mound at *Barrow Bottom*, the site of the earlier digs.

Two barrows stood on Risby Heath (Suffolk), and were partially excavated before 1869 by Greenwell.[306] One yielded an Anglo-Saxon cremation urn. A second excavation in 1959 produced only one small find: a blue glass bead of probable 5th c. date.

---

[302] Penn, 1998; O'Brien, 1999, ref.2087

[303] Meaney, 1964, p.177; O'Brien, 1999, ref.117

[304] Meaney, 1964, p.180

[305] Meaney, 1964, p.224

[306] Meaney, 1964, p.232

Smallburgh Labourers levelling a small mound at Smallburgh (Norfolk) in 1856 discovered pottery and glass and amber beads.[307] The site was known locally as *The Battleground* or *The Burnt Field*. The beads were intact and had not been cremated, so an inhumation accompanied by a pottery vessel is more likely than a cremation.

Soham There were at least three Anglo-Saxon cemeteries at Soham (Cambridgeshire).[308] The one dug in 1931 by Lethbridge, Tebbutt and Leaf was unusual in that the outer burials were all laid out as if on the circumference of a circle, and the parish boundary respects this spot: from this, it was deduced that the burials had been placed in a low barrow. The burials themselves were unusual in that the only male with weapons had an axe and a spear (an uncommon combination) and a Roman coin in his hand; another male had smith's tools in his grave; an older female was buried beneath limestone slabs and flints, and was covered with a band of charcoal; two cremations were buried in broken pots near the inhumations; an ox's head was buried face-down in a small pit nearby.

South Acre A large prehistoric round barrow at South Acre was identified by aerial photography.[309] Although the feature was greatly disturbed, there were more than a hundred shallow satellite burials of Anglo-Saxon date on the site, many of them decapitated. It seems likely that the barrow had been used as a *cwealmstow*, and that it had been chosen for its heathen associations.

Sporle An antiquarian named Johnson assisted with the opening of some barrows at Sporle (Norfolk) in 1820.[310] One mound contained seven skeletons, some with their faces covered by shields made from leather stretched over thin laths of wood. Spearheads lay by their sides, and each was covered with a woollen cloak or covering, fastened with a brooch, which disintegrated on contact with the air. One of the shieldbosses had been damaged by a spear-thrust. Another skeleton had a string of beads, and others had girdlehangers and buckles. In another mound the skeleton of a horse and some small bones was detected. Further small finds were retrieved between 1847 and 1851.

Stanton see **Ixworth**

---

[307] Meaney, 1964, p.181

[308] Meaney, 1964, p.69-70

[309] Wymer, 1996

[310] Meaney, 1964, p.181-2; O'Brien, 1999, ref.124

Thetford A possible barrow was present in the Thetford (Norfolk) cemetery, discovered in 1863 when trees were removed and human remains were found in the roots.[311] The burials were not accompanied and there were no flints or other inclusions. However a large inhumation cemetery of Anglo-Saxon date is known from the site.

Weasenham In 1886, Chester presented to the British Museum a series of items allegedly taken from a Bronze Age barrow at Weasenham (Norfolk).[312] The items were a silver pin; part of a scutiform disc; a bronze (belt?) plate; an iron knife; three glass beads; a broken bronze hand-tool. These goods are consistent with a female inhumation.

Woodbridge The riverside town of Woodbridge (Suffolk) is famous as the spot from which the Sutton Hoo mounds can be seen across the River Deben.[313] However, the town had its own barrow: on the site of Junior House, near Haugh Lane, vestiges of a barrow were discovered within which were the remains of an adult male with a spear.

---

[311] Meaney, 1964, p.182; O'Brien, 1999, ref.34

[312] Meaney, 1964, p.184

[313] Meaney, 1964, p.236; O'Brien, 1999, ref.740

Thames Valley – (includes Oxfordshire & Berkshire)

Asthall

The landowner, G.S. Bowles and the archaeologist, E.T. Leeds excavated this prominent mound on two occasions in 1923-4.[314] It is situated in a prominent position by the present A40 road near Witney, on land attached to Barrow Farm. (A later Anglo-Saxon find from the same area is the 'Minster Lovell jewel' a mid-Saxon gold fitting, perhaps for a 'wand' used to keep one's place when reading.) The finds were deposited in the Ashmolean Museum, Oxford, of which Leeds was then Assistant Keeper of Antiquities.

The barrow stood to a height of about 12' (3.5m) when Leeds excavated it, but is about half this height today. The perimeter is 55' (16.75m) in diameter, but it is understood that the barrow used to be larger, although this may have been due to the soil having slipped due to partial collapse of the wall. A notable feature is the use of a dry-stone walling technique to create the barrow's perimeter; this is understood to have been added in the post-mediaeval period in order to stabilise the structure.[315] The availability of usable local stone must have suggested this method of barrow reconstruction, and some other barrows locally have the same feature e.g. Squires Clump at Sarsden. A large wooden post had once stood in the soil, possibly before the cremation burial was inserted; it was not centrally placed and its function is unknown, although Swedish parallels suggest that a stake might be used to guide the builders in constructing the mound.

The Asthall barrow is unusual in containing just cremated remains and no evident chamber or high-status inhumation.[316] This is also the case at some of the Sutton Hoo barrows, nos.3, 4, 5, 6, 7 and 18. The deposit was considered undisturbed by Leeds, due to the lack of cremated remains in the covering soil. At Asthall, there was no surviving container for the bones, which were placed on a layer of clay, possibly brought from the Windrush

---

[314] Ellis Davidson, 1950; Meaney, 1964, p.203; Speake, 1980, p.39; Dickinson & Speake, 1992; O'Brien, 1999, ref.432

[315] Wigg, 1999, p.42. There are parallels for this construction technique in the Rhineland, Central Germany and eastern France in the early Roman period but it is considered an introduced Gallic tradition.

[316] MacGregor & Bolick et al., 1993. Yeates, 2008, p.136 suggests that the incumbent was represented as a victorious rider in the manner of the horsemen on Roman tombstones, but there is nothing in the remaining evidence to support this (e.g. no spurs, saddle, bridle or other equestrian equipment).

valley; the inclusion of clay inside the grave is a noted feature of some English examples, with parallels in Sweden. The cremated remains – vegetable, human and animal – were deposited on the clay in a layer up to 6" (15cm) thick in parts. Wooden postholes were located in the soil, which may even have formed part of the pyre itself. However, it cannot be excluded that one or other of the larger vessels originally contained the human remains before it disintegrated.

The grave-goods were fragmentary but still impressive, including fourteen bone and antler gaming pieces, fragments of pottery, various metal belt fittings, fragments of silverware, at least two imported copper alloy bowls and Merovingian Frankish wheel-made pottery, but they were not in the same league as those from the majority of 7th c. mound burials. There were at least three pottery bowls (possibly more). The quantity and range of vessels suggest that the occupant ranked among the most powerful people in the community at the time of his or her death: a high number and wide range of vessels is associated with only the very wealthiest inhumation burials and the same may have been true of cremations.[317]

A copper-alloy strap-end with ropework and herringbone decoration was among the few surviving objects of the belt-set, which also included copper-alloy strap fittings. A small pear-shaped mount consisting of two birds of prey emerging from a teardrop-shaped plate was one of the better preserved items. One of the belt-mounts featured a complex swivel arrangement, similar in intention, if not execution, to the swivelling strap attachment on the Sutton Hoo sword-belt.

Some fragments of repoussé foils with Style II decoration were found, which may have come from a bowl. They are formally very similar to those on the Sutton Hoo Mound 1 helmet, but there are no traces of any iron skull to which they would have been attached had they come from a helmet. However, use on a drinking horn or small cup (as at Sutton Hoo Mound 1) could not be excluded. Fragments of bone may have come from a casket, a comb-case or possibly the edges of a gaming board.

A 'Coptic' bowl was the main item suggesting a link with the general run of early 7th c. princely burials. The cremation probably took place in the first half of the century, at a time when cremation was already exceptional, although some traces of Style I decoration indicate the presence of articles which were probably at least half a century old at the time they were placed

---

[317] Dickinson & Speake, 1992, p.113-5

on the pyre.[318] However, the fact that the incumbent had been cremated must have influenced the choice and range of grave-goods. The remaining bones and teeth showed that the person was above 15 years of age. Leeds believed that the remains were those of a female, but this has been contested; certainly, there is nothing specifically female in the assemblage (no brooch or chatelaine) and it would be unusual (but apparently not unique) for a female to be buried with gaming pieces.[319] The presence of drinking horns and cups also points to a male rather than a female burial, as also does the presence of cremated animal bones. However, as Dickinson & Speake note, it remains possible that the mound covered a double burial, one of either sex, for which there is a parallel at Sutton Hoo (mound 4).[320]

The barrow at Asthall was carefully located to be visible from Akeman Street, a Roman road, as it crosses the River Windrush.[321] It does not appear to have been a re-used existing structure, but there are many examples of this practice in the Wychwood area to the north; this led Sonia Chadwick Hawkes to associate the burial with the Hwicce, a local Anglian group who were subject to the overlordship of the Mercians.[322] As such, like Taplow, the Asthall barrow should probably be seen as a sentinel barrow dominating and controlling the main routes into the local area. The Wansdyke is situated in this area, and the barrow's location may have been chosen to dominate that structure. The rite chosen – accompanied cremation – was a typically Anglian rite and it may be that the use of this (Anglian – Mercian) burial in a region which was contested by the Mercians and West Saxons was a statement of allegiance.[323] If so, the eventual relocation in 685 AD of the West Saxon ecclesiastical centre from Dorchester-on-Thames in the Thames Valley south to Winchester may have been a move to protect the central religious authority of the West Saxon kingdom from the power of their Mercian rivals.[324] (see fig.2)

---

[318] Dickinson & Speake, 1992, p.107. Style I ornament appeared on a fragmentary disc or ring.

[319] Dickinson & Speake, 1992, p.109. There are no females buried beneath large 7th c. mounds with gaming sets. Three definite Anglo-Saxon female burials with gaming pieces are known, but at least one was a multiple burial (and therefore the pieces did not necessarily belong with the female) and another was a curated Roman piece used as an ornament.

[320] Dickinson & Speake, 1992, p.112

[321] Hawkes, 1989, p.90-1; Williams, 2006a, p.202-4

[322] Hawkes, 1989, p.91 The *Hwicce* gave their name to the Wychwood itself.

[323] Hawkes, 1989, p.91

[324] Dickinson & Speake, 1992, p.123 The tribal lands to the north of the barrow belonged to the *Feppingas*, of whom little is known. Perhaps the burial was that of the lord of

Cuddesdon

The Oxfordshire village of Cuddesdon was chosen as the site for the episcopal palace of the bishop of Oxford, and extension work on an existing building in 1847 unearthed a quantity of skeletons accompanied by Anglo-Saxon material including swords, two blue glass bowls, a bronze fragment and a bronze bucket. The finds were published by Ackerman.[325] Subsequent investigation of the site, the palace having been demolished in 1962, produced only one find which might be of Anglo-Saxon date, a small copper-alloy lace-tag.

The skeletons were arranged radially and the grave-goods were placed nearby, but the report is not precise enough to indicate how the skeletons and goods were associated; the implication seems to be that the goods were recovered from a spot close to the bones. The burials were laid out prone, which is unusual in Anglo-Saxon contexts. The report mentioned two swords, which would be remarkable in a single male burial but not without parallel if the second sword was in fact a seax, since sword-and-seax combinations are known from Sutton Hoo Mound 17 and elsewhere.

The blue glass jars are similar to the examples from Broomfield and Prittlewell (both Essex) and fragments from Sutton Hoo Mound 2 and Snape (both Suffolk). The bronze vessel was one of the "Coptic" type which were popular as grave-goods in Anglo-Saxon England in the 7th c. – examples were found at Sutton Hoo Mound 1, Prittlewell, Taplow and the fragment from Asthall (Oxfordshire).[326] A fragment of gilded bronze resembles the bird-mounts on the Sutton Hoo lyre.

The radial burials may have been placed around the circumference of a burial mound, for which there are parallels at Sutton Hoo and elsewhere. The lack of an identifiable body with the grave-goods may have been due to the burial rite having involved cremation, or perhaps the barrow was robbed and disturbed before the 1847 construction. For these and other reasons Dickinson was inclined to infer that the Cuddesdon burial was a princely grave of early 7th c. date.

---

this folk, threatened on all sides by powerful neighbours and having to display political and cultural allegiance through material culture, including burial rites.

[325] Ackerman, 1855; Meaney, 1964, p.207; Dickinson, 1974; Speake, 1980, p.39; Hawkes, 1989, p.90; O'Brien, 1999, ref.420

[326] Meaney, 1964, p.92 records a Coptic bowl found on the seashore at Boscombe Chine (Hampshire) in 1807. It is likely that the bowl was once part of a rich chamber burial which was destroyed by coastal erosion, although other explanations are possible.

The earliest form of the place-name Cuddesdon is *Cuþenes dun* 'Cuthen's hill' in a charter of 956; a parallel *Cuþenes hlæw* 'Cuthen's barrow' lies behind the place-name *Cutteslowe*. A link between *Cuþen* and the West Saxon royal kindred is possible: *Cuþ-* is the single most productive prefix in the series from 550 to 680 in names such as *Cuða, Cuðwine, Cuðwulf, Cuðgils, Cuðræd* and *Cuðburh*.[327] (*Cuþenes* is a passable spelling of *Cuþwines* as far as the records allow.) Cuddington, a place-name of Oxfordshire and Buckinghamshire, probably reflects *Cudesdon* i.e. *Cuðes dun* 'Cuth(a)'s hill'. In 1261 AD, two strangers were found murdered in the 'how' of Cutteslowe, a haunt of brigands, and the Sheriff of Oxford ordered it levelled. It is likely that the 'how' (i.e. burial mound) was a Neolithic long-barrow, of which the chamber provided a convenient shelter for the robbers. It therefore remains possible that the royal burial mound survives, its tumulus levelled but its grave-cut protected, on the land called Old Cutchlow.[328]

It seems likely that **Cuþen* was a byname for one of the West Saxon royalty, but since the history of the West Saxon house is wracked with internal strife it may be that the burial at Cuddesdon was of one of the lesser members, a local leader albeit a wealthy one.

Lowbury Hill

The barrow at Lowbury Hill (Oxfordshire) is an isolated Anglo-Saxon mound of late 7th c. date on an elevated spur and with a commanding view over the Thames Valley to the north.[329] The hilltop is covered with an earthworks complex, part of which is probably the remains of a Romano-British *temenos* or sacred enclosure; the walls of this structure were slighted in the 6th or 7th c., presumably at the same time as the barrow was raised. The mound is now about 54' (16m) in diameter but only 3' (0.9m) high. The presence of Roman remains had attracted antiquaries in the past, and the barrow was dug in 1859 but only "Roman coins and ashes" were found. The site was known locally as *Oyster Hill* and large quantities of oyster shells were found, which had presumably been brought from the south coast in the Roman period.

The earthwork complex including the mound was formally excavated in 1913-4 by D.A. Atkinson, who found a large quantity (115) of Roman coins within the barrow. The inhumation was placed centrally on a south-north

---

[327] Dickinson, 1974, p.32-3; Hawkes, 1989, p.89-90

[328] Hawkes, 1989, p.89-90

[329] Ellis Davidson, 1950; Meaney, 1964, p.49; Fulford & Rippon et al., 1994; O'Brien, 1999, ref.510

alignment, with grave-goods consisting of: a knife; a spearhead; a sword; a shield boss; a decorated bronze hanging bowl; a bone comb in an elaborate wood and leather case; a pierced bone plate on the left shoulder; a small bronze buckle at the waist; a small pair of shears and a buckle were placed under the backbone. Other small iron fragments were found in the grave fill. The burial was presumably male, and dated to the mid-6th to mid-7th c. The skeleton was 5'9" (1.77m) tall and aged 45 or older; there was evidence of trauma to the right arm, which may have been the result of a wound, and his health was generally poor at the time of death. (A second skeleton, probably female, aged at 45 years or older, and of 6th or 7th c. date, was found in a grave next to the wall of the *temenos*.)

A further excavation was mounted in 1992, after the site had been subjected to damage by ploughing. Part of the purpose was to determine whether the barrow was an Anglo-Saxon structure or a re-used Bronze Age feature. The spread of fragments of Roman pottery through out the barrow and the surrounding soil suggested that it had been constructed from relatively loose and easily workable soil drawn from around the Romano-British *temenos*. The numerous Roman coins were all small, of rather low value, many badly worn, and it has been suggested that they were the remains of offerings made at the *temenos* site which had been accidentally included in the soil used in the barrow's construction. There were many other small and odd inclusions, such as:

fragments of bone, mainly sheep, and teeth;

- in copper alloy: a 1st c. BC bow brooch; the bezel from a 4th c finger ring and other parts of rings; a fragment of a late 3rd c. facetted bracelet; a small complete 4th c. finger ring; 4th c. pin terminals;

- in iron: mostly nails and hobnails; some pieces of farmyard tools; at least ten socketed spearheads, some of Roman date, but others possibly Anglo-Saxon;

- in ceramic: a mix of mainly Roman fragments, but with some Iron Age and some Anglo-Saxon inclusions (there was no Anglo-Saxon pottery in the *temenos*, only in the barrow);

- in glass: some clear and some blue-green vessel fragments of Roman date (but no evidence for Anglo-Saxon glassware such as clawbeakers or palm cups).

The presence of Anglo-Saxon pottery in the barrow implies that there was activity in the area into the 7th c., but as this material was absent from the temple enclosure the activity presumably did not include visiting that site, other than for the purpose of demolishing the wall and removing its usable stones. The shield boss is datable to the third quarter of the 7th c.[330]

The Lowbury Hill barrow was not the focus for a cemetery, nor a wealthy chamber-grave, nor was it a prominent landmark for the Anglo-Saxon population of the area, as the nearest settlement was 3 miles (5km) away in the valley. It is however quite close to the Ridgeway, and may have been chosen both for its high location and its association with the Romano-British temple enclosure, which provided the material used in its construction. The name 'Lowbury' properly refers to the 'enclosure by the barrow' (*hlæw-burh*) and must have been applied to the remains of the *temenos*. The burial should probably be associated with the West Saxon polity in the region, in opposition to the Anglian presence at Asthall, Lew and elsewhere.[331]

The spearhead from the grave is interesting, in that it is of a standard 5th c. Anglo-Saxon type (Swanton's Type C1) but it has traces of enamel decoration on the lower edges of the blade. Enamelling was not a decorative technique which the Anglo-Saxons or other Germanic folk of this time normally used, although there is some evidence for its adoption in East Anglia.[332] The use of enamel was common in the Pre-Roman Iron Age, but had fallen away by the later Roman period. The normal enamel colour was in the red to orange range, but the spearhead also showed some green, which is very rare at this time. It is therefore possible that the spearhead was made by an Anglo-Saxon smith but for reasons unknown the owner decided to have an enameller add decorations to it. The presence of Britons in the area is signified by the place-name 'Wallingford' (ford of the Welsh people), but there is at present no evidence for continuity in the use of enamel decoration.

It appears that the barrow was located on the Romano-British sacred site in order to show dominance over both the territory and its history, thus legitimising the rule of the Anglo-Saxon élite over both the Anglo-Saxon communities and the remnants of the Welsh in the area.

---

[330] Hawkes, 1989, p.91
[331] Hawkes, 1989, p.91
[332] Brown, 1981, p.230-1

Scutchamer Knob

There is a shire meeting point in Berkshire known as *Scutchamer Knob* or *Cuckhamsley Barrow* on Cuckhamsley Hill which is intriguing: the name Cuckhamsly is derived from *Cwichealmes hlæwe* (ASC, s.a. 1006) 'Cwichelm's barrow'.[333] There are two monuments named *Cwicelmes hlæw* – one in the region of Ardley (Oxfordshire) mentioned in a charter of 955 AD, and the other the Cuckhamsley site. There were also two leaders named Cwichelm in West Saxon tradition: one of them, brother of King Cynegils, was an active defender of West Saxon territory against the Mercians, and in Bede's story it was this king who sent an assassin to try to kill Edwin of Northumbria. The other Cwichelm was Cynegils's son who fought with him at *Feðanleag* (Stoke Lyne?) in 584 and died in 593 AD.[334] Excavation has failed to find any 7th c. burial within the structure but there are remains of this date in the area.

The *ASC* s.a. 1006 relates a tradition concerning *Cwichelmes hlæw*:

> *and wæron him ða ane niht æt Ceoles ege, and wendon him ða andlang Æsces dune to Cwichelmes hlæwe, and ðær onbidedon beotra gylpa, forðan oft man cwæþ, gif hi Cwichelmes hlæwe gesohton, ðæt hi næfre to sæ gangan ne sceoldan*

> and they [the Danish army] were then one night at Cholsey, and then went along Ashdown to Cuckhamsley hill, and there they waited from a daring boast, because it had often been said, if they came to Cuckhamsley hill, that they would never get back to sea

The notion that no army could reach this spot and escape alive suggests that it held great importance in local tradition, and may have been one of the sacred sites for the West Saxon royal house. The Cuckhamsley site dates from the Iron Age but may have held some West Saxon secondary inhumations.

A ruinous excavation took place in 1842, but produced no tangible results other than the destruction of a large part of the mound. An oak stump bound with willow wands was found, but could not be dated and may have been associated with mediaeval use of the mound as a beacon hill. The meetings at *Scutchamer Knob* ceased when nearby East Ilsley received a licence for a market and fair.

---

[333] Grinsell, 1936, p.102; Meaney, 1964, p.45-6; Williams, 2006a, p.209-12
[334] Hawkes, 1989, p.90

Taplow

Taplow barrow was for a long time the richest Anglo-Saxon burial known in England, and usually cited in early 20th c. books as showing the only examples of the kinds of wealth described in poems such as *Beowulf*. The poets of the OE tradition were widely supposed to have invented the idea of the king or leader buried with his treasures, as most Anglo-Saxon burials – even those with weapons - were quite modest compared to the literary tradition of the treasure-filled burial chamber. This position was only reversed in 1939 with the discoveries at Sutton Hoo.[335]

The name 'Taplow' is derived from OE *Tæppan hlæw* 'Tæppa's barrow', referring to the mound which is at the top of 'Berry Hill', probably from *burh hyll* 'stronghold hill'. The site has a commanding outlook over the Thames Valley. It is not certain that the association of the name with the location means that Tæppa was the person buried there: it may be that the name was that of the owner of the land and builder of the early church. The mound itself is 15' (4.5m) high and 80' (24m) in diameter, although Victorian or earlier landscaping had altered the profile which may explain the regular, conical shape in early images.[336] The mound may indeed have been based on an earlier structure, as it stood on the highest point within an Iron Age hillfort.[337] The spot was no doubt chosen because of its prominence and the fact that it dominated the access routes from and to West and East Saxon territory. The grave mound may have been placed here as a 'sentinel' burial, protecting the lower Thames from the activities of the *Gewissæ* and the later West Saxon kingdom. As Hawkes noted, "Taplow is well outside West Saxon territory and remote from any other major kingdom in the late sixth or early seventh century."[338] However, instead of seeing Tæppa as a local headman, the strong Kentish parallels for his grave-goods should imply that he was a local viceroy or *ealdormann*, a proponent of Kentish interests even if not directly controlled from Canterbury.[339]

---

[335] Smith, 1923, p.63-45; Ellis Davidson, 1950; Meaney, 1964, p.59; Speake, 1980; Hawkes, 1989, p.85, 89; Fitch, 1996; O'Brien, 1999, ref.491; Cook, 2004, p.47

[336] Williams, 2006a, p.147

[337] Williams, 2006a, p.202-4. Kerr, 2004 notes that the mound replaced three earlier Bronze Age mounds on the summit, and that it is possible the Anglo-Saxons used the material from all three in the construction of their imposing chamber-grave & barrow.

[338] Hawkes, 1989, p.85

[339] Welch, 2007, p.193. Kerr, 2004 notes that the name Tæppa is also found in two Kentish place-names, *Tapners* and *Tappington*. This must strengthen the Kentish connection of the Taplow burial, even if it does not prove that Tæppa was the occupant.

The imposing monument was too tempting a prospect for Victorian antiquarians, and in 1883 a local collector by the name of James Rutland undertook the digging of the barrow. An ancient yew on the mound's summit with a girth of about 20' (6m) was left in place while digging commenced, but the destructive intervention of the workmen caused the tree to collapse into the trench, injuring one of the excavators and damaging the chamber. The fabric of the barrow was gravel (with occasional inclusions of bone, ceramics and flints) and the burial chamber was finally located about 5' (1.5m) below the original ground surface, and measuring 12' (3.5m) by 8' (2.5m). The roots of the great tree appear to have penetrated the chamber, and probably contributed to the collapse of the wooden structure.

The human remains within the collapsed chamber were fragmentary – some pieces of femur and mandible, and some vertebrae. However, the grave-goods were spectacular: the gold and gilded fittings had survived very well even though the organic components had often decayed. The inventory included a gold buckle; gold thread, originally woven into a textile garment; two gilt-bronze clasps; six paired drinking horns of different sizes with silver gilt fittings; a Coptic vessel; a sword blade; four glass claw beakers; bone gaming pieces; three spearheads; two shield bosses; a large bronze cauldron; two bronze-mounted wooden buckets; a wooden harp. The grave-goods are consistent with a date roughly contemporary with Sutton Hoo Mound 1, which puts the date of the mound in the first quarter of the 7th c.

Near to Tæppa's barrow at the foot of the escarpment is a spring-fed pool called *Bapsey Pond* which local tradition associates with the missionary activity of St. Birinus who, in 642, used this spot for baptisms; possibly *Bapsey* is a derivative of 'baptism'. A small Anglo-Saxon church with an apse and two side porticus once stood by the mound, its presence revealed by parch-marks in 1995.

The Taplow excavations have never been published adequately and little is known of the details of the process undertaken, nor of the layout of the grave and its contents. The principal individuals overseeing the dig were James Rutland, Dr. Joseph Stevens of Reading, Major Cooper King and Walter Money. King drew plans of the grave while Rutland and Stevens reported the subsequent research findings to the Maidenhead Naturalists' Field Club and British Archaeological Association respectively.

Recently, an evaluation of the fabric remains and clothing accessories in the mound has been published by Penelope Walton Rogers, including a painting of the barrow's occupant wearing the characteristic kaftan or cross-over jacket which became fashionable in the later 6th c..[340] (see drawing page 171)

---

[340] Walton Rogers, 2007

Taplow Chamber Contents

1. Group of three shields with studded iron bosses. Only one of the handgrips survived.

2. Bronze and iron-bound yew wood bucket.

3. The warrior. He lays on a feather mattress and wears a fine woollen tunic trimmed with gold braid and secured at the waist with a pair of gold wrapped bronze clasps. At his left shoulder is a buckle of solid gold inset with garnets and opaque blue glass. It was possibly forty years old when buried. By his right shoulder is a pattern-welded iron sword 32" long bound at the scabbard with fine woollen tapes. No traces of the pommel or scabbard fitting were found.

4. Cast-bronze Coptic pedestal bowl with a scalloped rim and twelve protruding knobs. Grouped underneath is a small drinking horn, a glass claw-beaker and a reconstructed vessel with a silver rim (position unknown).

5. Wooden casket (conjectural).

6. Large bronze cauldron two feet in diameter. Inside are placed two large drinking horns, four maplewood drinking vessels and two claw beakers. The horns were already old when buried. Other fragments found suggest a fifth, undecorated horn (shown here incorporating a silver tripod foot found in the tomb).

7. Textiles (conjectural).

8. Unidentified iron complex, possibly the remains of a tub or bucket.

9. Small drinking horn and glass claw-beaker.

10. Six-stringed maplewood lyre. Only the bridge and the two gilt-bronze mounts survived. Also found were some leather scraps and two bronze attachment plates, possibly the remains of a holding strap or carrying pouch for the lyre.

11. Bone gaming pieces. Approximately fifty-four were found, apparently laid out as if on a board.

12. Two iron spears of unclassified type. A small iron buckle was found corroded onto one of the spearheads.

13. Barbed angon or throwing spear of Swanton Type A2. It could have been laid on top of the sealed chamber or on a wooden coffin within.

14. Bronze and iron-bound yew wood bucket.

15. Iron bladed knife.

Other Thames Valley Barrows

Abingdon At Abingdon (Berkshire) an extensive Anglo-Saxon cemetery was excavated in the 1930s while pipe-laying was taking place in Saxton Road. On the eastern edge was a Bronze Age mound in which some Anglo-Saxon secondary inhumations had been placed.[341]

Aston A grave discovered in a domestic garden at Aston (Berkshire) in 1921 is not recorded to have been enclosed by a mound but the quantity and quality of the grave-goods is suggestive of early 7th c. burial rites: a shieldboss, 3 spearheads, 3 knives, 2 bronze pieces from a horse-harness, 3 saucer brooches.[342] There is record of only a single skeleton, and the bulk of the grave-goods are masculine-gendered, so the saucer-brooches are something of a puzzle.

Bampton see **Lew**

Chilton At Chilton (Berkshire) the then-new practice of aerial photography revealed the presence of a probable Anglo-Saxon barrow to the south of the track from East Hendred Down.[343] It appeared to be undisturbed at the time (1936).

Chinnor A workman digging for stone in twin barrows at Hempton Plain, Chinnor (Oxfordshire) in 1885 opened one of the mounds and found within a wall of flints containing some metal remains: two spearheads, an angon-head and a U-shaped sword-chape; another spearhead was found in the same area after a landslip.[344]

Cock Marsh see **Cookham**

Cookham At Cookham (Berkshire) on Cock Marsh a series of four mounds was opened by A. Heneage Cocks in 1888; three of the barrows contained cremations (identified as 'British' by this rite) and the fourth contained an Anglo-Saxon inhumation of an adult male with a dog.[345] If the burials were identified as 'British' solely on the basis of the burial rite, there is at least a fair chance that they were Anglo-Saxon and the group formed a cluster of barrow burials. The report notes that the inhumation was primary rather than secondary, which must strengthen the case for an Anglo-Saxon date for the group as a whole.

---

[341] Meaney, 1964, p.43
[342] Meaney, 1964, p.44
[343] Meaney, 1964, p.45
[344] Meaney, 1964, p.206; O'Brien, 1999, ref.423
[345] Meaney, 1964, p.45; O'Brien, 1999, ref.499

Crawley A possible Anglo-Saxon barrow was dug in 1858 at Crawley (Oxforshire).[346] The only remains were a human skeleton with a small metal buckle by the hips.

Didcot Excavations in 1975 at the site of the Didcot power station (Oxfordshire) revealed a small Anglo-Saxon cemetery based on a Bronze Age pond barrow.[347]

Dorchester In 1946 a small cemetery was excavated at Dorchester (Oxfordshire) consisting of nine inhumations around the periphery of a Bronze Age tumulus.[348] The grave-goods included glass and amber beads, disc brooches and a spearhead. A quantity of further burials was destroyed when the site was mechanically cleared for gravel extraction.

Eynsham An Anglo-Saxon cemetery at Eynsham (Oxfordshire) contained a single possible burial mound.[349]

Frilford A large Anglo-Saxon cemetery was discovered at Frilford (Berkshire) in 1864-5. In 1939, an outlying grave was found in Noah's Ark Field near a Romano-British temple.[350] The grave does not appear to have been associated with the cemetery, and its isolated position makes it likely that it was once covered by a mound.

Great Tew A burial mound at Great Tew (Oxfordshire) is alleged to be of Anglo-Saxon date.[351]

Heyford Purcell During enclosure of the parish of Heyford Purcell (Oxfordshire) in 1801, part of an earthwork called *Harborough Bank* was levelled.[352] The bank was found to contain a large quantity of human bones, both adults and children. Some discreet burials were discernable, including one with notable grave-goods which were passed to the rector: two spearheads, one on each shoulder; a knife on the right hip; two bronze fibulae at the neck; some (amber and glass) beads at the neck. The presence of this single, well-equipped burial with satellite graves under an earthwork points to a barrow burial. The name *Harborough* could commemorate the element *–beorg* 'barrow'.

---

[346] Meaney, 1964, p.207; O'Brien, 1999, ref.421

[347] Boyle, Dodd, Mills & Mudd, 1995; O'Brien, 1999, ref.2266

[348] Meaney, 1964, p.208

[349] O'Brien, 1999, ref.2192

[350] Meaney, 1964, p.47; O'Brien, 1999, ref.505

[351] O'Brien, 1999, ref.2143. Neither Blair's nor Dickinson's notes on the barrow have been published. The only reference appears to be in *Oxoniensa* for 1966 (not consulted)

[352] Meaney, 1964, p.209

Hempton Plain see **Chinnor**

Ilsley A barrow (mound 3) at East Ilsley (Berkshire) is an isolated Anglo-Saxon mound of late 7th c. date containing an inhumation. The village was once the site of a large sheep fair and may have been of some importance in the more remote past, perhaps as the site for the local administrative meeting (*gemot*) as at some other barrows. A group of four mounds to the east of the village, known as the *Cross Barrows* were excavated in 1843.[353] One of the group contained the remains of a tall man with an iron knife at his waist; another yielded a buckle, 2 spearheads, an ornamental 'shield boss', some pieces of metal and unbaked pottery. The third contained six skeletons laid out side-by-side with poor grave-goods (a brass pin, some pottery and some beads), all very tall and oriented with their heads to the south-east. The fourth was apparently empty.

Inkpen At Inkpen (Berkshire) a series of three barrows was investigated in 1908; the westernmost contained fragments of Anglo-Saxon pottery placed beneath the topsoil, which may represent either secondary cremation burials on top of the mounds, or the remains of Anglo-Saxon period activity on the site.[354]

Lambourne Downs A site called *Seven Barrows* on Upper Lambourne Downs (Berkshire) was investigated in 1879 and in the smaller of two barrows opened, a penannular brooch was found dating to the late 6th c.[355]

Leafield There is a large earth mound called *Barry Tump* (barrow tump?) at Leafield, 4 miles northeast of Asthall, which appears to be an Anglo-Saxon barrow, but is so far unexcavated.[356] It is sited with perfect visibility in every direction and must have been a highly emphatic mark of its builder's presence in the landscape; a modern concrete triangulation post disfigures the monument. Both this tumulus and that at Lew appear to be sited in relation to the Asthall monument and perhaps commemorate members of the royal line of the *Hwicce*.

Lew A round barrow at the hamlet of Lew (Oxfordshire) near the later major Anglo-Saxon town of Bampton, is believed to be of early Anglo-Saxon date but has not been excavated in modern times. The mound is about 4 miles southeast of the Asthall barrow and was both larger and more prominently sited.[357] The name Lew is derived from OE *æt hlæwe*

---

[353] Meaney, 1964, p.45; O'Brien, 1999, ref.501

[354] Meaney, 1964, p.48

[355] Meaney, 1964, p.43; O'Brien, 1999, ref.756

[356] Hawkes, 1989, p.91

[357] Hawkes, 1989, p.91

'at the barrow', which appears in a land-grant of 984 by King Æþelræd to his *minister* or thane, Ælfwine.

Lyneham At Lyneham (Oxfordshire) human remains were recovered during quarrying for stone in 1842 in a pit on the south side of Lyneham Camp.[358] In 1872 a burial with an iron knife was found in the same area. More bones appeared in 1875 at a spot known as *The Roundabout*, and they were taken to the church for reburial. Two spearheads were found while planting trees on the edge of the Camp in 1884, and ten years later excavation took place of Lyneham barrow, a long barrow near the road to Chipping Norton. Two secondary inhumations were found in the centre: one with a spearhead and knife, the other with just a knife. There were other burials in the edges of the mound, some perhaps of Anglo-Saxon date. Between the long barrow and the edge of the Camp there were as many as six mounds, some of which may have been Anglo-Saxon barrows.

Radley A site known as *Barrow Hills* at Radley (Oxfordshire) consisted of five barrows of Romano-British date which were respected by two Anglo-Saxon inhumations: an adult female with a knife, iron buckle and bronze pin, and a new-born infant.[359] The Anglo-Saxon use of the site was dominated by a cluster of sunken-featured buildings.

Reading During construction of ballast pits on the railway sheds at Reading (Berkshire) in 1891 the burial was discovered of a man accompanied by a horse, with a sword by his side.[360] There was no recorded trace of a mound, but the burial was undisturbed. The pommel of the sword was decorated with human and animal ornament, and was dated to the early 9th c. However, inhumation accompanied by both a horse and a sword is a characteristic early 7th c. rite found also at Lakenheath (Suffolk) and Sutton Hoo Mound 17.

---

[358] Meaney, 1964, p.210; Meaney & Hawkes, 1970, p.31

[359] Chambers & McAdam, 2007

[360] Meaney, 1964, p.50

Sarsden At Sarsden, Oxfordshire, a round barrow known as *Squire's Clump* is believed to date from the early Anglo-Saxon period. Excavation took place in the late Victorian period, and allegedly exposed two skeletons, sitting side by side in a chamber with their hands raised to their faces. Leeds, the excavator of Asthall, tried to trace the diggers or records of the operation in the 1920s, but was apparently unsuccessful.

Shipton-under-Wychwood At Shipton-under-Wychwood, an early Anglo-Saxon mound known as *Shipton Barrow* forms part of a multi-period earthwork which may have been started in the Bronze Age.[361] This lies about 3 miles northwest of Asthall barrow, in a landscape sprinkled with mounds of various dates, mostly unknown.

Stanton Harcourt At Stanton Harcourt (Oxfordshire) a Bronze Age bowl-barrow was under excavation in 1940.[362] Twenty two Anglo-Saxon secondary burials were found in the barrow, as well as one further possibility. Only six were adults, and there were some 'empty' graves which may once have contained children's remains. The provision of grave-goods was very sparing: a silver pin with an elderly female; knives and other small tools with three of the children; a spearhead. The barrow may date to the 7th c. and have been selected for burial by a group already experiencing the transition to the Final Phase tradition of few and small grave-goods.

Swinbrook The barrow at Swinbrook, to the north of Asthall, was assumed to be of Bronze Age date, like the majority of mounds in this area, but some Late Roman coins were discovered in the fill which must indicate either an Anglo-Saxon structure, or perhaps a secondary burial within a Bronze Age tumulus.[363]

Uffington *White Horse Hill* at Uffington on the Berkshire Downs is famed for its large chalk-cut hill figure of a running or prancing horse.[364] In 1858 two barrows on the hill were opened: one contained Romano-British material while the other was Anglo-Saxon, with six carelessly inhumed skeletons of which the central one was an adult male. Two detached skulls placed either side of the male may have belonged to the jumbled skeletons in the mound or may have been trophies of other

---

[361] O'Brien, 1999, ref.2193

[362] Meaney, 1964, p.213

[363] Dickinson & Speake, 1992, p.115 Several other barrows in the Thames Valley which are believed to have contained cremations are noted. Some at least may have been of Anglo-Saxon date.

[364] Ellis Davidson, 1950; Meaney, 1964, p.53-4; O'Brien, 1999, ref.522

individuals. The combination of injuries, decapitation and an adult male laid out with human remains around him may indicate the aftermath of a battle; if so, the Romano-British mound may be contemporary. At a villa site at the foot of the hill at Woolstone, a male burial was found in 1884, accompanied by a large knife, as well as a female and young male.

Worton At Worton (Oxfordshire) a mound lies on the border of the present church graveyard. This has sometimes been identified as an Anglo-Saxon barrow, but the possibility that it might be a later defensive earthwork cannot be excluded.

Wessex (The West Country)

This section includes Hampshire, Wiltshire, Isle of Wight and Dorset.

Rodmead Hill

The barrow at Rodmead Hill (or Rodmead Down), near Maiden Bradley (Wiltshire) was dug by Sir Richard Colt Hoare and published in *The Ancient History of Wiltshire*, a narrative of that gentleman's voyages round the byways of the West Country in search of tumuli to dig into.[365] As with Bateman in the Midlands, we do at least have a record of his progress and of some of his finds.

The barrow was the more northerly of two on the site, and was dug by Colt Hoare in October 1807. The remains consisted of a skeleton laid supine with its head to the northeast, and accompanying grave-goods. A bronze vessel, 7 ½" (19cm) in diameter, lay at the feet of the skeleton, with internal gilding and its exterior "protected by wood and small strips of brass". The vessel was probably a bronze pan, and the wood and brass perhaps belonged to a stave-built bucket on which the pan had rested.

The grave-goods were all of the usual masculine type. Shield fittings in the grave included two silver studs and a large sugar-loaf shield boss. Another silver plate and buckle, which Colt Hoare associated with the shield, were more probably belt fittings. An iron two-edged sword was placed by the warrior, 2'6" (75cm) long and 1 ¾" (4.5cm) wide, as well as a longer and a shorter knife, 11" (29cm) and 3" (7.5cm) respectively, and two spearheads of 11" and 6 ½" (29cm and 17cm). Colt Hoare knew that such barrows were attributed to the Saxons, but he preferred to see the remains as belonging to a Belgic warrior of the time of Caesar or before. The neighbouring mound was dug but yielded no burial.

The presence of the sugar-loaf shield boss places this barrow in the mid-7th c. according to the typology of Dickinson and Härke.[366] Ref The contents of the gravemound are not exceptional for Anglo-Saxon high-status burials of the earlier 7th c., and given the late persistence of barrow-burial in this part of the country, as shown by Swallowcliffe Down, there is no reason to doubt that this was the last resting place of one of the West Saxon kings or nobles.

---

[365] Colt Hoare, 1812, p.46-7 and plate IV; Meaney, 1964, p.273; O'Brien, 1999, ref.618; Cook, 2004, p.102-3

[366] Dickinson & Härke, 1992

Roundway Down

In 1805 Hoare and Cunnington opened two mounds on Roundway Down (Wiltshire).[367] The first, on the right side of the road, contained a skeleton but no grave-goods. The second, off to the east, contained a burial with an ivory ring and a set of ivory playing pieces and some decayed wood which may have been the gaming board. In 1855 Cunnington re-opened the barrows. The first contained a cist and fragments of a drinking vessel; the skeleton was of a tall young man. The second barrow revealed nothing new but a piece of antler.

Another small barrow on Roundway Down (Wiltshire) was dug by Lord Colston and Stoughton Money in 1840; this is the barrow near Oliver's Castle.[368] The grave goods retrieved included some garnet-and-gold pendants, gold beads and a set of hair-pins, all of which suggest a high-status female burial of the later 7th c. A second barrow on the site (Roundway Down II) contained a quantity of animal bones which the excavators identified as a dog, cat, boar and horse.[369]

The grave was cut into the chalk and surmounted by a mound which was at a height of 7' (2.1m) when the excavation took place. There was a large quantity of ironwork around the edges of the grave, which may have been the remains of a coffin but might equally indicate a former bed-burial.

An attempt by Semple and Williams in 2000 to identify the barrow on the ground was unsuccessful. The place-names expert, Grinsell, had suggested that the likely site was a partially destroyed barrow on the Wiltshire Downs, but excavation revealed only a complex of Bronze Age structures. The Victorian records imply that the Anglo-Saxon female was a secondary inhumation within an earlier mound, but there was no evidence that any of the mounds detected in 2000 had ever held an Anglo-Saxon interment. (see fig.7)

Swallowcliffe Down

The mound known as Swallowcliffe Down stood on the boundary of two parishes (Swallowcliffe and Ansty) in southwest Wiltshire and was excavated in 1966.[370] The mound was a re-used Bronze Age structure, sited in a

---

[367] Meaney, 1964, p.273-4; O'Brien, 1999, ref.584; Semple & Williams, 2001

[368] Meaney, 1964, p.273-4; Speake, 1980, p.65; Speake, 1989, p.107-10; O'Brien, 1999, ref.585; Semple & Williams, 2001; Cook, 2004, p.103; Semple & Williams, 2006

[369] Dickinson & Speake, 1992, p.111

[370] Speake, 1980, p.65, 93; Speake, 1989; O'Brien, 1999, ref.1111; Cook, 2004, p.104; Williams, 2006a, p.27-35

prominent position on the Downs, and stood at around 43' (13m) in diameter and 3' (90cm) high, with a causeway on the eastern side. There are many other barrows in this area, including one in Alvediston parish excavated in 1926 which included a Saxon primary inhumation: the grave-goods included an iron spearhead and ferrule; an iron knife; a sugar-loaf shield boss. All these items are typical of a mid 7th c. male burial.[371]

The chamber was partially disturbed, perhaps even robbed, but it still contained one of the most complex female burials ever unearthed in England. The human remains point to an adult female of an age between 18 and 25 years old. The date of the burial is assumed to be in the later 7th c., which is towards the end of the period in which chamber burial was practised.

The body was laid with her head to the west, surrounded by five groups of objects. At the western end of the grave were two vessels: an iron-bound bucket made from yew wood, and an iron pan or skillet. At the eastern end, beside her feet, was a bronze-mounted bucket, placed on a small ledge cut into the end of the grave. To the south, by her right forearm, lay two small glass palm cups, and by her leg a bag made from wood and leather with an openwork disc mount with gold and silver repoussé decorative foils, and with metal mounts on the strap; its buckle had two tongues. To the north by her left leg was a maplewood box containing some small items (a silver strap end, a silver spoon, two knives, a bronze sprinkler, four silver brooches, three small beads, an iron spindle, a decorated bone comb).

None of these objects is without parallel in the Anglo-Saxon burial records, but to find them in the grave of an adult female is unusual. The feasting equipment – the cups and buckets for pouring and drinking – are usually associated with lords and kings as patrons of feasts; however, the role of noble ladies at these occasions is alluded to often in the literature and it may this aspect that we see here: she is portrayed as 'the lady with the mead cup' to use Enright's phrase. [ref] If so, the sprinkler/strainer may have formed part of the equipment used to serve the mead or beer to guests. These items convey her status as the primary female of her community, responsible for overseeing daily tasks of production (the spindle whorl) and food preparation (the skillet), for presenting a tidy and hospitable appearance to guests (the comb and dress fastenings) and for offering drink and food to guests in her hall (the buckets, palm cups and sprinkler).

---

[371] Meaney, 1964, p.264; Speake, 1989, p.1, 120; O'Brien, 1999, ref.610 Swallowcliffe report

The brooches and strap-end were not in place on her costume and appear to have been hidden away from view in the casket; if so, this may be due to the late date of the burial when such displays were no longer acceptable to the Christian élite. The lady is presumed to have been either Christian herself or buried by Christians, since one of the emblems on her openwork disc was a *chi-rho* symbol which was commonly used as an expression of religious allegiance. The west-east alignment and supine posture are typical of Christian burials at this time, but are also common among heathens. The contents of the casket may equally have been small personal items which were kept in a private chest, and which were not considered worthy of display. However, it is also possible that some of the grave-goods were removed when the chamber was opened, and the assemblage we have today may simply be what was not immediately recognisable as treasure to the excavators. The absence of a showy brooch, for example, is odd in so rich a grave.

The physical remains of the body were badly disturbed but it was possible to ascertain that she had been an adult aged between 18 and 25, and about 5'3" tall. There was no indication on the skeleton of the cause of death, which may mean that it was due to disease or soft tissue infection. The body was surrounded by corroded iron fittings which have been reconstructed as the remains of an iron-bound wooden bed with an angled headboard.[372]

The chamber was timber-lined, with four timber posts at the corners, and clay was used to seal it. This clay was not local, and must have been brought to the burial spot from the river valley below. The timber may have been decorated or painted, and the chamber itself was hung with textiles, and soft furnishings were laid on the floor and bed. Above the chamber a large timber post may have been erected to mark the site of the burial. As was usual in the Final Phase, the items interred at Swallowcliffe Down had been concealed rather than displayed: the jewellery items were apparently held in a bag on the chest or in the maplewood box, and the various groups of vessels were placed around the body, perhaps as final gifts from the mourners.[373]

It is possible that there were other burials surrounding the barrow, although the only evidence for contemporary activity was a find of an Anglo-Saxon spearhead nearby. Williams notes that another barrow burial was situated just 250 metres away from the chamber burial, across the parish boundary, and with good all-round views meaning that the site could be seen from many

---

[372] Williams, 2006, p.31. The grounds for reconstructing this furniture as a bed are not beyond challenge. See Pollington (forthcoming).

[373] Williams, 2006, p.76

different points in the vicinity.[374] The date was again later 7th c., at a period when the area was already under the control of an élite with a Christian ideology. It was near the route of a Saxon military road (*herepæð*) which would also have allowed its significance to be recalled every time the king and his warband rode by; this would necessarily have kept the memory of the deceased alive for a long time.

An Anglo-Saxon charter for the area, recording a land-grant by King Edmund in 940 AD, uses a barrow in the description of the boundaries:

...of þære hane on þone herepæþ to Posses hlæwe, of þæm hlæwe to lytlan crundelle ....

…from the stone on the Herepath to Posse's barrow, from the barrow to the little quarry …

The boundary apparently corresponds with that of the modern parish of Swallowcliffe, although the presence of two main routes in this area – an upper and a lower *herepæð* – means that we cannot be certain. It is a pity that the boundaries of the neighbouring parish of Ansty have not survived. If *Posses hlæw* is the name of the barrow, then *Poss* cannot be the name of the occupant because it is a masculine term while the burial was that of a female. It may be that *Poss* is the name of a subsequent landowner, and although the name is not recorded there are other place-names which seems to contain it, such as Posingford, Possingworth, Posbury and others. It appears to be related to the word *pusa* ' a bag or pouch'. The lady in the mound had with her a magnificent metal-framed leather satchel, and it may be that the barrow was actually named 'the satchel barrow' in memory of the grave-goods rather than the person interred.[375] However, it is not known how far back the name *Posses hlæw* goes, only that a barrow in the vicinity bore this name in 940 AD, according to the existing document which is itself a 14th c. copy.

Other West Country Barrows

Ablington A mound known as *Cicencutt Barrow* at *Barrow Clump* near Ablington (Wiltshire) was revealed to contain an Anglo-Saxon secondary inhumation when a spearhead was revealed through the burrowing of rabbits in 1935.[376]

---

[374] Williams, 2006, p.32-3 Presumably this second barrow is Barrow 1c at Alvediston, referred to above.

[375] Speake, 1989, p.12-3

[376] Meaney, 1964, p.264

Alvediston A barrow at Alvediston (Wiltshire) on Middle Down was opened in 1925.[377] It contained the grave of a young man with injuries to the jaw; the body had been covered in large flints. Grave-goods were an iron shieldboss, spearhead, knife and a fragment of a bracelet of shale. The barrow appeared to have been erected for the Anglo-Saxon occupant.

Amesbury see **Boscombe Down**

Andover A Bronze Age complex at Andover (Hampshire) was excavated in 1975.[378] Aside from the Bronze Age and Roman features on the site, a series of Anglo-Saxon secondary inhumations was found in six Bronze Age round barrows. There were sixty-nine inhumations and an estimated eighty-seven cremations on the site. The cemetery was moderately wealthy with a quantity of jewellery and weapons.

Arreton Down see **Carisbrooke**

Ashton Valley see **Codford St. Peter**

Bedhampton A long barrow at Bedhampton (Hampshire), known as *Bevis's Grave*, was opened in 1815.[379] It contained three skeletons, and a broken Anglo-Saxon spearhead.

Bokerley Ditch see **Pentridge**

Boles Barrow A Neolithic barrow on Salisbury Plain known as Boles Barrow was opened by William Cunnington in 1801 and it is famous for the human remains found there, which show considerable evidence of cranial injuries.[380] Among the interments were some metal buckles, reported by Richard Colt Hoare, which are presumed to have belonged with secondary Anglo-Saxon burials on the site.

Boreham In 1800 Cunnington opened the *King Barrow* at Boreham (Wiltshire). The mound then stood 206' long, 56' wide and 15' high.[381] Only 18" deep in the barrow's summit were found three skeletons. One had at his side a corroded iron sword with an oak hilt. The original Bronze Age burial had been disturbed in the barrow's re-use.

---

[377] Meaney, 1964, p.264

[378] Cook & Dacre, 1985; O'Brien, 1999, ref.1110

[379] Meaney, 1964, p.94

[380] Smith & Brickley, 2007

[381] Meaney, 1964, p.269

Boscombe Down A Bronze Age barrow on the border of Boscombe Down and Amesbury was being removed in 1930.[382] Several items were found in the disturbed earth, including a bronze belt-fitting, a split-socketed spearhead, a fragment of iron shears and a small bronze ring. Probably an Anglo-Saxon secondary inhumation had been placed in the mound.

Bowcombe Down see **Carisbrooke**

Bower Chalke see **Pentridge**

Bradley Hill see **Somerton**

Bratton Camp The earthworks known as Bratton Camp (Wiltshire) were investigated some time before 1812 and a large mound was opened by Cunnington.[383] Three skeletons were found near the top at the larger end of the barrow, perhaps Anglo-Saxon secondary inhumations.

Brigmerston A high and prominent barrow on Silk Hill near Brigmerston (Wiltshire) was opened by Cunnington before 1812.[384] An Anglo-Saxon secondary burial was discovered with an iron spearhead.

Broad Town see **Clyffe Pypard**

Cannington The earthworks at Cannington Park Quarry (Somerset) were excavated in 1969 by Rahtz. There was at least one barrow on the site.[385]

Carisbrooke On Arreton Down, Carisbrooke (Isle of Wight) Mr. Cooke of Newport opened a barrow in 1815.[386] It contained the skeleton of a 6' male with an iron knife, and a child of about 9 years old accompanied by a buckle and knife. Five more skeletons accompanied by knives, a spearhead, a bone comb, an iron buckle and other goods were found, as well as horses' teeth and boars' tusks. At Bowcombe Down, in the same area, eleven small barrows were excavated in 1854.[387] The barrows respected a much larger Bronze Age mound, and the burials were unusual: for instance, the two intact inhumations were both headless. Other inhumations had been almost entirely dissolved by the soil. The four cremations were all urned and packed in the hollow with flint and

---

[382] Meaney, 1964, p.266

[383] Meaney, 1964, p.266

[384] Meaney, 1964, p.276

[385] O'Brien, 1999, ref.606 (Rahtz, Hirst & Wright: forthcoming – not consulted)

[386] Meaney, 1964, p.94; Arnold, 1982, ch.3; O'Brien, 1999, ref.640

[387] Meaney, 1964, p.94-5; Arnold, 1982, ch.11; O'Brien, 1999, ref.639

brickearth as if they had been fired in situ. In 1858, during construction of the racecourse, a large barrow was excavated. It contained a central burial of an adult male with a sword in a wooden scabbard with bronze fittings, two iron spearheads, a bronze buckle, an iron knife and a bronze clasp. About twelve more inhumations were included in the mound, containing weapons and bronze vessels. It is not clear whether this barrow was part of the same group as the 1854 excavations.

Chessel Down The site of Chessel Down (Isle of Wight) is an important Anglo-Saxon cemetery with many significant finds, including a runic plate attached to the reverse of a sword scabbard.[388] The cemetery was probably a barrowfield in part. Before 1816 when Dennet began his investigations, a skeleton had been found accompanied by a sword and a 'brass helmet'; the latter may have been a bronze bowl, perhaps of Coptic type. Around 30 graves were opened containing swords, knives, spearheads, buckles and brooches. Further graves were dug subsequently into the 1850s. Many of the graves were very regularly spaced and laid out, perhaps in the *Reihengräber* tradition of Merovingian Francia, and the regularity of layout suggests the presence of low barrows.

Clyffe Pypard Labourers removing the top of a mound at Broad Town, Clyffe Pypard (Wiltshire) in 1834 discovered some skeletons with an iron arrowhead, some beads and the rim of a glass vessel.[389] An Anglo-Saxon date is presumed from the presence of iron.

Codford St. Peter A mound (number 3 of the group) excavated some time before 1812 at Codford St. Peter (Wiltshire) contained a probable chamber-grave.[390] The mound itself was only about 18" high, but the excavation revealed Roman pottery in the fill, and beneath the mound a 'room' was formed to a depth of 11' in the chalk. A body lay within, in a wooden coffin which remained intact in parts, held by iron nails. Also in the Ashton Valley, a burial site excavated in 1801 contained several tumuli, one of which (number 7) contained a secondary inhumation of Anglo-Saxon date, accompanied by a copper-bound stave bucket.[391] The skeleton was unusually placed with one arm extended backwards and the finger bones displaced. A mass of iron by

---

[388] Meaney, 1964, p.95-7; Arnold, 1982, ch.1; O'Brien, 1999, ref.641 *Chessel* was recorded in 1278 as *Chestull*, probably from *ciest hyll* 'coffin hill'.

[389] Meaney, 1964, p.266-7 The barbed arrowhead may have belonged to an angon.

[390] Meaney, 1964, p.264; O'Brien, 1999, ref.815. This was probably part of the 1801 excavation project.

[391] Meaney, 1964, p.264-5; Cook, 2004, p.100-1

the body's side was probably the remains of a sword, covered with cloth. Below this Anglo-Saxon burial was a stone cist with the bones of the original Bronze Age occupant.

Compton During the 1913 excavation of the English Civil War fieldwork known as Oliver's Battery at Compton near Winchester (Wiltshire), an Anglo-Saxon inhumation was discovered in the north-east corner of the revetment; the burial was beneath a barrow which had been a prominent earthwork visible from the valley below, and it may have been this which drew it to the Parliamentarians' attention.[392] The grave contained the skeleton of an adult male accompanied by a bronze bowl, an angon head, and a seax.

Coombe Bissett At Coombe Bissett (Wiltshire), Cunnington opened two barrows in 1803.[393] They stood at the junction of the Roman road from Old Sarum with the road from Salisbury to Shaftesbury – a prominent location. The larger one contained a very disturbed inhumation but no grave-goods. The smaller mound covered a pit cut into the chalk which contained some interesting grave-goods: an iron sword with a wooden hilt and traces of the wooden scabbard; three iron spearheads with traces of the ash shafts; two knife blades; a shieldboss and mounts; a copper alloy buckle with leather and some small iron buckles; some rings of silver and gold wire; copper alloy sword pyramids; a gilded copper alloy drinking vessel; two glass vessels, one a claw-beaker. There was no trace of a body. This grave is sometimes called the Salisbury Race Course burial, due to the later use of the site.

Crichel Down At Crichel Down (Dorset) some Anglo-Saxon secondary inhumations were discovered in the excavation of a Bronze Age barrow in 1960.[394]

Deanland An isolated find of a piece of iron from a horse trapping was made at a site known as *Wor Barrow* near Deanland in Dorset, by Pitt-Rivers in 1898.[395] Whether it was ever part of a secondary inhumation or a casual loss is not known. Six burials were found within the barrow itself, without dating evidence. The excavation process effectively destroyed the barrow.

---

[392] Meaney, 1964, p.98-9; O'Brien, 1999, ref.546

[393] Meaney, 1964, p.274-5; O'Brien, 1999, ref.586; Cook, 2004, p.103

[394] Meaney, 1964, p.81

[395] Meaney, 1964, p.82; O'Brien, 1999, ref.134

Durrington A barrow at Durrington, near Stonehenge (Wiltshire) was opened in about 1865.[396] A small skeleton, probably female and Anglo-Saxon, was found within.

East Grafton At East Grafton (Wiltshire) a barrow was opened in 1910 on the edge of Shalbourne.[397] It contained a skeleton with an iron spearhead and a bronze buckle; beneath it were parts of another skeleton, and the original cremated remains. Another barrow nearby revealed a secondary inhumation, without grave-goods and of indeterminate date.

East Kennet In 1643 Aubrey reported that a barrow at East Kennet (Wiltshire) contained a human skeleton between two long side-stones, with a third stone covering the grave.[398] The grave-goods were a sword and a knife.

East Meon In 1842, an inhumation burial was discovered at East Meon (Hampshire) during construction of the road from Winchester to Bramdean.[399] A gilt-bronze buckle plate with a central garnet was among the grave-goods, as well as other objects, all subsequently lost. The presence of a barrow is implied by the digging of a cutting in the flat valley bottom; a stony barrow exists in the vicinity of the boundary with the adjoining parish of Privett.

Ebbesbourne Wake In 1926 an Anglo-Saxon inhumation burial was found at Ebbesbourne Wake (Wiltshire) during pipe-laying.[400] The grave contained a human skeletoin, a shieldboss and fittings, and a spearhead. The site was known as *Barrow Hill*.

Everley The Everley (Wiltshire) barrow group was investigated by Thurnam and in 1853 he opened the most westerly of them.[401] An Anglo-Saxon date was assigned to the grave, despite no obvious Anglo-Saxon material being present and the discovery of some fragmentary Roman pottery in the mound.

Ford see **Laverstock**

---

[396] Meaney, 1964, p.267

[397] Meaney, 1964, p.268

[398] Meaney, 1964, p.269; O'Brien, 1999, ref.785

[399] Meaney, 1964, p.98

[400] Meaney, 1964, p.265

[401] Meaney, 1964, p.267

Hardown Hill A barrow on Hardown Hill (Dorset) accidentally yielded a spearhead to a boy hunting rabbits, and was subsequently excavated in 1916 by a Dr. Wingrave.[402] Another spearhead was found at a depth of 1' (30cm), and further investigation uncovered an iron axe; eight spearheads with split sockets; a knife; a shieldboss; a square-headed small-long brooch; a flint pebble with a natural hole.

Heddington At Heddington (Wiltshire) on *King's Play Down* a barrow was opened in 1907.[403] The mound contained a large grave and a coffin, but the male skeleton was unaccompanied by any grave-goods. An Anglo-Saxon primary inhumation was deduced from the clean nature of the grave cut. (see fig.3)

Heytesbury Near Heytesbury (Wiltshire) by the ancient trackway stood a long mound 150' long and 94' wide, standing to a height of 10 ½ feet, called *Bowl's Barrow*.[404] The name was previously recorded as *bodelusburg3e* 'Bodel's barrow'. Cunnington opened it in 1801 and found a grave in the broader end, containing a human skeleton with a copper alloy buckle and two thin pieces of metal. Two more skeletons were placed in the centre of the mound. In 1864, Thurnham re-opened the barrow and found another Anglo-Saxon secondary burial near the surface. Further excavations found only Bronze Age remains.

Hinton Down About 1890, Greenwell opened the only known barrow on Hinton Down (Wiltshire).[405] A male skeleton was discovered, with an iron spearhead by the skull.

Horndean In 1947 a grave was discovered at Snell's Corner, Horndean (Hampshire) beneath a flat mound just north of the crossroads.[406] The mound's burial was of Bronze Age date, but graves of Iron Age and Roman date were found nearby, and 33 Anglo-Saxon burials. The Anglo-Saxon graves all respected the mound, but none seemed to have been placed within it; grave-goods were not few but the quality was poor. Influence from the South Saxon region was detected in some of the pottery. The flattened barrow and its position near a crossroads are suggestive of a meeting point.

---

[402] Meaney, 1964, p.81; O'Brien, 1999, ref.603. The split-socket is characteristic of early Anglo-Saxon spearheads. This barrow has not subsequently been identified, but there are several in the area.

[403] Meaney, 1964, p.269; O'Brien, 1999, ref.786

[404] Meaney, 1964, p.266

[405] Meaney, 1964, p.269

[406] Meaney, 1964, p.100

King's Play Down see **Heddington**

Knook The long barrow at Knook (Wiltshire) was investigated by
Cunnington in 1801.[407] Four headless secondary inhumations in the
upper levels may indicate Anglo-Saxon re-use of the barrow.

Knoyle At East Knoyle (Wiltshire) a neat barrow stood on the brow of the
hill.[408] Hoare opened it in 1802 and discovered a male skeleton in the
upper levels, above the remains of the Bronze Age occupant. At West
Knoyle (Wiltshire), on the downs stood two low tumuli which Hoare
opened in 1807.[409] In the smaller of them were the skeleton of a male,
a shieldboss, a spearhead and iron knife. The other mound yielded only
disturbed burnt material.

Laverstock A middle-range barrow was excavated at Ford, Laverstock
(Wiltshire) in 1969, having been detected when a cultivator disturbed a
cremation and some associated finds: a pair of tweezers and the tip of a
sword blade.[410] There were two barrows on the site, one Anglo-Saxon
in date and the other Bronze Age (possibly having had a secondary
Anglo-Saxon burial, subsequently destroyed); both had been ploughed
flat before Colt Hoare surveyed the area in search of such monuments
in the early 19th c. A skeleton was present in the grave as well as some
splendid grave-goods, including an unusual seax in a metal-edged
sheath, two spears, a shieldboss, an iron belt buckle with two tongues,
a bone comb and a hanging bowl.

Maiden Castle The imposing monument of Maiden Castle is a well-known
prehistoric site in Dorset, with a Neolithic long barrow; near the
eastern end of this highly visible monument, excavations in the 1940s
revealed a shallow grave with a human skeleton, a 5'9" tall male.[411] On
his left thigh was an iron seax and a smaller knife, which had been
carried in the same sheath. There were also fragments of iron, perhaps
belt fittings, in the waist area. The burial is dated to the 7th c.

Middle Down see **Alvediston**

---

[407] Meaney, 1964, p.269-70

[408] Meaney, 1964, p.270; O'Brien, 1999, ref.617

[409] Meaney, 1964, p.270

[410] Musty, 1969; O'Brien, 1999, ref.1168

[411] Meaney, 1964, p.81 The mounting of a larger and a smaller knife in a single sheath is
paralleled in Kent (Buckland, grave 93) and elsewhere.

Netheravon The site of Netheravon (Wiltshire) was chosen for an aviation school, and excavations for cellars on the site in 1931 produced a male skeleton accompanied by an iron spearhead.[412] In 1938, further work nearby revealed a skeleton surrounded by iron nails from a coffin, long since decayed; the depth of soil above the grave was greater than usual on the site and it is possible that a mound had once stood over it.

Newport Near Newport (Wight) stands a mound known locally as *Michael Moorey's Hump*. It was disturbed during road-widening in the 19th c. and among the artefacts recovered were seven skeletons and an iron knife of Anglo-Saxon date. The barrow had been used as the site of a gibbet into early modern times, and the excavators removed the stone block which housed the gibbet's post.

Normanton Cunnington opened a long barrow at Normanton (Wiltshire) before 1812, and discovered a skeleton 18" below the surface at the broad end.[413] Although there was no direct evidence for Anglo-Saxon activity, the situation is reminiscent of other secondary burials which are known to be Anglo-Saxon in date.

Oakley Down see **Pentridge**

Ogbourne St. Andrew The barrow at Ogbourne St. Andrew (Wiltshire) near the churchyard was dug in 1885 and was found to contain remains of many burials, one from the Bronze Age and others possibly from different periods, one of which was in a wooden coffin and may have been Anglo-Saxon in date.[414]

Oliver's Battery see **Compton**

Pentridge At some point before 1812, Hoare was staying at Woodyates, Pentridge and observed some barrows on the Bokerley Ditch.[415] Two of these he opened and in one discovered two skeletons and several iron objects, including a spearhead and two knives, and a bone object. The same area produced a rare Anglo-Saxon bed-burial (see next para.). Some barrows at Bower Chalke near Woodyates (Wiltshire) were

---

[412] Meaney, 1964, p.270-1; O'Brien, 1999, ref.576

[413] Meaney, 1964, p.271

[414] Meaney, 1964, p.271

[415] Meaney, 1964, p.8; O'Brien, 1999, ref.489, 953. The nature of the bone object is intriguing. Bone and antler combs are not uncommon in Anglo-Saxon graves, but occasionally flat plates occur; one such, used as a wrist-guard while shooting a bow, was found at Boveney (Oxfordshire)

investigated in 1842.[416] One was apparently undisturbed, 2' high and formed from gravel. A skeleton lay in a cist within, with an iron dagger at the right side; a green substance on the upper part may have been the hilt. Remains of a probable spear were also found in the grave.

A barrow burial of Anglo-Saxon date at Woodyates, Pentridge (Dorset) was similar to Swallowcliffe Down in some respects:[417] it was a bed-burial holding an adult female with beads and other decorative items, including a millefiori pendant, a gold chain and an ivory ring which the excavator took for a bracelet but which would probably have been one of the purse-rings found in late 6th and 7th c. high-status graves. In the same area, at Oakley Down, Hoare records the digging of a roadside barrow which contained the remains of a female accompanied by many glass and amber beads, and two finger rings, some iron fragments and a button brooch.[418]

Portsdown At Portsdown (Hampshire) twelve skeletons were found sometime before 1817, placed in both sides of a long barrow as secondary inhumations.[419] An Anglo-Saxon date has been suggested for these burials.

Preston Candover A barrow in *Long Barrow Field* at Preston Candover (Hampshire) yielded evidence of Anglo-Saxon secondary inhumation:[420] before 1893 a spearhead with a split socket had been recovered from the mound; before 1939 a seax was found from near the same site.

Roche Court Down An earthwork at Roche Court Down (Wiltshire) was investigated by Stone in 1931.[421] The site was complex due to the presence of three barrows, a battlefield cemetery of possible Anglo-Saxon date and a small Anglo-Saxon period cemetery about 40 yards north of the barrows. The two small barrows also stood about 40 yards from where the battlefield graves were sited; they were low at 6" (15cm) high, but did not appear to have been ploughed or damaged. The first barrow had a rounded hole in the centre, but contained nothing but some flints and a fragment of pot and some charcoal. The

---

[416] Meaney, 1964, p.266; ; O'Brien, 1999, ref.561

[417] Meaney, 1964, p.82; Speake, 1989, p.107

[418] Meaney, 1964, p.81-2

[419] Meaney, 1964, p.99

[420] Meaney, 1964, p.99

[421] Meaney, 1964, p.272-3; O'Brien, 1999, ref.582

second held a large grave, aligned with the hole of the first barrow. The grave's sides had been lined with turf, and in it rested the skeleton of a man 6' tall, with a seax under his right wrist still in its leather sheath. Some iron fragments lay by the left hip, and the leg-bones of a sheep. The third barrow contained only Bronze Age remains.

Salisbury Race Course see **Coombe Bissett**

Shalbourne see **East Grafton**

Shalcombe Down In 1816 a barrow on Shalcombe Down (Isle of Wight) yielded a bronze disc brooch among items of Bronze Age date.[422] Another barrow had stood nearby but had been undermined by industrial activity and collapsed; in its debris were found a long sword, tweezers, silver-gilt openwork brooches with central garnets, and some pieces of glass.

Sherrington A prehistoric long barrow at Sherrington (Wiltshire) featured an Anglo-Saxon secondary inhumation accompanied by a spear and shield, a belt buckle and a piece of bronze strip, possibly from a stave bucket.[423] The initial dig took place in 1804, conducted by Cunnington; a later dig by Thurnam in 1856 yielded no new information.

Somerton An Anglo-Saxon cemetery at Bradley Hill, Somerton (Somerset) contained fifty seven inhumations.[424] There were ring-ditches which may have formed part of barrows.

Snell's Corner see **Horndean**

Stonehenge (see also **Durrington**) Before 1740, Stukeley investigated the pair of barrows north of Stonehenge in Wiltshire.[425] The western mound contained a male skeleton at a depth of 14", the bones badly decayed. It seems likely that this was a secondary inhumation in a Bronze Age mound, and of Anglo-Saxon date.

Tilshead Lodge At Tilshead Lodge a mound named *Kill Barrow* was opened before 1958.[426] Two secondary inhumations were found, of probable Anglo-Saxon date. The *Tilshead Lodge Long Barrow* was already opened by Hoare and Cunnington before 1812, and revealed a

---

[422] Meaney, 1964, p.99-100

[423] Meaney, 1964, p.275-6; Cook, 2004, p.104

[424] O'Brien, 1999, ref.2186

[425] Meaney, 1964, p.264

[426] Meaney, 1964, p.269; Cook, 2004

skeleton in the upper layers, but unaccompanied.[427] In 1860 Thurnam re-opened the barrow and found a skeleton with a shieldboss and fittings on its chest and with a small wooden vessel by the head.

Ventnor At Ventnor (Isle of Wight) an Anglo-Saxon secondary inhumation was found in a cairn or barrow in 1904.[428]

Whitchurch A long barrow at Twinley Farm, Whitchurch (Hampshire) revealed an iron sword of Anglo-Saxon date during ploughing in 1918.[429] A secondary inhumation in a Neolithic barrow seems likely.

Wilsford At South Wilsford (Wiltshire), near Stonehenge, a barrow stood in Lake Field.[430] In 1763 a drawing was handed to Stukely of a spearhead taken from this barrow as well as an object identified as a helmet but more likely a shieldboss placed over the face. The remains came from the top of the barrow, and were probably an Anglo-Saxon secondary inhumation. The *Ell Long Barrow* at North Wilsford was opened by Thurnam some time before 1865. Within was a large male skeleton, with a deep cleft in the skull apparently from a sword blow.[431]

Winkelbury Hill A barrow at Winkelbury Hill (Wiltshire) was 4.5km distant and visible from the Swallowcliffe Down site, and the two monuments may have formed part of a landscape of memorial burials.[432] Both sites (Swallowcliffe Down and Winkelbury Hill) were complexes of barrows and other earthworks, sited for intervisibility.[433] Again, a Bronze Age mound had been re-used by the local West Saxons, and the site was very close to an Iron Age hillfort and other landscape features. (There were at least 30 further inhumations of Anglo-Saxon date placed around the barrow, and a second re-used barrow stood nearby containing a skeleton with an Anglo-Saxon knife.) The grave cavity contained a bed burial, of which the iron fittings remained, but the grave had been robbed before Pitt Rivers excavated it in 1881.

---

[427] Meaney, 1964, p.277

[428] Meaney, 1964, p.101

[429] Meaney, 1964, p.101

[430] Meaney, 1964, p.270

[431] Meaney, 1964, p.267

[432] Meaney, 1964, p.277-8; Speake, 1989, p.105; Williams, 2006, p.32

[433] Welch, 2007, p.198 notes a similar phenomenon in respect of east Kentish barrows.

Winterbourne Stoke The small village of Winterbourne Stoke (Wiltshire) has at least three Anglo-Saxon barrows.[434] The first was part of the West Conygar group, opened by Cunnington in 1809, about a mile north of the village. The Bronze Age remains were displaced to make room for a secondary burial, which was in turn disturbed by the insertion of a cist. An iron knife was associated with either the second or third burials. The same year, Cunnington opened the second mound, a small barrow to the east of the enclosure, which appeared to have been disturbed. The only identifiable inclusion was a small bead of Anglo-Saxon type. The third barrow revealed five or more skeletons in the upper layers when Hoare opened it before 1812.

Winterslow Hut In 1814 Hutchins opened a barrow at Winterslow Hut (Wiltshire) near the enclosures. About 2' from the surface was a skeleton accompanied by a shieldboss and grip, and a bronze-bound wooden bucket.[435] An Anglo-Saxon secondary inhumation seems likely. Nearby was a bell-barrow which he also opened to reveal a bronze spearhead and four iron arrowheads; the latter may also be the remnants of a disturbed Anglo-Saxon secondary inhumation.

Woodyates see **Pentridge**

Yatesbury The village of Yatesbury (Wiltshire) is the site of several tumuli. One opened by Bray before 1743 held a large stone in the top, which was found to be the cover of a stone cist holding a skeleton with a gold ring, some indeterminate metal object and some iron spearheads.[436] About 1833 a workman was employed to demolish two barrows about 20' (6m) in *Barrow Field* in the same village. Once reduced to a height of 9' (2.7m) one of the barrows revealed a small metal workbox (pyxide), some beads, a knife and two complete skeletons. (see fig.9)

---

[434] Meaney, 1964, p.278

[435] Meaney, 1964, p.279

[436] Meaney, 1964, p.279; O'Brien, 1999, ref.599

Mercia & Middle Anglia (East & West Midlands)

Under the heading 'Mercia and Middle Anglia' I include the present West Midlands, the East Midlands and the southern Central counties north of the Thames, and the area bordering Wales.

Benty Grange

Benty Grange is the name of a barrow situated in the Peak District, near Monyash. Local antiquarian Thomas Bateman dug the mound in 1848, but his record of the dig was mainly concerned with the objects found in the grave rather than the construction and layout of the barrow itself, which was "of inconsiderable elevation, perhaps not more than two feet at the highest point".[437] The burial was placed "about the centre and upon the natural soil" but no human remains could be detected other than some fibrous matter identified as human hair.

The grave-goods were unusual: the silver fittings for a cup; three enamelled escutcheons, perhaps from a cauldron; a quantity of fine wire, part of a textile garment; an iron chain, badly rusted; a "six-pronged instrument of iron"; a unique helmet with an iron frame and a covering of horn plates, also badly corroded. If this was the burial of a leading warrior, as the helmet suggests, then the absence of weapons is remarkable; it may be that the mass of corroded iron which was later shown to be a suspension chain, may also have contained unrecognised spearheads and knives which Bateman thought to be a single "six-pronged" item.

Bateman was at pains to comment on the decorations: "a yellow interlaced dracontine pattern, intermingled with that peculiar scroll design, visible on the same class of ornaments ... and used in several manuscripts of the VIIth century for the purpose of decorating the initial letters."

The helmet had a boar figure on the crest and a small, inlaid silver cross on the nasal, suggesting that it may have been a heathen item re-branded for a Christian convert. However, it seems unlikely that a newly-converted Christian would have allowed a heathen *insignium* to remain on his personal helm, and the cross was in any case not a popular Christian symbol at this time. Indeed cross-shaped designs are among the commonest forms of stamp on heathen funerary urns. These two facts together suggest that the helmet belongs to the heathen period, although perhaps to the end of it. The

---

[437] Bateman, 1861 (1978), p.28-33; Meaney, 1964, p.72; O'Brien, 1999, ref.307

silver cross had originally been equal-armed, like a +-sign, but the lower limb had been extended with additional silver at some stage. The helmet showed no sign of wear or battle-damage, and may never have been worn in a fight.

We cannot be sure that this burial was in fact in a chamber, although the quality of the grave-goods and the provision of a suspension chain suggest that it may have been. The only parallel for the chain is in the Sutton Hoo Mound 1 burial, and the helmet is one of perhaps only three found in Anglo-Saxon graves, of which the one found in Sutton Hoo Mound 1 is the most famous (but see p.200 below).

Caenby

In 1850 a four-day excavation began into a barrow near Caenby (Lincolnshire) in the former kingdom of Lindsey.[438] The site is close to the junction of the Roman Ermine Street, running north-south and connecting Lincoln to the River Humber, with an east-west route to the coast. There is evidence for Roman period and later activity in the area, and the barrow was well placed to be seen by travellers. The tumulus measured 340 feet in circumference and stood about 8 feet high, which makes it larger (though lower) than the largest mounds at Sutton Hoo.

The excavation account is confused. The barrow had been robbed at some previous period but the excavators were able to ascertain that it had contained a remarkable burial: a body in a seated position with a wooden stool, made of timbers an inch (25mm) thick and decorated with gilt-bronze, with his shield on his knees and his sword at his right side. The shield was decorated with gilt-bronze mounts in circular and pelta shapes, bearing knotwork designs. The peltas were placed radiating from a circular silver mount bearing Style II animal decoration; the lobes of the pelta plates were formed with the heads of birds of prey. The decoration is very reminiscent of the designs used on the *Book of Durrow* a 7th c. Gospel book, probably made in Northumbria.

Moreover, in the area some fragments of decorated silver bearing Style II design, like that found at the contemporary Sutton Hoo Mound 1 burial, have been discovered; they may have been part of the decorative plates from a helmet. (The date of the barrow was considered contemporary with Sutton Hoo Mound 1 by Speake on art-historical grounds.) Some bones and pieces of metal are believed to be the remains of a horse buried with its trappings in the barrow.

---

[438] Smith, 1923, p.86; Meaney, 1964, p.152-3; Speake, 1980, p.39, 42; O'Brien, 1999, ref.374; Cook, 2004, p.62

It has been speculated that the barrow once housed a member of the Lindsey royal house. Conversely, Plunkett suggests that the Caenby mound may have been the tomb of Rægenhere, son of Rædwald, who died at the Battle of the River Idle on the Mercian border fighting Æðelfrið of Northumbria.[439] While this is certainly possible, the presence of East Anglian style decorated fittings in the mound would be unusual unless we assume that Rægenhere was buried on or near the site of the battlefield. The practice seems to have been for the dead (of the winning side, at least) to be retrieved and taken away for honourable burial, and large mounds of this kind are usually sited on the borders of their home territories. Therefore, unless we assume that East Anglian power reached into Lindsey at this time (which is not impossible following a great military victory, but seems improbable nonetheless) the choice of a location so far from the Suffolk heartland appears rather odd for the barrow of a prince of the Wuffingas.[440]

Loveden Hill

Loveden Hill in Lincolnshire was formerly a wapentake (hundred) meeting spot.[441] Evidence for Anglo-Saxon activity in the area was first discovered in 1921 when a cremation urn was unearthed during ironstone extraction. Excavation of the site commenced in 1925 with the digging of the barrow on the hilltop, standing 4' high and 28' in diameter. A skeleton lay on the north side, with the skull placed over the midriff, surrounded by a ring of stones and with an urn at both hips and both shoulders, and a cremation urn beyond where the head should have been.

Further excavation the following year revealed three more skeletons, their heads placed close together and their bodies radiating, on the barrow's southern side where a series of 34 cremation urns were also found, most having been covered with a stone each. Occasional typical Anglo-Saxon finds such as bronze tweezers were in some of the urns. Rows of stones marked the northern and south-eastern edges of the barrow.

In 1955 deep-ploughing on the hill-top turned up broken urn-rims and a squad of fieldwalkers spent several weeks gathering as much of the recently-damaged ceramics as possible. A concentration of finds was plotted near the barrow. The following year, during the gathering of the harvest, the end of a large whetstone was discovered in the field, probably having stood upright

---

[439] Plunkett, 2005, p.80-1

[440] Plunkett, 2005, p.80 notes that two place-names point to a Wuffingas presence in the east Midlands: Uffington, near Stamford and Ufford, near Barnack.

[441] Meaney, 1964, p.158-9; O'Brien, 1999, ref.333

among the graves as a marker. One end of the stone was carved with a human head and the suggestion of clothing, a hollow having been ground into the crown of the head. (This parallels the large stone sceptre found in Sutton Hoo Mound 1 which had metal fittings with cup-shaped terminals, as if to rest on the knee.) The stone may have come from Dumfries, again as with the Sutton Hoo find, but the Loveden Hill example is much smaller.

Rescue excavations between 1955 and 1959 traced a broken ring of stones which may have marked another barrow on the site, long since ploughed away. Eight inhumations and more than 100 cremations were found in this area; the inhumations had grave-goods including a shieldboss; two small shield appliqué plates; two decorated combs; a knife and the remains of a drinking horn with a bronze terminal. A cist burial was the most unusual inhumation, and a double burial had been covered with part of a column from a Roman building.

 Two bodies lay under the second mound, covered with limestone blocks. A male had a circle of upright stones near his head. A female had some grave-goods – part of a knife; a large flat bronze dish with attachments riveted to the rim; a hanging bowl with three silver-gilt escutcheons containing a cremated human as well as an iron nail and a glass palm-cup; fragments of an iron-bound wooden bucket. More ironware, including a horse's bit, was found with a bronze cauldron containing a spearhead, a bucket handle and piece of fused glass. Several triangular drinking horn mounts and a rectangular handle were found nearby. Another hanging bowl was found containing a cremation, and a tall ceramic urn. A third, small bronze bowl was found with twisted bronze loops above it. All the bronze bowls had been deliberately stabbed or pieced before burial.

A further area to the east contained over 100 cremations in urns, some with pieces of fused glass and bronze, and bone counters for game-playing, as well as the usual tweezers and bone combs. Southwest of the barrow were 170 cremations in urns, some with brooches, girdle-hangers, wrist clasps and so on.

The cemetery at Loveden Hill is one of the largest cremation groups ever found in England with around 1700 urns – only Spong Hill (Norfolk) is known to be larger with over 2000. One of the urns bears a curious runic text on the shoulder: although poorly executed, most of the characters can be either read directly or narrowed down to one of two possibilities. The text may most probably be read as "Siþibæld receives a barrow" or "Siþibad (the) maid's grave".[442]

---

[442] Looijenga, 2003, p.261-2

It seems likely that the barrows at Loveden Hill once contained the remains of a series of community leaders who were accorded the rite of barrow-burial while the majority of the folk continued to use accompanied cremation in urns.

Lapwing Hill

On 3rd August 1850, Bateman opened a barrow on Lapwing Hill, near Brushfield (Derbyshire).[443] The barrow was 51' (15m) across and 4' (1.25m) high in the middle, composed of earth but with a stone setting in the centre. A shallow grave-cut contained the badly decayed remains of a male with his head to the west, resting on a textile base, with 'a considerable quantity of decayed wood, indicating a plank of some thickness, or the bottom of a coffin.' A broad iron sword with remains of its leather sheath lay to the body's left, with a smaller knife beneath the hilt; above the right shoulder were two angon heads. There were many objects of corroded iron in the grave, including nine hoops of about 1" (25mm) breadth and various staples and other fittings disposed about the body.

It seems likely that the remains of wood and iron were indeed part of a bier or coffin, and the textiles would thus be explicable as part of the grave furniture. However, Speake is inclined to see these more elaborate fittings as part of a bed-burial.[444] The hoops would suggest a stave-built bucket of the standard type.

Bateman noted that the same farm had previously yielded a sword and shield boss in 1828, and it seems likely enough that these might have been found in an accompanying burial. He conjectured that the land was identical with *Beorhtrices feld* (recorded as *Brighterighefield*) in a 16th c. land conveyance and that Beorhtric was the name of the 'noble Saxon' in the barrow. A nearby tumulus, known as "Gospel Hillock" he supposed to have been the site of early missionary activity in the area, but his excavation revealed only some bone and pottery fragments. A third barrow, closer to that of the nobleman, excavated on 14th August in the same year, had previously been disturbed and yielded just an undatable piece of human skull and some human and animal bones.

---

[443] Bateman, 1861 (1978), p.68-70; Meaney, 1964, p.74; O'Brien, 1999, ref.310
[444] Speake, 1989, p.103-5

NewhavenLow

While Benty Grange is a justly famous Anglo-Saxon barrow, in which one of the few known existing Anglo-Saxon helmets was discovered, less well known is the barrow at Newhaven which was dug by Thomas Bateman in the following year on 27th April.[445] The tumulus was known locally as *The Low* and it stood by Newhaven House at Hartington Middle Quarter; it had been previously dug which, as Bateman himself acknowledged, " is much to be regretted, as the contents appear to be late in date, and different in character from anything we have before found in tumuli." Bateman recognised that the mound was similar to that at Benty Grange in its construction, and it was similarly devoid of human remains apart from some "fragments of calcined bone" which could not be ascribed to a human or animal source.

This barrow also produced what may have been the remains of a similar helmet, in the form of "many small pieces of thin iron straps or bands, more or less overlaid with bronze, which are by no means unlike the framework of the helmet found at Benty Grange." The description fits rather better with a helm of the Sutton Hoo type, made of an iron bowl to which tinned bronze plates were attached with copper alloy strips.

It is worth recording here that in 1844, workmen digging at Leckhampton Hill (Gloucestershire) discovered a skeleton in a roadside grave.[446] Around the skull were several tight-fitting bronze bands, surmounted by a knob; this has been interpreted as the frame of a helmet. A length of chain was attached to it, which might be the remains of an aventail similar to that found on the 8th c. Coppergate helmet from York. However, an Anglo- Saxon date is only evidenced by some aspects of the pottery. The bronze bands could possibly have been the reeded strips which held the helmet's outer decorative plates in place, as at Sutton Hoo. At the same site, another inhumation was discovered; the earth around the skull was found to contain many iron studs, as if there had been a cap studded with iron on his head at the time of burial. The finds associated with this skeleton were of Roman date (Samian ware and coins of Constantine).

Another item in the Newhaven Low grave was " a boss of thin bronze, three inches diameter, pierced with three holes for attachment and divided by raised concentric circles, between which the metal is ornamented with a dotted chevron pattern, in the angles of which are small roses punched by a

---

[445] Bateman, 1861 (1978), p.45-6; Meaney, 1964, p.77; O'Brien, 1999, ref.956; Pollington, 2002

[446] Meaney, 1964, p.90

die." This sounds like an Anglo-Saxon composite disc brooch, which is usually associated with female burials. Another find was a small round bronze container, which from its description may have been a pyxides, a small needlework container found in Anglo-Saxon graves in the east and south-east. Other objects included an iron ferrule, "some shapeless pieces of melted glass which from their variegated appearance might be the product of fused beads" and many pieces of charred wood throughout the mound.

Although Bateman's clumsy attempt at excavation may have destroyed the helmet, its subsequent fate is not recorded and it is possible that the broken remains were replaced in the mound as it was back-filled.

The grave appears to have held the remains of a cremated female (the pyxides and beads and the possible brooch point to a female, while the fused state of the glass is likely the result of cremation), but the helmet (if such it was) would naturally be associated with a male. However, as the grave had previously been robbed it may be that it originally contained a male with helmet and weapons, and the remains of a cremated female in a perishable, organic container. The grave having been opened, the weapons and any recognisable artefacts would have been removed, leaving only an iron spear ferrule, the rusted helmet and the remnants of the female cremation. The burnt wood is not uncommon in Anglo-Saxon graves and is believed to have been part of a purification ritual.

Wollaston

In 1997 during gravel extraction a 7th c. princely burial was unearthed on land near Wollaston (Northamptonshire).[447]

The grave contained an iron sword, a fragmentary bronze hanging bowl and skeletal remains including teeth, a six-inch piece of leg bone, and a skull fragment. The bronze bowl was decorated with an inlaid millefiori escutcheon and may have been incomplete when placed in the grave. The sword blade, pattern-welded from four bundles of iron rods, is about three feet long. It may have had a horn, antler or wooden hilt which does not survive. Traces of a leather-covered wooden scabbard lined with fleece were found adhering to the blade.

However, the outstanding element in the burial was the remains of an iron helmet, only the third certain example from the Anglo-Saxon period to have been excavated from a barrow. (The fourth, from Coppergate, York, was deposited in a well.) The soil block containing the helmet was extracted for

---

[447] O'Brien, 199, ref.2257

laboratory examination. Apart from the iron skull, nasal and cheek-pieces, there were other remains. Organic materials found inside the helmet may be the remains of its leather lining, while traces of feathers and textiles on the outside of the helmet suggest that the body had been placed on a bolster. The top of the helmet is decorated with an iron boar figurine, rather plainer than the only other surviving example on the Benty Grange helmet. The helmet was probably secured close to the face with a leather strap fastened between the crescent-shaped cheek pieces and tied off beneath the chin.

The teeth showed no evidence of poor health or deformity, and the leg and skull fragments suggested that the occupant was slender and not tall. The deceased was probably around 25 years old when he died, which would place him at the end of his military career. Fly pupae cases on the helmet indicated that it may have been buried after a period of being transported to the grave site. It is tempting to speculate that the young man fell in battle and was brought home to rest with his armour and weapons in a mound on the border of his homeland.

Wollaston lies on the southern edge of Mercia, between the East Anglian and Mercian polities which were both very important in the 7th c. The nearby village of Earl's Barton boasts a very well-preserved church tower dating from the 10th c., with many original Anglo-Saxon features.

The evidence of the Mercian *Tribal Hidage* document indicates that there were numerous small chiefdoms in surrounding Mercia which acted as 'buffer states' between the larger, more centralised power blocs and it may be that the young man belonged to one of these.

Other Midlands Barrows

There are several examples of secondary inhumation in the Peak District, including the barrows at *Galley Low, Wigber Low, White Low, Cow Low*. Each of these names and several others appears to feature the local continuation of the OE *hlæw* 'mound, barrow', but most are probably of Bronze Age date. *Arbor Low* – a stone circle and barrow – is derived from *eardburg hlæw* 'earth-barrow mound' [or Eadburg's mound?]. *Wigber Low* is a re-used Bronze Age cairn, into which three females and four males had been inserted in the 7th c.[448] The grave-goods were of good quality but generally unremarkable – a sword, five spearheads, combs, buckles, some copper alloy strip, knives, a firesteel. The unusual items were a beaver's tooth mounted in a gold binding, a fragment of a gold bracteate and two silver pins with cross-shaped gold sheet heads. These

---

[448] Meaney, 1964, p.79; Collis, 1983; O'Brien, 1999, ref.1181

are consistent with one high-status female burial in the group, but even so there is not enough high-status material for this assemblage to be classified as a princely grave, and the burials were too close together in the cairn for a chamber to have been constructed around any one of them.

Abington At Abington (Northamptonshire) a mound was destroyed, which the local archaeologist believed was Anglo-Saxon in date.[449] A female skeleton and iron knife were recovered from a roadside mound here in 1933, and it is possible that there was once either a large mound with many burials, or a series of small tumuli.

Akeman Street *Chavenage Sleight* is the name of a barrow overlooking Akeman Street in Gloucestershire.[450] In 1847, a labourer was levelling part of the mound when he discovered the remains of seven inhumations arranged radially, with ashes and stones placed in the centre. Beads, spearheads, buckles, a knife, a shieldboss, annular brooches, earrings and some bronze items were all consistent with an Anglo-Saxon date for the burials.

Alsop In 1845 Bateman opened a barrow called *The Lowe* above Alsop (Derbyshire) which contained a skeleton with an iron shield boss, and some small metal fragments, perhaps corroded iron buckles.[451] It was probably a secondary inhumation.

Alstonefield In 1848, Carrington mounted a two-week campaign on *Steep Low*, Alstonefield (Staffordshire), which had previously yielded no material.[452] A large quantity of charcoal was unearthed, as well as the skull of an ox and a small Roman coin. An iron spearhead was found and an iron arrowhead, but neither in association with any human remains.

Baggrave In 1784 a barrow was accidentally opened by a labourer at Baggrave (Leicestershire).[453] It contained an iron shieldboss, a spearhead, a turned bone disc used as a brooch, bronze and iron fittings from a bucket and some bone.

---

[449] Meaney, 1964, p.193; O'Brien, 1999, ref.456

[450] Meaney, 1964, p.90

[451] Meaney, 1964, p.72 Although dug by Bateman, this excavation does not appear in his *Ten Years' Diggings*, presumably due to the date (1845) which falls outside the parameters of his book.

[452] Meaney, 1964, p.222

[453] Meaney, 1964, p.144; Cook, 2004, p.70

Ballidon *Galley Lowe* at Ballidon (Derbyshire) was visited by Bateman in 1843.[454] The name *Galley Lowe* is sometimes attributed to a mound where a gallows stood, but the alternative local name *Callidge Lowe* belies this explanation in this case. Human, rat and horse remains were found mixed together with iron objects such as coffin fittings, 2 arrowheads, a whetstone, a bone pin, an earthenware vessel, some beads and pendants. The finds appear to be normal 7th c. Anglo-Saxon female grave-goods with the exception of the arrowheads and hone.

Barton-on-Humber The Castledyke cemetery at Barton-on-Humber (Lincolnshire) was first discovered in 1939, when air-raid shelters were being dug.[455]

Beacon Hill see **Cleethorpes**

Bingham In 1863 a skeleton was found at Parson's Hill, Bingham (Nottinghamshire).[456] It was accompanied by a sword and shieldboss, and an object described as a 'helmet'. While helmets do occur in Anglo-Saxon barrows, it is more likely that the object was a metal bowl (perhaps one of the 'Coptic' bowls of the 7th c. graves), which would also point to a high status burial. There is no mention of a barrow, but if the burial did indeed contain such costly items it would probably originally have been covered with a mound.

Bishopstone A destroyed tumulus is supposed to have covered three human skeletons discovered at Cursley Hill, Bishopstone (Buckinghamshire) in 1866;[457] there were spearheads and shieldbosses associated with the human remains. Further graves found in 1875 were probably associated burials respecting the barrow.

Bledlow-cum-Saunderton *The Cop* is a barrow near Bledlow-cum-Saunderton (Buckinghamshire);[458] the original structure is of Bronze Age date, but Anglo-Saxon remains from the site include an inhumation and at least five cremation burials. The barrow was sited close to the Icknield Way.

---

[454] Meaney, 1964, p.75

[455] Meaney, 1964, p.151; Drinkall & Foreman, 1998; O'Brien, 1999, ref.661

[456] Meaney, 1964, p.202

[457] Meaney, 1964, p.56

[458] Meaney, 1964, p.56-7

Blore In 1849, Carrington opened a barrow at Blore (Staffordshire) in a field called *Nettles*.[459] A disturbed secondary inhumation was found, with a ceramic vessel and an iron ring.

Borough Hill see **Daventry**

Borrowash In the construction of the Midland Railway some time before 1851, workmen digging near Borrowash (Derbyshire) disturbed a barrow containing around 80 recognisable human skeletons.[460] The finds were mostly items of stone but a Roman coin of Constantinian was found in a pot, implying a Roman or post-Roman date for this vessel. Secondary burial is the most likely explanation here.

Brundcliff see **Hartington**

Burgh-le-Marsh In 1933 a trench was cut through a mound called *Cock Hill* at Burgh-le-Marsh (Lincolnshire).[461] The lower part of a human skeleton was found, with a bronze buckle of late 6th or early 7th c. type.

Bury Bank see **Cannock Chase**

Buxton *Cow Lowe* at Green Fairfield near Buxton (Derbyshire) was opened by Bateman in 1846; it contained a secondary Anglo-Saxon inhumation of which only the teeth and part of the skull remained.[462] Two gold pins with garnet settings and a blue glass bead found near the skull imply that this was a 7th c. burial of a high-status female. A small wooden box found nearby contained a glass vessel; an ivory comb; some iron and brass tools (perhaps a toilet set?); 11 pendants for a necklace of which one was a canine tooth; a perforated bone (a needle?). A red deer's horn was placed above the body.

Calton In 1849, at Calton (Staffordshire), Carrington opened a barrow which contained an inhumation accompanied by flint.[463] A further skeleton within the mound was supine and accompanied by a 'short, thick-backed iron knife, which had been inserted into a wooden haft', presumably a 6th or 7th c. *seax*.

---

[459] Meaney, 1964, p.220

[460] Meaney, 1964, p.73; O'Brien, 1999, ref.951

[461] Meaney, 1964, p.152; O'Brien, 1999, ref.136

[462] Meaney, 1964, p.74-5

[463] Bateman, 1861 (1978), p.128-9; Meaney, 1964, p.220-1

Cannock Chase *King's Low* and *Queen's Low* are a pair of barrows at the northern end of Cannock Chase (Staffordshire); despite their evocative names, they do not appear to have held any Anglo-Saxon material and it may be that the names were given for legendary reasons. Equally picturesque is the name *Saxons' Low* near Bury Bank (Staffordshire) which tradition associates with King Wulfhere of Mercia.

Carlton Scroop Before 1930, a barrow at Carlton Scroop (Lincolnshire) was excavated and several brooches and ornaments were recovered.[464] A series of beads and bronze tweezers from the same site were recovered separately.

Castern In 1845, Bateman excavated a barrow at Castern (Staffordshire) which contained some prehistoric burials, Roman material and a knife with a horn handle, implying at least one Anglo-Saxon secondary inhumation in the mound.[465]

Castle Hill see **High Wycombe**

Castledyke see **Barton-on-Humber**

Cauldon Hills A damaged barrow on the Cauldon Hills (Staffordshire) was opened by Carrington in 1849; it stood only 3' (1m) high with a diameter of 18 yards and was at some distance from the other mounds at this site.[466] A skeleton was found, with a ceramic vessel alleged to be similar to Frankish ware of the 7th c.

Chelmorton Near *Nether Low* at Chelmorton (Derbyshire) a small, low mound was opened by Bateman in 1849; it contained a stone-lined grave which held the skeleton of a tall man, with an iron knife across his pelvis. A primary inhumation of Anglo-Saxon date is most likely.[467] On 9th September 1859, Bateman opened a mound at Chelmorton, a mere 27' (8.25m) across and 2' (62cm) high.[468] A male skeleton lay extended, supine, with an iron buckle and two small knives at his waist, but the burial was badly decayed.

---

[464] Meaney, 1964, p.153; O'Brien, 1999, ref.376

[465] Meaney, 1964, p.221

[466] Meaney, 1964, p.221; O'Brien, 1999, ref.977

[467] Meaney, 1964, p.74

[468] Bateman, 1861 (1978), p.105-6; O'Brien, 1999, ref.313

Churchover An Anglo-Saxon cemetery was discovered at Gibbet Hill, Churchover (Warwickshire) in 1823 when a shieldboss and spearhead were found near Watling Street.[469] A group of burials by the roadside, equipped with weapons, brooches, pottery, etc. excavated the following year may have been covered by a barrow, since in 1730 Dugdale described a very large tumulus in this area, which travellers had to walk round. It is even possible that the burials were each covered originally by a single mound which was later levelled.

Cleethorpes At Cleethorpes (Lincolnshire) a barrow was excavated on Beacon Hill in 1935.[470] The mound was 45' long, 25' wide and 10' high – hence a probable long barrow. Most of the burials dated from the Bronze Age but an Anglo-Saxon cremation urn had been inserted in the 6th or 7th c.

Cold Eaton In 1851, on 9th August, Carrington discovered two low, flat barrows lying between the mounds of *Net Low* and *Green Low* at Cold Eaton (Derbyshire), which had been opened in 1845.[471] The mound nearer *Net Low* was 60' (18m) across but only 18" (45cm) high and had previously been overlooked. The report mentions that the bones and objects, found in a circular hole 18" (45cm) in diameter, were cremated, and the grave otherwise appears to have been typical of such burials except that no urn was found. With the bones were some fragments of iron with attachments of some perishable material and including a loop; parts of two bone combs; and "twenty-eight convex objects of bone, like button-moulds." These were evidently bone gaming pieces. The iron was presumable from either a stave-bucket or some other vessel, and the combs were decorated, one with ring-and-dot patterns and the other with herringbone hatching. The grave appears to have been a primary cremation burial.

Cossington Three barrows stood above the River Wreake by Cossington (Leicestershire).[472] All three were of Bronze Age date, but the northerly one had been re-used in the 6th c. to house five separate burials, among which were found the remains of three buckets, an annular brooch and a glass bead, all suggestive of high-status female inhumations. Two iron knives and a spearhead were found just outside the ring-ditch.

---

[469] Meaney, 1964, p.259-60; O'Brien, 1999, ref.1169

[470] Meaney, 1964, p.153

[471] Bateman, 1861 (1978), p.179-81; Meaney, 1964, p.74; O'Brien, 1999, ref.314

[472] Thomas, 2008

Croxall see **Lichfield**

Cursley Hill see **Bishopstone**

Darwen Moor In 1780 a mound called *Bone Low* on the edge of Darwen Moor (Derbyshire) was dug by workmen looking for re-usable stone, and was found to contain some pots filled with human bones which, from the description, may have been Anglo-Saxon cremation urns. If so, they would have been a secondary interment in the barrow.[473]

Daventry A mound on Borough Hill, Daventry (Northamptonshire) was dug in 1823 and revealed some Roman objects as well as an Anglo-Saxon bronze pin, a small-long brooch; a buckle with rectangular plate; glass, ceramic and amber beads; a bronze stud; two perforated Roman coins.[474] These grave-goods are consistent with an early Anglo-Saxon female burial. The location of the barrow is not recorded accurately, and there are several earthworks on the hill. Human and animal remains were visible on the surface at this time, and a cist burial of a male accompanied by an iron spearhead had previously been discovered by fieldworkers.

Dunstable At *Five Knolls*, Dunstable (Bedfordshire) a barrow overlooking the vale of Aylesbury, nearly 100 Anglo-Saxon burials were placed within a large tumulus of Bronze Age date; they were mostly young men and women, and many had their hands tied behind their backs. It is possible that the burials took place over a period of time and that a pre-existing barrow was used as the focus for a gallows or *cwealmstow* (place of legal execution). The earliest Anglo-Saxon activity may have been an urned cremation in the barrow, of which fragments were recovered in the 1882 excavation.

Eddlesborough At Eddlesborough (Buckinghamshire) workmen digging at *Gallows Hill* found several human skeletons;[475] it is likely that these are the remains of hanged criminals, but the possibility remains that this was an Anglo-Saxon barrow later re-used.

Gallows Hill see **Eddlesborough**

Gibbet Hill see **Churchover**

---

[473] Meaney, 1964, p.73
[474] Meaney, 1964, p.187; O'Brien, 1999, ref.440
[475] Meaney, 1964, p.57

Great Addington At Great Addington (Northamptonshire) a site called *Shooters Hill* was found to contain an Anglo-Saxon cemetery in 1847.[476] None of the burials were in mounds, but investigations in the adjoining field revealed a (ploughed out?) barrow with some skeletons beneath.

Green Fairfield see **Buxton**

Hampnett At Hampnett (Gloucestershire) a mixed cemetery was discovered at the *Burn Ground* site in 1940-1.[477] The Anglo-Saxon burials were on the edge of a group of round barrows skirting the eastern end of a long-barrow. There were ten inhumations and four cremations with occasional grave-goods such as a disc brooch and an iron knife, some beads and bonework.

Hartington In 1847, Bateman opened a mound at Brundcliff, Hartington (Derbyshire) which contained a collection of animal bone and a human skeleton in a shallow grave cut into the rock surface.[478] A small iron knife at the pelvis marks the burial out as Anglo-Saxon, with further unidentified iron and wood remains also present, including those of coffin planks. A red earthenware jug from the grave is of an unusual type, perhaps Romano-British or Frankish. Another grave in the same vicinity at *Carder Low* yielded human skeletal remains, an iron knife and three sandstone whetstones.[479]

In 1848, Bateman dug the feature called *Vincent Knoll* in Hartington Middle Quarter. It contained the remains of four humans, one of which was accompanied by an iron spearhead. The latter may have been an Anglo-Saxon secondary inhumation in the mound.[480] Three more barrows in the Hartington area were opened in 1849 by Bateman.[481] The first, at Hurdlow, contained an iron knife, a bronze work-box containing thread, bronze pins and a chatelaine. The grave also contained sections of hazel sticks, and the impression of woven fabric could be detected on the iron. Two further barrows nearby but closer to Buxton were less well-equipped: one contained an iron knife and some wooden remains, but no skeleton, while the other held the skeleton of a young man without grave-goods. Also in the Hartington area, *Waggon Low* was dug

---

[476] Meaney, 1964, p.186; O'Brien, 1999, ref.436

[477] Meaney, 1964, p.90

[478] Meaney, 1964, p.73-4; O'Brien, 1999, ref.309

[479] Meaney, 1964, p.74

[480] Meaney, 1964, p.79

[481] Meaney, 1964, p.76; O'Brien, 1999, ref.320

by Bateman in 1852. Among the human remains were two large iron knives. The possible Anglo-Saxon date for the mound is uncertain.[482]

High Wycombe In 1901 a high-status barrow was excavated at Castle Hill, High Wycombe (Buckinghamshire), near the present parish church.[483] It contained a skeleton accompanied by a gold filigree pendant, a necklace of glass beads and an iron object, identified as a sword. It is however more likely that the object was a weaving slay, of which some examples were fashioned in the same manner as swords, as the grave-goods are otherwise indicative of a female burial.

Hurdlow see **Hartington**

Ingarsby At Ingarsby (Leicestershire) a barrow was discovered during plantation in about 1830.[484] Several skeletons were revealed and some grave-goods, one of which was a fragment of a garnet-and-glass brooch of probable 7th c. date. An iron sword in Leicester Museum is also known to have come from Ingarsby, but whether it came from the same barrow or another is unknown. Meaney describes the burial as probably a secondary inhumation.

Kegworth In about 1930 an Anglo-Saxon pin was found at Kegworth (Leicestershire);[485] the site may have been a ploughed-out barrow.

Kempston At Kempston (Bedfordshire) a mixed inhumation and cremation cemetery was examined at several times from 1856 onwards.[486] There are discrepancies in the accounts of the digs, but one contemporary writer described a burial in a seated position accompanied by a knife, urn and spearhead. Although a rarity, this is not the only example of a corpse reported to have been buried as if seated – see Caenby (p.196).

Kirton-in-Lindsey During road-building at Kirton-in-Lindsey in 1856 a barrow was discovered on the parish boundary.[487] A series of cremation urns – perhaps as many as sixty – were dug out, and found to contain bones and other odd inclusions such as tweezers. Such burials are typical of Anglo-Saxon cremations, and may have been primary within a purpose-built barrow as at South Elkington.

---

[482] Meaney, 1964, p.79

[483] Meaney, 1964, p.59; O'Brien, 1999, ref.492

[484] Meaney, 1964, p.146

[485] Meaney, 1964, p.146

[486] Meaney, 1964, p.36-7 O'Brien, 1999, ref.57

[487] Meaney, 1964, p.156-7; O'Brien, 1999, ref.331, 332(?)

Lechlade At Butler's Field, Lechlade (Gloucestershire) an Anglo-Saxon cemetery excavated in the 1980s produced some extraordinarily rich finds.[488] About 217 inhumations were found and a further 32 cremations. Secondary inhumation in a Bronze Age feature – perhaps a mound but more likely a circular bank – was detected.

Leighton Buzzard At Leighton Buzzard (Bedfordshire) a small Anglo-Saxon cemetery was discovered in 1931.[489] One of the graves was surrounded by shallow ditch which may have been the trench for a mound.

Lichfield A mound at Croxall, near Lichfield (Staffordshire) is sited near the churchyard and is thought to be of Anglo-Saxon date. It was dug in the 19th c. and some human skeletal remains were found, but no other finds were reported.[490]

Long Itchington A large mound, presumed to have been a barrow, was dug in 1864 during recovery of stone at Long Itchington (Warwickshire).[491] An urn with bones was found within, of Anglian form.

Medbourne Medbourne Field at Medbourne (Leicestershire) was a known 'productive site' for Roman coins and other items, when in 1794 several skeletons were discovered, each covered by a cairn.[492] A spearhead was found with the remains.

Middleton Moor In 1788 a farmer digging in a field called *Garratt's Piece* at Middleton Moor (Derbyshire) discovered a human skeleton accompanied by a bronze bowl with enamelled escutcheons, a probable Anglo-Saxon primary inhumation within a barrow.[493] In 1787 a barrow was discovered on the moor: it contained a skeleton with an iron spearhead, and there were other discoveries nearby.[494]

Bateman opened a barrow called *Kenslow Knoll* in the Middleton area in 1821 and discovered a bronze penannular brooch among the human remains; he re-opened the same mound in 1848 and concluded that the original construction was Bronze Age in date, but the presence of an iron knife and a ceramic vessel also suggested Anglo-Saxon

---

[488] Boyle, Jennings, Miles & Palmer, 1998; O'Brien, 1999, ref.1237

[489] Meaney, 1964, p.37-8; O'Brien, 1999, ref.486

[490] English Heritage Record of Scheduled Monuments, no. 21536

[491] Meaney, 1964, p.217

[492] Meaney, 1964, p.147; O'Brien, 1999, ref.468

[493] Meaney, 1964, p.75; O'Brien, 1999, ref.318

[494] Meaney, 1964, p.77; O'Brien, 1999, ref.322, 323

interference.[495] Another barrow in the area was opened in 1825; it contained two iron knives with traces of the wooden hafts, and some fragments of iron and bone.[496] In 1827 labourers digging holes found a barrow containing a skeleton laid into a natural rock depression, and an iron knife with wood remaining on the tang.[497] A similar knife and part of a stone cist were found on the spoil heap. Bateman undertook a dig on the same spot in 1848 and dicovered disturbed human remains accompanied by a flint spearhead, a flint arrowhead and an antler tine. A Roman coin and a comb riveted with iron were also in the soil. A Roman date seems most likely for this barrow, but the possibility of a badly disturbed Anglo-Saxon grave alongside or above a Bronze Age interment cannot be excluded.

Monsal Dale At Monsal Dale, Bateman conducted an excavation into a tumulus on 23rd May 1851 which unearthed some Bronze Age remains.[498] On the north side of the mound, at a shallow depth were found some human bones and an iron spear, 9 ½" (24cm) long with a broken socket, and a blue glass bead with a white spiral trail. Locals told him that the mound had been dug some years before by someone hoping to find minerals and the remains had been brought to the surface at that time. However, no further Anglo-Saxon material was found in the barrow.

Musden Hill In 1848, Carrington investigated a group of barrows on Musden Hill (Staffordshire).[499] The 'second barrow' of the group contained a skeleton with two ceramic vessels similar to cremation urns found at e.g. Sleaford (Lincolnshire). The 'fourth barrow' contained two skeletons, one with a pair of annular brooches.

Newport Pagnell A small Anglo-Saxon cemetery on the Tickfield Park Estate at Newport Pagnell (Buckinghamshire) consisted of several bodies laid out radially around a central inhumation;[500] this layout would normally be expected where the central burial was covered with a barrow, although no trace of one is mentioned.

---

[495] Meaney, 1964, p.76 The more likely origin is Roman, according to Meaney.

[496] Meaney, 1964, p.76-7

[497] Meaney, 1964, p.77-8

[498] Bateman, 1861 (1978), p.75; Meaney, 1964, p.77

[499] Meaney, 1964, p.221

[500] Meaney, 1964, p.58

Newton Grange *Stand Low* at Newton Grange was dug by Bateman in 1845.[501] It contained an iron knife and a bronze work-box on the left side of where the skeleton had lain and nearby another knife; two bronze rings and some fragments of iron from a chatelaine; sherds of a yellow glass vessel; eleven glass beads and another of twisted silver wire; a silver needle. A female primary inhumation seems likely.

Northampton A barrow stood in *Cow Meadow*, Northampton (Northamptonshire) until the mid-1950s when it was levelled in urban redevelopment.[502] It had been opened in 1844 and found to contain two small urns and a swastika disc brooch. Some small finds including tweezers are now in the county museum.

Norton About 1855 a low long barrow at Norton (Northamptonshire) overlooking Watling Street, was being levelled.[503] The labourer discovered five or six skeletons and some pieces of metal within, as well as a red amber bead. In 1863, Watling Street was being straightened at this point, taking the road over the site of the burial mound; the previously disturbed bones were rediscovered, and a further skeleton accompanied by a saucer brooch, a disc brooch, a great square-headed brooch, two bronze rings, three iron hooks, an iron knife and a bone spindlewhorl. The Anglo-Saxon burial is presumably secondary within a Bronze Age barrow.

Oddington In 1787 a small barrow was discovered at Oddington (Gloucestershire) formed from layers of flat stones with earth between.[504] A number of skeletons (either six or ten depending on the source of information) were found beneath. Grave-goods included an iron disc, a shieldboss with silvered rivet-heads, two bronze pins, two spearheads, beads, a disc brooch and a saucer brooch with zoomorphic decoration.

Oldbury In about 1835, a barrow was opened at Oldbury in the Hartshill hills.[505] Apart from some human remains, a spearhead and shieldboss of iron were found.

Over Haddon In 1849, Bateman dug a mound called *Grind Low* (or *Grindlow*), near Over Haddon (Derbyshire).[506] The barrow was sited at

---

[501] Meaney, 1964, p.78; O'Brien, 1999, ref.326

[502] Meaney, 1964, p.193; O'Brien, 1999, ref.457

[503] Meaney, 1964, p.194

[504] Meaney, 1964, p.92

[505] Meaney, 1964, p.262

the meeting of three field-walls and must have pre-dated the layout of fields in the area. It contained a small bronze bowl and an escutcheon. (In the same area workmen opened a stone-lined cist in 1887 which contained a crouched burial. An iron hook found nearby in the fill of the mound was probably not related to this grave, which would be of pre-Iron Age date.)

Oxton A large barrow in the forest about a mile from Oxton (Nottinghamshire) was opened in 1789.[507] It stood 7½' high and was 159' in circumference. Finds included a shieldboss, sword, iron knife in a wooden sheath, some fragmentary iron objects, a section of bronze rim (from the shield?) and glass gaming counters. The shieldboss was said to contain 'ashes' but these may have been the decayed wood from the shield, or the organic liner used to help secure the user's hold on the shield-grip.

Pegsdon Common see **Shillington**

Pilsbury At Pilsbury (Derbyshire) Bateman opened a stone cairn in 1847; a smaller barrow on the cairn contained a skeleton and an iron knife.[508]

Pitsford At Pitsford (Northamptonshire) in 1882 an Anglo-Saxon barrow was discovered, containing fourteen cremation urns with some small inclusions.[509]

Pole's Wood In 1874-5 two barrows in Pole's Wood (Gloucestershire) were excavated.[510] The South Barrow, a long barrow, contained an adult female buried with two bronze buckles, an iron knife and a spindle-whorl, as well as the two original occupants. The East Barrow contained three Anglo-Saxon secondary inhumations, probably accompanied by a knife and spearhead.

Puddlehill At Puddlehill, near Dunstable (Bedfordshire) a human skeleton was discovered in 1955.[511] A spearhead had been broken before burial and a shieldboss was also present; the back of the man's skull had been smashed. A later burial had been inserted into the barrow, accompanied by a comb, and the remains of four more unaccompanied inhumations were close by.

---

[506] Meaney, 1964, p.75; O'Brien, 1999, ref.952

[507] Davies-Pryce, 1908; Meaney, 1964, p.201-2; O'Brien, 1999, ref.303

[508] Meaney, 1964, p.77

[509] Meaney, 1964, p.195; O'Brien, 1999, ref.461

[510] Meaney, 1964, p.93

[511] Meaney, 1964, p.39; O'Brien, 1999, ref.63

Readon Hill (Derbyshire) At Readon Hill, on 4th September 1848, Carrington opened a barrow which contained the remains of two males, one of whom may have been the original Bronze Age occupant.[512] The later burial was of a young man, and there were remains of an iron spearhead (13", 33cm long) and a narrow iron knife (8", 10cm long). The remainder of the shaft within the spearhead was examined by microscope and it was determined that it was made from ashwood, and the knife-blade had been mounted in a hilt of horn.

Repton At Repton (Derbyshire) a large mound in St. Wystan's church was found to contain the probable remains of a slaughtered Danish army.[513]

Saxby An Anglo-Saxon cemetery was discovered at Stapleford Park, Saxby (Leicestershire) in 1827.[514] The first indications were four cremation urns, unearthed during gravel digging. Further work in the area connected with the construction of the railway in 1890-1 revealed further burials, mainly cremations but some inhumations. The site was on a slight elevation and may once have comprised a series of mounds, levelled out by ploughing.

Shooters Hill see **Great Addington**

Shillington An Anglo-Saxon primary barrow was erected on Pegsdon Common, near Shillington (Bedfordshire).[515] It was opened in 1879 by Ransom and found to contain a single inhumation, a 6'4" male buried in a sitting posture, with a knife near his left hand. A shieldboss and spearhead from the grave were recovered. The leg bones of three other burials were also present in the mound.

Sleaford The village of Sleaford (Lincolnshire) was the site of a large Anglo-Saxon cemetery, mainly of inhumations but with a few cremations; excavations began in 1824.[516] The majority of the graves were arranged in neat rows, and the land surface was low-lying but undulating; there were significant blank areas among the graves which were probably due to the presence of barrows which have subsequently been ploughed out.

---

[512] Bateman, 1861 (1978), p.123-4; Meaney, 1964, p.221-2. The name is also spelt 'Wredon'.

[513] O'Brien, 1999, ref.1210

[514] Meaney, 1964, p.148-9; O'Brien, 1999, ref.348

[515] Meaney, 1964, p.39; O'Brien, 1999, ref.62

[516] Meaney, 1964, p.162-3; O'Brien, 1999, ref.145; *British Archaeology*, no.98, 2008

South Elkington A sizeable cremation cemetery was discovered during ploughing at South Elkington (Lincolnshire) in 1946, and subsequent excavation revealed an artificial mound of post-Roman date into which the urns had been inserted.[517] The majority of the ceramic was quite plain and poor in quality, and a 5th-6th c. date has been suggested for it.

Southworth Hall see **Winwick**

Stanshope (Derbyshire) On 31st August 1851, Carrington opened a barrow near Stanshope; the internal structure was constructed from stones and may have resembled the dry-stone walling at Asthall.[518] The excavator initially thought that the slabs represented a stone cist, but the central burial had been disturbed and all that remained were some fragments of human skull and other human bones; numerous rats' bones; fragments of some urns, one of "very hard black ware" and another of red pottery; two small pieces of bronze, warped by the heat of a fire; a small iron awl in wooden handle; a piece of a "thick cup or bason [sic] of green glass". The latter is possibly a description of a green-glass palm-cup, typical of 7th c. interments, although a date in the 17th c. has also been suggested.

Stapleford Park see **Saxby**

Stenigot Deep ploughing at Stenigot (Lincolnshire) in a field on a spur of land overlooking a valley produced several Anglo-Saxon objects, collected by the ploughman, but subsequent harrowing of the soil caused destructive disturbance of the site.[519] The remains of three adults – at least two of which were male – could be discerned, and the grave-goods included a bronze plate, an iron firestriker, an iron knife, three smaller iron blades, fragments of curved iron plate (a shieldboss?).

Stoke Golding A low barrow overlooking Watling Street at Stoke Golding (Leicestershire) was found to contain a hanging bowl and some flints; it was excavated in 1931.[520] The bowl was very similar to the one recovered from Asthall (Oxfordshire).

---

[517] Meaney, 1964, p.154

[518] Bateman, 1861 (1978), p.187-8; Meaney, 1964, p.222

[519] Meaney, 1964, p.164; O'Brien, 1999, ref.147

[520] Meaney, 1964, p.149; O'Brien, 1999, ref.470

Swarkeston The *Swarkeston Lowes* is the name of a group of four barrows near the River Trent in Derbyshire. Partial excavation 1955 due to plough and animal damage revealed the presence of an Anglo-Saxon cremation cemetery.[521]

Thenford A large pile of earth and rubble at Thenford (Northamptonshire) was dug before 1830 and found to contain human bones and ceramics.[522] Two skeletons lay at the upper part of the mound, and to the south side five more were discovered in three tiers, one with an iron knife-blade.

Thor's Cave see **Wetton**

Thurmaston The village of Thurmaston (Leicestershire) was the site of a cremation cemetery, discovered in 1954.[523] At least one of the urns was covered with a cairn to form a small mound.

Tickfield Park see **Newport Pagnell**

Tissington *Bowers Low*, Tissington (Derbyshire) was opened in 1863 by Mr. Lucas.[524] The barrow – also called *Rose Low* or *Boars Low* – stood at the crossroads of the road from Tissington and the major road from Buxton to Ashbourne; it was at that time 40' in diameter and 10' tall but apparently slighted and reduced from its original size. The barrow contained the remains of a shield with a sugarloaf boss; traces of cloth; an iron sword 34" in length, in a wooden sheath with silver fittings; an iron spearhead. The sugarloaf shield boss dates the grave to the later 7th c. A heap of burnt human bones was found at another spot in the mound. The burial appears to have been a primary inhumation. Also at Tissington, Bateman opened the *Sharp Low* mound in 1848; among the various human remains was an iron knife, suggesting Anglo-Saxon re-use of an existing monument.[525] About 1 mile away, another barrow revealed to Bateman disturbed remains of two humans, and some fragments which may have been a shield with iron fittings.[526]

---

[521] Meaney, 1964, p.78

[522] Meaney, 1964, p.196

[523] Meaney, 1964, p.149; O'Brien, 1999, ref.349

[524] Meaney, 1964, p.73; O'Brien, 1999, ref.959

[525] Meaney, 1964, p.78

[526] Meaney, 1964, p.77-9 This barrow may be the feature called *Cromwell's Low*.

Twyford A Leicestershire grave discovered in 1958 was named *Burrough Hill*.[527] Although the site has not been identified for certain, it is likely that it was part of the Twyford cemetery. *Burrough* here is presumably a variant of *beorh* 'barrow'.

Walton Some time before 1899 'bones and things' were discovered in a field near Walton (Staffordshire) although what these 'things' were is not recorded.[528] The estate to which the field belonged has the suggestive name *Borough Fields Farm*.

Welton-by-Lincoln A possible mound at Welton-by-Lincoln (Lincolnshire) excavated in the late 1960s formed part of an Anglo-Saxon gravefield with eleven inhumations.[529]

Wetton A small mound covering an inhumation with an iron knife and spearhead was destroyed in 1845, on land called *Borough Fields* at Wetton (Staffordshire).[530] Close by, on the supposed site of a British village, a further burial came to light: a female with glass beads and an annular brooch. Some small iron tools and pieces of antler were also in the grave, which was a cist. Some suggestive remains in the surrounding earth (a Roman coin, a boar's tusk, a possible angon head, etc.) were inconclusive as the soil had been cut away drastically. Also in Wetton, in 1850 Carrington opened a barrow at *Thor's Cave*; it contained some probable Bronze Age ceramics and a bronze vessel which might be Roman or Anglo-Saxon in date (i.e. a 'Coptic' bowl).

Willoughby-on-the-Wold A prominent tumulus called *Crosshill* in Top Field near Willoughby-on-the-Wold (Nottinghamshire) was excavated in 1947-8.[531] The tumulus was probably substantially Roman, but there were at least five secondary inhumations in the top. Only two of the burials had been carefully handled, and was of an adult male accompanied by pottery of late 4th c. date. Another was buried on a stone slab. It is possible that the 4th c. burial was of a Roman period inhabitant of the area, although a *foederatus* stationed locally might also be suggested. The burial on the stone slab might be from the same group, but could equally date from the Danish incursions. The mound had been used as the site of a gallows, and the careless nature of the remaining burials suggests graves of those hanged on the spot.

---

[527] Meaney, 1964, p.145

[528] Meaney, 1964, p.220

[529] O'Brien, 1999, ref.1238

[530] Meaney, 1964, p.223; O'Brien, 1999, ref.361

[531] Meaney, 1964, p.200

Winceby At Winceby (Lincolnshire) skeletons were found during road-widening in 1931 at a spot called *Round Hills Holt*, a name suggestive of round barrows but not otherwise known to have been the site of mound burials.[532] (An alternative name *Round Heads* is also recorded.) Accompanying grave-goods included two iron spearheads and wooden bowls, and some other items too decayed for identification. The battle of Winceby Field took place here in 1643 and it may be that the items should be connected with that event, but there is mention of iron bowls with the skeletons, which may indicate Anglo-Saxon shieldbosses.

Winster Moor *White Low* on Winster Moor (Derbyshire) was dug in ca. 1767 and was found to contain a bronze-bound casket containing a silver-gilt disc-mount with garnet and filigree decoration, and two light-green glass vessels, possibly pouch bottles. It is likely that this was the burial of an aristocratic Mercian lady of the 7th c.[533] A small gold cross decorated with filigree was found in a nearby field and is presumed to have come from the burial.

Winwick A large Anglo-Saxon cemetery was discovered at Southworth Hall, Winwick (Cheshire) in the late 1970s. There was evidence for barrows among the graves, which numbered around two hundred.[534]

Wold Newton In 1828 a cremation cemetery was discovered at Wold Newton (Lincolnshire) during road-mending.[535] The large barrow consisted of a mound of gravel on the local chalk geology, and on top of this had been placed a smaller mound in which the cremations were found.

Wyaston On 10th September 1851, Carrington and his men opened "the gravehill of a Saxon lady, at Wyaston" (Derbyshire).[536] The mound was 39' (11.75m) in diameter and 4' (1.25m) high in the centre. The body had decayed so that only the crowns of the teeth were still detectable. Among the grave-goods were a necklace of 27 beads, of amber and opaque glass; a length of silver wire twisted into a finger ring; silver ear-rings; a disc or annular brooch.

---

[532] Meaney, 1964, p.165

[533] Speake, 1989, p.124; Meaney, 1964, p.79; O'Brien, 1999, ref.329

[534] O'Brien, 1999, ref.1152

[535] Meaney, 1964, p.166

[536] Bateman, 1861 (1978), p.188-9; Meaney, 1964, p.80; O'Brien, 1999, ref.330

Northumbria (Northern England)

Barrows of certain Anglo-Saxon date are not plentiful in northern England, but this has to be seen in the context of a general low incidence of Anglo-Saxon material from all graves in this region. There are many place-names including the element 'low' or 'law' from OE *hlaw, hlæw* but none appears to have contained an Anglo-Saxon burial, as either a primary or secondary inhumation. Round barrows are less common here than long barrows and cairns, and there is therefore no presumption that a circular bump in the landscape might be artificial, as for example the seemingly artificial mound at Stockley Beck (County Durham) which does not appear to have been investigated.

Aldborough At Upper Dunsforth near Aldborough (Yorkshire), a mound called *Devil Cross* was opened in about 1785.[537] A collection of human bones and vessels was revealed; one was illustrated in the *History of Knaresborough* and is much like an Anglian cremation urn.

Barrasford At Barrasford (Northumberland) a cairn of stones on the escarpment above Barrasford Burn was opened some time before 1875, in the making of the railway cutting.[538] A shieldboss with six silver studs, a sword and a knife were recovered. Lower in the mound a (Bronze Age?) urn was found; an Anglo-Saxon secondary inhumation seems likely.

Beacon Hill see **Garrowby Wold**

Beggarbog Barrow see **Housesteads**

Capheaton A barrow stood south of the road near Capheaton (Northumberland) and was opened at some point before 1813.[539] It held a copper vessel containing two 'fibulae', a finger ring, some copper fragments and a quantity of human bones. The fibulae were later identified as escutcheons from the bowl.

Carthorpe During gravel extraction human bones were found at *Howe Hill*, Carthorpe (Yorkshire) in 1865.[540] Four burials were excavated – an adolescent female with beads; an elderly female with an iron knife and bronze tags; a crouched burial with an iron knife and bronze buckle;

---

[537] Meaney, 1964, p.287

[538] Meaney, 1964, p.198

[539] Meaney, 1964, p.198

[540] Mortimer, 1893; Garson, 1893; Meaney, 1964, p.283-4

the fourth, crouched, was unaccompanied. An iron knife was recovered from the gravel spoil. The mound was apparently a natural feature, but the burials have the attributes of Anglo-Saxon secondary inhumations.

Castle Eden An isolated grave was discovered at Castle Eden (County Durham) in 1775 by workmen uprooting a hedge near the stream which formed the boundary between the church and the castle.[541] The grave was covered by a cairn to form a mound. A blue glass clawbeaker was the most startling find.

Cheesecake Hill see **Driffield**

Copt Hill see **Houghton-le-Spring**

Cowlam *Kemp Howe* at Cowlam (Yorkshire) near Driffield was excavated by Mortimer in 1878.[542] Five burials had been placed in the top of the mound and a sixth in the ditch. Mortimer considered them to be Anglo-Saxon from the construction of the grave-cuts.

Crosby Garrett A mound burial was found in an Anglo-Saxon period cemetery at Crosby Garrett (Cumbria).[543]

Dinnington In 1862, Althorpe opened a mound of stones on his estate at Dinnington (Yorkshire).[544] There were twenty two skeletons beneath it, but no associated finds and it is not certain that they belong to the Anglo-Saxon period.

Driffield At Driffield (Yorkshire) a series of tumuli are known as *The Danes' Graves*, supposedly being the remains of a slaughtered invading Viking army.[545] In the 1820s, some of the barrows were opened and found to contain human remains but no record of any grave-goods is preserved. It is possible that these are Final Phase burials with few or no grave-goods, although the possibility that they were previously robbed cannot be discounted. In the same area is *Cheesecake Hill*, a large flat mound.[546] Workmen began removing soil in 1845 and found several human skeletons about 3' (1m) below the surface. The skeletons were carelessly buried, with some accompanying finds: beads, brooches,

---

[541] Meaney, 1964, p.83; O'Brien, 1999, ref.256

[542] Mortimer, 1880; Meaney, 1964, p.292

[543] O'Brien, 1999, ref.2272

[544] Meaney, 1964, p.285-6; O'Brien, 1999, ref.932

[545] Meaney, 1964, p.287

[546] Meaney, 1964, p.285

clasps, a shieldboss and fittings, a spearhead. Elsewhere in the mound were found an arrow- or angon-head, two knives, a pair of scissors, more brooches (cruciform and radiate-headed), clasps, tweezers, a bone disc. A cremation urn was also present, of Anglo-Saxon type. A full investigation was mounted in 1849 and it was determined that some of the burials had been disturbed previously. In 1871 Mortimer re-opened the mound and discovered the primary Bronze Age burial. About eight of the Anglo-Saxon graves were female, and only one male and the cremation were without grave-goods. Bones were also ploughed up at Driffield, from a mound on a farm called Kelleythorpe.[547] The barrow was investigated in 1851, having been reduced to 4' in height, and more human remains were revealed: some Bronze Age burials, but also an intrusive skeleton with an object of iron and bone in its hand. Some cremated remains were also present in the eastern portion. Remains of at least ten bodies were found buried in the mound, one with an Anglo-Saxon penannular brooch. Subsequent excavation by Mortimer in 1870-2 revealed twenty seven more Anglo-Saxon burials and one from the Bronze Age. The Anglo-Saxon graves all pointed towards the mound, and there were several grave-goods including spearheads, shieldbosses, buckles, brooches, shears, combs, a firesteel, and a flat bronze object. In 1887, two more graves were found near the mound by labourers; an extended investigation revealed a further eleven graves on the south side of the mound, accompanied by beads, an annular brooch, a silver buckle, a knife, a bronze hoop and fragments of another. Also in this area, a barrow had stood in King's Mill Road, Driffield, and its footprint was revealed when a recreation ground was laid out in 1893.[548] A small cemetery of twelve graves was discovered, as well as fragments of ceramic vessels. The barrow contained a cremation burial.

Duggleby Duggleby (Yorkshire) is the site of a barrow called *Howe Hill* or *Duggleby Howe*, a large isolated mound.[549] It was opened in about 1798 but no record exists of any finds. It was re-opened in 1890 by Mortimer, who found some stray finds: some nails, some corroded iron, part of a pair of shears, part of a bone pin, part of a bone comb. About 250 ceramic fragments were also recovered, some Anglo-Saxon. Animal bones were also present, with a horse buried in the top of the mound. Some human bones were still discernable in the upper layers –

---

[547] Meaney, 1964, p.286

[548] Meaney, 1964, p.286

[549] Meaney, 1964, p.291-2

part of a female jaw and some arm bones; more of the same skeleton and an iron knife were buried deeper, which suggests that the 1798 dig disturbed them. However, the top of the mound may have been levelled in Anglo-Saxon times to make it serve as the local Moot Hill.

Ferrybridge In 1811 the tenant began to open a barrow in *Roundhill Field*, Ferrybridge (Yorkshire) but the quantity of bones within proved too daunting and he gave up; one of the skeletons was said to be a warrior in armour.[550] Further investigation in1863 revealed three skeletons in an extended position.

Filey The barrow of *Spell Howe* on private land near Filey (Yorkshire) appears to have been used as a meeting place for local government in Anglo-Saxon times rather than as a burial mound. The name means 'speech mound'.

Fimber The church in Fimber (Yorkshire) was built on a mound which may have been a Bronze Age barrow, later re-used by the Anglo-Saxon inhabitants of the region.[551] Investigations in 1863 while digging foundations for a cottage revealed six or more human skeletons. Two more were discovered in 1870 near the church porch itself. Fragments of iron and ceramics found in association with the first group implied an Anglo-Saxon date, while a penannular brooch was found with the later pair.

Ganton Wold Greenwell found a secondary inhumation in a barrow at Ganton Wold (Yorkshire) before 1877.[552] The only surviving human remains were a single tooth, but the burial contained woollen fabric, three cruciform brooches, a belt-clasp, a necklace of amber and glass beads, a spindlewhorl, and two urns. The burial appears to be mid-6th c. from the grave-goods.

Garrowby Wold The *Beacon Hill* barrow at Garrowby Wold (Yorkshire) was opened in 1866 by Mortimer, when it was 44' (14m) across and 1' (30 cm) high.[553] A skull and part of the arm were found in the centre at only 6" (15cm) deep. An iron spearhead with split socket lay by the skull, and the blades of a pair of iron shears lay further down the grave. The burial had been disturbed in the construction of the beacon. It was a secondary inhumation in a Bronze Age mound.

---

[550] Meaney, 1964, p.288; O'Brien, 1999, ref.270

[551] Ellis Davidson, 1950; Meaney, 1964, p.288

[552] Meaney, 1964, p.288

[553] Meaney, 1964, p.288-9

Garton Slack A barrow of 70' diameter at Garton Slack (Yorkshire) was excavated by Mortimer in 1868. The surrounding ditch contained four secondary burials – two adults and two children, without any grave-goods, and one of them very fragmentary.[554] Another skeleton in the mound was accompanied by two iron objects, perhaps a knife and sharpening tool; they were carried at the waist. When the large cemetery 200 yards distant was discovered in 1872, the excavated area was extended to the barrow to determine whether there were any further burials. The skeleton of an adolescent was found, with some pig bones; whether this was Bronze Age or Anglo-Saxon in date could not be determined, although Mortimer considered the latter more likely.

Garton Station At Garton Station (Yorkshire) an Anglo-Saxon cemetery of about thirty-four inhumations was discovered.[555] Although the graves were generally not of high status, there was evidence for mound burial on the site.

Goathland At Goathland (Yorkshire) on Fylingdales Moor, a Bronze Age mound called *Lilla Howe* yielded some Anglo-Saxon material before 1871: four silver strap-ends, two with interlaced ornament; two roundels of gold filigree; some plain gold rings; a gold brooch with a plain white stone inset.[556] The barrow is associated in local tradition with the thane called Lilla who stopped an assassin's knife from killing King Edwin in 625 AD according to Bede. The *ASC* for AD 626 says:

Her com Eomer fram Cwichelme Westseaxna cininge; þohte þet he wolde ofstingan Eadwine cininge, ac he ofstang Lillan his ðegn 7 Forðhere 7 ðone cining gewundode. 7 þære ilcan nihte wes Eadwine dohter acenned, seo wæs gehaten Eanfled.

ASC, MS.E

Here (in this year) Eomer came from Cwichelm, King of the West Saxons; he thought that he would stab to death King Edwin, but he stabbed Lilla his thane, and Forþhere, and wounded the king; and that same night a daughter was born to Edwin, who was called Eanfled.

The description of the objects fits in with this date, which is roughly contemporary with Sutton Hoo Mound 1. The mound sports an

---

[554] Meaney, 1964, p.290

[555] O'Brien, 1999, ref.2187

[556] Meaney, 1964, p.293-4

ancient stone cross – allegedly the oldest Christian monument in northern England – which was moved here in 1962 to prevent destruction by artillery fire at its previous location on the moor.[557]

Great Tosson In 1858 a barrow at Great Tosson (Northumberland) was opened.[558] It revealed four cist burials from the Bronze Age. A bronze buckle and iron spearhead accompanied some separate inhumations, presumably of Anglo-Saxon date.

Hawnby Close to Hawnby (Yorkshire) was the site of several mounds.[559] A large one, 120' (30m) in circumference and 4' (1.3m) high was opened before 1865. It contained the skeleton of a young female wearing a decorated leather belt, decorated with garnets and closed with gold rivets. She also had two hairpins (one silver and one gold), four silver annular brooches, a bronze annular brooch, glass beads and a stone spindle whorl. A bronze hanging bowl with three escutcheons was by the head; it had a wooden cover decorated with bronze strip. Some iron fragments included part of a knife. There were only two other tumuli with burials in the group, neither of them Anglo-Saxon.

Houghton-le-Spring *Copt Hill* at Houghton-le-Spring (Durham) is a prominently-sited barrow of Neolithic date which also yielded Bronze Age material and an unfurnished inhumation which would be consistent with an Anglo-Saxon date.[560] (see fig.4)

Housesteads *Beggarbog Barrow*, near Housesteads (Northumberland) was excavated in the 1830s, but whatever was found there was not reported and the location of the finds is unknown. At 28m diameter and about 10' (3m) height it would be at the larger end of the scale for known Anglo-Saxon mounds.

Howick Heugh In 1928 an inhumation cemetery was discovered at Howick Heugh (Northumberland).[561] The site was on a steep hillside and the graves were close to the surface. Some showed signs of having been covered by cairns (piles of stones) to make burial mounds. Grave-goods included iron knives, a spearhead and some beads. There were some unassociated finds on the site, including a horse-bit.

---

[557] Points, 2007, p.148-51

[558] Meaney, 1964, p.199

[559] Meaney, 1964, p.290-1; O'Brien, 1999, ref.278

[560] Meaney, 1964, p.83

[561] Meaney, 1964, p.199; O'Brien, 1999, ref.252

Hull Melton Hill was the site of a grave from which a bead and a brooch of Anglo-Saxon date were recovered before 1907.[562] *Melton Hill Barrow* is a tumulus at South Cave, near Kingston-upon-Hull (Yorkshire). It is understood to be of Anglo-Saxon date. Curiously, a nearby outcrop called *Saint Austin's Stone* is alleged to be the site from which St. Augustine preached Christianity to the local Deirans in the 7th c. before baptising them in a nearby pool.

Kingthorpe see **Pickering**

Kirby Moorside A tumulus stood at *Howe End*, Kirby Moorside (Yorkshire) but was destroyed when an inn was built on the site before 1949.[563] Twelve skeletons were allegedly recovered, as well as three urns. There is no reliable dating evidence, but the possibility cannot be excluded that these were Anglo-Saxon secondary inhumations.

Kirkburn A mound at Kirkburn (Yorkshire) was investigated by Mortimer in 1870.[564] A large cruciform brooch brooch was found on the surface, probably the only remnant of a ploughed-out Anglo-Saxon secondary inhumation.

Langton A scatter of broken Anglo-Saxon pottery was found on an earthen bank at Langton race course (Yorkshire) in 1877.[565] Probably ploughing and other earthworks had disturbed a shallow cremation cemetery in an existing long barrow.

Lissett At Lissett (Yorkshire) a number of skeletons were recovered from an elliptical mound with post-holes and pits.[566] The graves may be Anglo-Saxon in date but there were no supporting finds.

Loftus The mound called *Stang Howe* near Loftus (Yorkshire) is connected in local tradition with a form of public humiliation of wrongdoers, in which the miscreant was ridiculed in verse by a crowd at his door on three successive nights and a straw effigy of him was burnt on the last night; this continued into the early 20th c. The *howe* or mound is not known to be Anglo-Saxon in date, but its connection with the dispensing of justice must point to its importance in Anglo-Saxon times. The *stang* was a pole to which the straw man was tied while it

---

[562] Meaney, 1964, p.295

[563] Meaney, 1964, p.292

[564] Meaney, 1964, p.292-3

[565] Meaney, 1964, p.293

[566] Meaney, 1964, p.294

was being burnt. This tradition seems to have a Scandinavian predecent: such a device was erected by the Icelander Egil Skallagrimsson against King Eiríkr Blóðöx in the 930s before leaving Norway.

Hann tók í hönd sér heslistöng ok gekk á bergsnös nökkura, þá er vissi til lands inn; þá tók hann hrosshöfuð ok setti upp á stöngina. Síðan veitti hann formála ok mælti svá: "Hér set ek upp níðstöng, ok sný ek þessu níði á hönd Eiríki konungi ok Gunnhildi dróttningu," - hann sneri hrosshöfðinu inn á land - "sný ek þessu níði á landvættir þær, er land þetta byggva, svá at allar fari þær villar vega, engi hendi né hitti sitt inni, fyrr en þær reka Eirík konung ok Gunnhildi úr landi." Síðan skýtr hann stönginni niðr í bjargrifu ok lét þar standa; hann sneri ok höfðinu inn á land, en hann reist rúnar á stönginni, ok segja þær formála þenna allan.

Egilssaga Skallagrimsonar, ch.57

He took a hazel-pole in his hand and went to a certain cliff which faced in towards the land; then he took a horse-head and set it up on the pole. After he uttered a curse and spoke thus: "Here I set up a scorn-pole and I direct this scorn towards King Eirik and Queen Gunnhild" - he turned the horse-head towards the land – "here I direct this scorn towards the land-spirits there, who dwell in that land, so that they may leave their dwellings and become lost, and may not find their homes, neither by chance nor through searching, until they have expelled King Eirík and Queen Gunnhild from the land." Then he fixed the pole in a crack of the rock and it left it standing there; he then turned the head of the horse towards the mainland, and he scratched runes on the pole and spoke all that curse there.

This *niðstöng* or scorn-pole was a powerful magical device which resulted in the exile of both the king and his queen; Eirík later became King of York and had further dealings with the truculent Icelander.

Norton-on-Tees A large Anglo-Saxon cemetery at Mill Lane, Norton-on-Tees (County Durham) excavated in the 1950s contained 117 burials and about six cremations.[567] There was evidence for mounds erected over some of the graves.

---

[567] O'Brien, 1999, ref.2040

Painsthorpe Wold A chalk pit at Pudsey Plantation, Painsthorpe Wold (Yorkshire) was extended in 1862.[568] The extraction revealed a burial mound, exposing two skeletons. In 1870 the centre of the mound was investigated and a disturbed burial was revealed with some fragments of Anglo-Saxon pottery. The following year, further chalk extraction uncovered another burial, missing its skull; this may have been due to the action of rabbiters or to the planting of trees. Full excavation of the remainder took place in 1876. A large skeleton was found in the upper layers, and a complete female skeleton in a crouched position, with a small bronze annular brooch, a necklace of beads, a pyxide containing needle and thread, a small knife, two bronze rings, some long pieces of bronze and iron from a chatelaine. The remains of a textile bag with a bronze fastener decorated with interlace, described by Mortimer, may actually have been the chatelaine and vestiges of the woman's dress. In 1877 Mortimer opened another barrow in the area; unfortunately, three bovines had been buried in it after the cattle plague of 1866-7, and this activity had destroyed the evidence for the barrow's previous occupants. The only remains were a bronze dish and the ferrule from an Anglo-Saxon spear.

Pickering A barrow at Pickering (Yorkshire) was dug by Bateman in 1850.[569] It contained a human skeleton accompanied by an iron knife, a canine tooth or tusk and an article of baked clay. James Ruddock was one of Bateman's colleagues. He was active in the Pickering area of Yorkshire, although he seems to have had little luck in detecting Anglo-Saxon period burials. On 20th September 1852 he opened a barrow at Kingthorpe.[570] Although the tumulus was originally of Bronze Age date, a secondary inhumation had been placed centrally within it over the primary. The burial was disturbed but still recognisable were some human bones; a bronze cruciform brooch; a boar's tusk; the edge of a dark pottery vessel. The pottery may have been black burnished ware, and the presence of an amuletic boar's tusk is known from other Anglo-Saxon sites. The grave-goods all suggest a high-status female.

Pudsey Plantation see **Painsthorpe Wold**

Pudding Pie Hill see **Sowerby**

---

[568] Meaney, 1964, p.296
[569] Meaney, 1964, p.296
[570] Bateman, 1861 (1978), p.235; Meaney, 1964, p.292

Roseberry Topping The hilltop site of *Roseberry Topping* (Yorkshire) is known to have been the location of a *hearh* or holy place which was sacred to the god Woden. A nearby settlement called Freeborough may commemorate the high-place of Frea, another member of the Anglo-Saxon pantheon. There have been numerous finds on the prominent hill, but nothing of Anglo-Saxon date has been reported.

Rudstone A Bronze Age mound at Rudstone (Yorkshire) dug before 1877 showed evidence for Anglo-Saxon re-use.[571] Three male skeletons lay parallel across the centre of the mound, and a fourth in a crouched position lay close by. A fifth near the feet of the row of three had been almost destroyed by ploughing. All were considered to be Anglo-Saxon secondary burials due to the attitudes of the bodies. A partner barrow nearby was investigated: it contained a quantity of broken Anglo-Saxon pottery at all levels down to the original ground surface.

Saltburn An unexpected find by a metal-detectorist in 2005 set off a full excavation programme at a site called Street House Farm, Saltburn, near Loftus (Yorkshire).[572] The cemetery was focused on a large barrow containing a bed-burial, only the eleventh known in England and the furthest north so far excavated.[573] The 109 graves contained no human bone or other organic material due to the adverse soil conditions. The interred female had with her a collection of fine garnet cloisonné jewellery including a curious pendant of which the central panel held a piece of ribbed purple translucent stone, delicately cut to resemble a scallop. The majority of the graves were focussed on the barrow, and were laid out in a very regular, rectangular array, which suggests that the cemetery was not in use for long. Few weapons, other than a splendid seax, were found in the cemetery. There was also a round structure on the site and a sunken-featured building which, it has been suggested, may have been a mortuary house. Due to the exceptional richness of the grave-goods, the lady has been identified as a probable cult-leader and three possible identifications have been proposed: the favourite is Æðelburh, the Kentish wife of King Edwin who first brought Roman Christianity to the north, based on the Frankish nature of the cloisonné items. Æðelburh came north with an entourage including Bishop Paulinus; it was he who baptised the new

---

[571] Meaney, 1964, p.296-7

[572] Sources include Sherlock & Simmons, 2008; Redcar Museum website (www.redcar-cleveland.gov.uk/museums.nsf/) and the *Yorkshire Post.*

[573] However, Mound 4 at Sutton Hoo has been suggested as a twelfth example.

Christian converts at the king's palace after the incident with Coifi the heathen priest reported by Bede. Alternatively Oswiu's wife, Eanflæd, or his daughter, Ælfflæd, may be the occupants.

Seaham At Seaham (Northumberland) a barrow was opened in the 1860s near St. Mary's church, which was interpreted at the time as being that of a Briton, but which contained Roman Samian ware in the fill, and a fragment of quernstone. The witness was one Angus Bethune, whose records were quoted by John Robinson in *Antiquities of Sunderland* (Vol.5) in 1904. While it is possible that the mound covered a Romano-British grave, that would be very unusual and it would be more likely that the burial was of an Anglo-Saxon, perhaps already opened and robbed of any metalwork before the Victorian dig began. Other chance finds of skeletons in the town of Seaham have been made, some of which date to the 7th c. The barrow report implies more than one body (or grave), which suggests that this might be a mound burial with adjacent graves, but that must be no more than speculation.

Sewerby In 1958 a major cemetery was excavated by Rahtz at Sewerby (Yorkshire).[574] One adult female grave was marked by a cairn of chalk blocks to form a mound. The grave-goods included a bronze vessel; over two hundred glass and amber beads in two necklaces; a great square-headed brooch; two smaller square-headed brooches; a pair of wrist-clasps; two girdle-hangers; an iron ring; an iron knife; a pair of triangular pendants; a wooden thread-box; there was a second skeleton above the main burial.

South Cave see **Hull**

Sowerby *Pudding Pie Hill* at Sowerby (Yorkshire) was popularly believed to be a fairy mound or 'hollow hill', while local historical opinion considered it the motte for a watchtower.[575] A dig was organised in 1855 to discover the truth of the matter, and in the centre of the mound was found the skeleton of a large male with his shield on his chest, of which only the boss and rivets remained. As Edmund Hogg noted in his work *The Golden Vale of Mobray*: "The mound has probably been the burial place of a small band of the first Anglian settlers in this district, say about early in the 6th century." Indeed the burial has the characteristics of an early Anglo-Saxon primary inhumation.

Sunny Bank see **Hawnby**

---

[574] Meaney, 1964, p.300-1; O'Brien, 1999, ref.657

[575] Meaney, 1964, p.296

Uncleby In 1868 Greenwell excavated an inhumation cemetery at Uncleby (Yorkshire).[576] The Anglo-Saxon cemetery was centred on and partly covered a Bronze Age tumulus, and the re-distribution of earth increased the barrow's circumference to 94' (28m). The cemetery had been laid out in rows for the most part, the bodies about 3' (1m) apart. Seventy-one graves were discovered, some with animal bones included, and in three graves there were heaps of bones from previous burials. All the graves contained quantities of charcoal, and one also held burnt earth. A curious feature of the cemetery is the presence of a small carved whetstone, placed upright in the earth but not associated with any graves. The cemetery was not rich in finds: seven knives, some annular brooches, pendants, beads, buckles; a sword and a seax were the only weapons.

Upper Dunsforth see **Aldborough**

Wharram Percy Mortimer opened a mound at Wharram Percy (Yorkshire) in 1868, although it had already suffered from a trench having been cut through it.[577] A male skeleton lay in the upper levels, 12" (30cm) below the surface, damaged by a posthole cut into the soil which had removed some of the chest and lower-back. The legs and hips of another skeleton lay nearby. They appeared to be secondary Anglo-Saxon inhumations.

Whitby *Knipe Howe* near Whitby was dug in 1856.[578] Only a single glass bead was found, perhaps the last remnant of a robbed Anglo-Saxon burial.

Wigan In 1770 a barrow was excavated at *Hasty Knoll*, Wigan (Lancashire).[579] It was found to contain various iron weapons. Although described as 'British' at the time, the likelihood is that it was either Anglo-Saxon or, perhaps more probably, Hiberno-Norse in origin.

Wilders Moor The *Two Lads* stone setting on Wilders Moor (Yorkshire) was held in local tradition to be the burial of two sons of a Saxon king, but the monument is a 'cairn'. A quantity of pale green broken glass from the vicinity might point to a Roman burial, although the possibility cannot be excluded that these were fragments of a claw- or cone-beaker of 7th c. type.

---

[576] Ellis Davidson, 1950; Meaney, 1964, p.302-3; Harrison, 1997

[577] Meaney, 1964, p.303

[578] Meaney, 1964, p.293

[579] Meaney, 1964, p.143; O'Brien, 1999, ref.802

York A mound called *Lamel Hill* outside York (Yorkshire) was planted with
trees in about 1824 and some human bones were found in the
upcast.[580] Thurman excavated it in 1847-8 and discovered some human
and animal remains, greatly disturbed. A Roman pot was in the centre
of the mound, with a male skeleton nearby, with many iron nails in the
grave. There were also three concentrations of burnt human bones. An
Anglo-Saxon secondary burial is perhaps most likely.

---

[580] Meaney, 1964, p.293

Lost Barrows

One must lament too the destruction of the ancient earth-works, especially of the barrows, which is going on all over the downs, most rapidly where the land is broken up by the plough. One wonders if the ever-increasing curiosity of our day with regard to the history of the human race in the land continues to grow, what our descendants of the next half of the century, to go no further, will say of us and our incredible carelessness in the matter! So small a matter to us, but one which will, perhaps, be immensely important to them!

W.H. Hudson, *A Shepherd's Life* (1910)

Hudson's words, published before the First World War, were a timely warning but one which was not widely heeded. The efficiency of modern agriculture and the need to feed the population of these islands came before matters of heritage and history for the greater part of the 20th c. More recently, pressure on the land has come not just from the need to produce food cheaply and in quantity, but also from housing developers and the construction industry as the modern population swells.

There are several known examples of barrows which were opened in the Victorian period without any substantial or detailed record having been made of the location (see the discussion of Roundway Down above). Some were discovered as part of the extension of the canals and construction of the railways, and in many cases the navigators who were involved in the laying of the track are believed to have appropriated any interesting finds for sale to collectors of antiquities.

A find of a garnet-and-gold sword pyramid at Forest Gate (Essex) of exceptional quality might be indicative of a forgotten barrow in this district, but such items occur frequently as casual losses and there are no other known high-status finds from this area to support this.[581] At Goldhanger (Essex) at some point before 1903, relics of "Saxon or Danish" provenance are said to have been taken from a series of mounds on the marshes.[582] A pair of tumuli at North Foreland, near Broadstairs (Kent) were said in local folklore to commemorate the dead from a violent clash between Saxons and Danes. No

---

[581] Jones, 1980, p.91

[582] Meaney, 1964, p.87; Jones, 1980, p.90; O'Brien, 1999, ref.1034

sign of the barrows remains today, and they may have been destroyed in the construction of a lighthouse in the mid-17th c.

Examples of 'looted' items are not hard to find, with many antiquities having been found in the course of agricultural activity. The lack of any provenance before they are first recorded in the hands of a dealer lends weight to the suspicion that they were taken from a grave, either as a chance find by a labourer, the spoil of a freelance barrow-opener or the legal property of a landowner taking the opportunity to extract gain from the contents of graves on his land.

Appendix 1.
Freyr's Burial Mound

From *Ynglingasaga* ch.12-3. Text from Garmonsway, 1928.

Freyr tók þá ríki eptir Njörð; var hann kallaðr dróttinn yfir Svíum ok tók skattgjafir af þeim; hann var vinsæll ok ársæll sem faðir hans. Freyr reisti at Uppsölum hof mikit, ok setti þar höfuðstað sinn; lagði þar til allar skyldir sínar, lönd ok lausa aura; þá hófst Uppsala auðr, ok hefir haldizt æ síðan. Á hans dögum hófst Fróða friðr, þá var ok ár um öll lönd; kendu Svíar þat Frey. Var hann því meir dýrkaðr en önnur goðin, sem á hans dögum varð landsfólkit auðgara en fyrr af friðinum ok ári. Gerðr Gýmis dóttir hét kona hans; sonr þeirra hét Fjölnir. Freyr hét Yngvi öðru nafni; Yngva nafn var lengi síðan haft í hans ætt fyrir tignarnafn, ok Ynglingar váru síðan kallaðir hans ættmenn. Freyr tók sótt; en er at honum leið sóttin, leituðu menn sér ráðs, ok létu fá menn til hans koma, en bjoggu haug mikinn, ok létu dyrr á ok 3 glugga. En er Freyr var dauðr, báru þeir hann leyniliga í hauginn, ok sögðu Svíum at hann lifði, ok varðveittu hann þar 3 vetr. En skatt öllum heltu þeir í hauginn, í einn glugg gullinu, en í annan silfrinu, í hinn þriðja eirpenningum. Þá hélzt ár ok friðr. ....Þá er allir Svíar vissu at Freyr var dauðr, en hélzt ár ok friðr, þá trúðu þeir at svá mundi vera meðan Freyr væri á Svþjóð, ok vildu eigi brenna hann, ok kölluðu hann veraldargoð, blótuðu mest til árs ok friðar alla ævi síðan.

Then Freyr took the kingdom after Njörð, he was called lord over the Swedes and took the tax-renders from them. He was blessed with friendships and blessed with harvests as his father had been. At Uppsala Freyr raised a great temple, and there he set his main dwelling. He endowed it with all his dues, lands and chattels. Then Uppsala's great wealth began, and it has kept it ever since. In his days began the 'peace of Fróði' and then were also good harvests in all the land; the Swedes attributed it to Freyr. He was worshipped more than the other gods because of this, to the extent that the land's people became in his days wealthy with peace and good harvest. Gerðr, the daughter of Gýmir, was his wife; their son was called Fjölnir. Freyr was known by another name, Yngvi; Yngvi's name was long after borne in his family as a title of honour, and the Ynglings were afterwards called his descendants. Freyr took a sickness, but when the illness came upon him, men took counsel together, and they had a few men come to him, and they built a great mound and they put in a door and three windows. And when Freyr was dead, they carried him into the mound in secret, and said to the Swedes that he still lived, and they kept him there for three years. And all the payments they placed into the mound there: gold through one window, and silver through another and through the third copper coins. The good harvest and peace continued then....When the Swedes all realised that Freyr was dead but the harvests and peace continued, then they believed that it should be so while Freyr was in Sweden and they did not want to burn him, and they called him the World-God, they sacrificed mostly for harvest and peace ever since.

Appendix 2.
Sigurð Hring's Mound

The funeral of Sigurð Hring forms part of *Skjoldungasaga* (the saga of the Danish dynasty known in English as the *Scyldingas*, descendats of "Shield"). The Scandinavian original is lost, but a Latin summary of it was made and is reproduced here (based on the text in Weston Wyly, 1997):

Qvi Alfsolae funere allato magnam navim motuorum cadveribus oneratam solus vivorum conscendit, seqve et mortuam Alfsolam in puppi collocans navim pice, bitumen et sulphure incendi jubet; atqve sublatis veils in altum, validis a continente impellentibus ventis, proram dirigit, simulaqve manus sibi violentas intulit ... bustum tamen in littore more sui sæculi congeri fecit, qvod Ringshaug apellari jussit; ipse veru tempestatibus ratem gubernantibus Stygias sine mora tranavit undas.

Having heard of Alfsola's death, he had a large ship laden with dead men and boarded it himself, the only living one. Placing himself and the dead Alfsola abaft, he had the ship fired with pitch, bitumen and sulphur, and with the raised sails pushed by the offshore winds he steered the prow while he harmed himself with his own hand ... according to the custom of the time he had a mound raised on the seashore, which he commanded to be named 'Ringshaug'; indeed he sailed the ship over the sea in raging storms to the Styx without delay.

Appendix 3.
Beowulf's Mound

Him ða gegiredan Geata leode
ad on eorðan unwaclicne,
helmum behongen, hildebordum,
beorhtum byrnum, swa he bena wæs;
alegdon ða tomiddes mærne þeoden
hæleð hiofende, hlaford leofne.
Ongunnon þa on beorge bælfyra mæst
wigend weccan; wudurec astah,
sweart ofer swioðole, swogende leg
wope bewunden (windblond gelæg),
oðþæt he ða banhus gebrocen hæfde,
hat on hreðre. Higum unrote
modceare mændon, mondryhtnes cwealm;
swylce giomorgyd Geatisc meowle
..... bundenheorde
song sorgcearig swiðe geneahhe
þæt hio hyre heofungdagas hearde ondrede,
wælfylla worn, werudes egesan,
hynðo ond hæftnyd. Heofon rece swealg.
Geworhton ða Wedra leode
hleo on hoe, se wæs heah ond brad,
wægliðendum wide gesyne,
ond betimbredon on tyn dagum
beadurofes becn, bronda lafe
wealle beworhton, swa hyt weorðlicost
foresnotre men findan mihton.
Hi on beorg dydon beg ond siglu,
eall swylce hyrsta, swylce on horde ær
niðhedige men genumen hæfdon,
forleton eorla gestreon eorðan healdan,
gold on greote, þær hit nu gen lifað
eldum swa unnyt swa hit æror wæs.
þa ymbe hlæw riodan hildediore,
æþelinga bearn, ealra twelfe,

woldon ceare cwiðan ond kyning mænan,
wordgyd wrecan ond ymb wer sprecan;
eahtodan eorlscipe ond his ellenweorc
duguðum demdon, swa hit gedefe bið
þæt mon his winedryhten wordum herge,
ferhðum freoge, þonne he forð scile
of lichaman læded weorðan.
Swa begnornodon Geata leode
hlafordes hryre, heorðgeneatas,
cwædon þæt he wære wyruldcyninga
manna mildust ond monðwærust,
leodum liðost ond lofgeornost.

Beowulf, l. 3136 - 3183

Then the nobles of the Geats made for him
mightily a balefire on earth
hung about with helms and battle-shields,
bright mailshirts as he had asked.
They laid in the middle then the famed leader,
the lamenting heroes their dear lord.
Then on the barrow the greatest of balefires
the warriors began to kindle; the wood-smoke rose up
black over the blaze, the roaring fire
surrounded by weeping – the wind subsided -
until it had broken the bone-house,
hot in its heart. With sad hearts
they mourned with grief the killing of the lord of men;
a sad song thus a Geatish girl
...... with bound-up hair
sang sorrowfully, frequently stated
that she greatly dreaded the armed attacks,
a deal of slaughter, the warband's terror,
humiliation and captivity. Heaven swallowed the smoke.
Then the Weders' nobles made
a barrow on a spur of land, it was high and broad,
widely seen by seafarers
and they built in ten days

the battle-bold man's beacon for the remains of the flames,
they made a wall about it as most worthily
the wisest men could devise it.
Into the barrow they put ring and circlet
all such adornments as from the hoard previously
cruel-minded men had taken out,
they left the wealth of the heroes for earth to keep
- gold in the soil where it still lies now
as useless to men as it was before.
Then around the mound rode the warriors,
sons of noblemen, twelve in all,
they wished to speak their sorrow and mourn their king
make a lament and speak of the man;
they praised his heroism and his brave deeds,
they deemed him doughtily as it shall be fitting
that a man may praise his friendly lord in words
love him in his heart when forth he must
be led from his body.
Thus the Geats' nobles grieved for
their leader's fall – his hearth-mates
said that he had been, among kings in the world,
the mildest of men and the kindest to folk,
gentlest to his people and keenest for a good name.

Appendix 4.
The Franks Casket Panel

The text on this side of the casket is unfortunately the most problematic of all.[583] For reasons unknown, the carver decided to divert from normal practice when laying out this design, including running the runes along the bottom panel upside down relative to the rest of the text. More curiously, he decided to substitute the normal runestaves for vowels with arbitrary characters. The result is a text which is only imperfectly understood. As if to confound the reader even more, the short texts within the picture use the normal vowel runes:

bita 'biter, wild animal' near the horse's head
risci 'rushes, thicket' over the horse's back
wudu 'woodland' beneath the horse's feet

As if to further complicate the text, the normal **e**-rune appears in the word *særden* and probably in the ligature **fa** in the word *sefa*. Below is a transcription of the surrounding text, using numbers to correspond to the vowel runes, and then a version with suggested vowel values inserted:

---

[583] Elliott, 1959; Becker, 1973

h1rh2ss3t4þ2nh4rmb1rg45gl…
dr3g3þsw4
h3r31rt51g3sgr5fs4rdens2rg45
nds1fat2rn4

This has been turned into standardised OE to give a short alliterative verse:

> Her hos sitæþ on hærmberge
> agl(ac) drigiþ swa hir i erta e gisgraf
> særden sorgæ and sefa tornæ

> Here a horse sits on the woe-barrow
> undergoes hardship as Erta shaped terror for her
> a grave of sorrow, mind's turmoil.

One of the many problems with this reading is that the word *hors* 'horse' is curiously misspelt, and the horse is shown standing next to the mound not sitting on it as the text implies. Amendments such as *herhos* 'god of the harrow' have been proposed to overcome this difficulty.[584] The text still defies a lucid explanation without recourse to runic cryptography, but the very fact that the runes on this panel were partly encrypted argues in favour of such an explanation.

---

[584] Becker, 1973

Appendix 5.
Some Barrow Place-Names

The list below is a summary of entries containing the word *hlaw* and *beorg* drawn from the English Place-Name Society's records and elsewhere. The descriptions include a presumed OE form which would give rise to the modern name. There is sometimes confusion in the early spellings between *hlaw* 'barrow' and *leah* 'woodland clearing', *beorg* 'mound' and *burh* 'stronghold'. Names in italics are pre-modern.

There are 94 *hlaw* names in the listing, most with a prefix. Vegetation is a common theme, with ten occurrences presumably denoting the type of tree or plant commonly found on the barrow (birch, briar, cress, dock, etc.); soil type (bare and soft) also appears. Bassetlaw may belong with this group, if it really denotes land cleared of woodland by burning. Animal associations are fairly common, with seven probable and one possible (*bucc* in Bucklow) occurrences. Animals may have been included in the name for their economic importance as food, in which case Butterlaw and Slingley should also appear here.

Construction details and location account for fourteen more names. Seven barrows have specifically military associations, either as part of a system of watching-points (Wardlow) or as army-mounds (Harlow). There are at least three examples of the simplex *hlaw* (Lew) and five of a simple derivative e.g. *hlawtun* (Lawton). Four barrows have supernatural connotations: Woden, Þunor, a dragon and a troll (Wenslow, Thunderlow, Drakelow & Buglawton).

It is interesting to note that less than half of the barrows appear to be named for the occupant: 34 probable cases and two more possible ones (*Hund* in Hounslow and *Winter* in Winterslow). Many of the names are simply the best attempt at explanation for the name that can be arrived at with our present knowledge: *Eatta* (Atlow), *Bassa* (Baslow) and many others are names which are not otherwise recorded or which only occur rarely. At the other end of the scale, there are a few names which look very intriguing. Challow is derived from *Ceawa*, a hypocoristic form, and there is at least one member of the West Saxon dynasty whose name would fit: *Ceawlin*, son of *Cerdic*. Cuttesloe appears to derive from *Cuðen* or *Cuðwine*, another typical West Saxon royal name. Huxloe, derived from *Hoc*, commemorates a figure from the *Hengest* cycle of legends. Kearsley, from *Cenhere* or *Cynehere*, relates to names in the Mercian royal family. Kenners Barrow is from a similar royal-sounding name, *Cyneheard*; a man of this name features as a pretender to the

West Saxon throne in the ASC s.a. 755. If Orsloe is really *Horsan hlaw*, then the history of the Kentish dynasty may have to be re-evaluated; *Horsa* is also bound up in the *Hengest* legends. Likewise Pentlow appears connected to the Mercian royal dynasty of *Penda* rather than to any local tradition. Queen Low from *Cyne* would seem to point to someone of importance. Wolferlow from *Wulfhere* also commemorates a Mercian royal name. It does not follow that the name associated with the barrow is that of the occupant – if such places were regularly used as meeting points, then it is likely that a name such as 'Wulfhere's barrow' would commemorate some notable visit by the king of that name to the spot.

The list includes three *beorg* names, although these are easily confused with *berg* 'mountain, hill' and *burh* 'stronghold'. Among the *beorg* 'barrow' names, personal names are common. The *Ælfred* commemorated at *Albretesberge* may even be the West Saxon king of this name.

Names containing the word 'barrow' are often base on OE *bearu* 'copse, grove' rather than *beorg* itself. There are seven entries, mostly from Dorset.

Modern name	County	Background
Albretesberge	Dorset	*Ælfredes beorg* 'Alfred's barrow' location unknown, a hundred gathered at this site
Alcomlow	Cheshire	*Ealhmundes hlaw* 'Ealhmund's barrow'
Ardsley	Yorkshire WR	*Eanredes hlaw* 'Eanred's barrow'
Atlow	Derbyshire	*Eattan hlaw*, Eatta's barrow. There is no known barrow in the area but the name may refer to a natural hillock.
Barrow	Rutland	*Beorg* 'barrow', a mound at The Green.
Barrow Hill	Dorset	*Beorg hyll* 'barrow hill'
Barrow Law	Northumberland	*Brer hlaw* 'briar-barrow', a barrow overgrown with briars.
Barrowden	Rutland	*Beorg dun* 'barrow hill'
Bartlow	Cambridgeshire	*Beorc hlaw* 'birch barrow'. The Bartlow Hills were a famous group of Roman mounds (p.129).
Baslow	Derbyshire	*Bassan hlaw* 'Bassa's barrow'. There is no known barrow in the area but the name may refer to a natural hillock.

Bassetlaw	Nottinghamshire	*Bærnetsæte hlaw* 'barrow of the settlers of the land cleared by burning'? Formerly the site of the hundred (wapentake) meeting place, so perhaps not a barrow at all but a moothill.
Biccan hlew	Wiltshire	*Biccan hlæw* 'bitch's barrow'; a Bronze Age barrow in the Anglo-Saxon boundary of Coome Bisset, revealed as a parchmark[585]
Bird's Barrow	Wiltshire	*Byrd beorg* 'burden (?) barrow'; a bowl barrow in the Anglo-Saxon boundary of Coome Bisset[586]
Blacklow	Gloucestershire	*Blæccan hlaw*, 'Blæcca's barrow'. The site of the hundred meeting, but where the barrow stood is not known.
Bledlow	Buckinghamshire	*Bleddan hlaw*, 'Bledda's barrow' (p.204)
Blidesloe	Gloucestershire	*Bliðes hlaw*, Blithe's barrow' Once a hundred meeting point, the name now rests with a farm, but no barrow is known.
Botloe Green	Gloucestershire	*Botan hlaw*, 'Bota's barrow'. Once the hundred moothill.
Brenkley	Northumberland	*Brincan hlaw*, 'Brinca's barrow' or possibly 'barrow on the edge'.
Brightwells Barrow	Gloucestershire	*Berhtwaldes beorg* 'Beorhtwald's barrow', site of the hundred moothill.
Brinklow	Warwickshire	*Brincan hlaw*, 'Brinca's barrow' as with Brenkley, once the hundred moothill.
Bucklow	Bedfordshire	*Buccan hlaw*, 'Bucca's barrow' or 'barrow of the buck'. Once the site of the moothill for the half-hundred.
Buglawton	Cheshire	*Buggan hlawtun*, 'estate of the troll-barrow'. *Bugge* 'troll, goblin' is Middle English; the name is distinct from Church Lawton.
Bul Barrow	Dorset	*Bulan beorg* 'Bula's barrow'?
Butterlaw	Northumberland	*Butere hlaw*, 'butter barrow'? perhaps a reference to dairy produce on the estate.

---

[585] Acornley, 1999, p.56
[586] Acornley, 1999, p.56

Callow	Derbyshire	*Cald hlaw*, 'cold-barrow' or *calu hlaw* 'bare barrow'
Castlow Cross	Staffordshire	*Ceastel hlaw*, 'cairn barrow'?
Cauldon Low	Staffordshire	The barrow at Cauldon (p.206)
Challow	Berkshire	*Ceawan hlaw* 'Ceawa's barrow'
Chidlow	Cheshire	*Ciddan hlaw*, 'Cidda's barrow
Church Lawton	Cheshire	*Hlawtun*, 'barrow-estate'
Cocklaw	Northumberland	*Cocc hlaw* 'cock barrow' – a barrow where wild birds could be caught
Cockle Park	Northumberland	*Cocc hlaw* 'cock barrow'
Cottesloe	Buckinghamshire	*Cottes hlaw* 'Cott's barrow', moothill for the hundred
Creslow	Buckinghamshire	*Cræs hlaw* 'cress barrow' a barrow covered in cress
Cutteslowe	Oxfordshire	*Cuðenes hlaw* 'Cuþen's barrow'. Cuþen may be a variant of Cuþwine (p.164).
Docklow	Herefordshire	*Doccan hlaw* 'dock barrow'- a barrow covered in dock
Drakelow	Derbyshire	*Dracan hlaw*, 'dragon barrow'
Dudslow	Buckinghamshire	*Dyddes hlæw* 'Dydd's barrow', a lost barrow, part of the boundary of Winslow manor[587]
Farlow	Shropshire	*Færnhlaw* 'fern barrow' – a barrow covered in ferns
Foolow	Derbyshire	*Fugol hlaw* 'bird barrow' a barrow where wild birds could be caught, or *fæg hlaw* 'colourful barrow'
Great Hucklow	Derbyshire	*Huccan hlaw*, 'Hucca's barrow'
Great Thurlow	Suffolk	Perhaps *Þryþe hlaw* 'Þryð's barrow', a female name
Grindlow	Derbyshire	*Grene hlaw* 'green barrow'(p.213)
Hadlow	Kent	*Hæð hlaw* 'heath barrow' – either 'barrow on the heath' or 'barrow covered in heather'
Hankelow	Cheshire	*Hanecan hlaw* 'Haneca's barrow'

---

[587] Bull & Hunt, 1996

Harlow	Essex	*Here hlaw* 'army barrow' the site of the moothill for the hundred, known as Mulberry Green from *gemot beorg* 'moot barrow' (p.131).
Harlow Hill	Northumberland	*Here hlaw* 'army barrow'
Hartley	Northumberland	*Heort hlaw* 'hart barrow'
Hauxley	Northumberland	*Hafoc hlaw* 'hawk barrow'
Henlow	Bedfordshire	*Henn hlaw* 'hen barrow' or (*æt þam*) *hean hlawe* '(at the) high barrow'.
Highlaw	Northumberland	*Heah hlaw* 'high barrow'
Highlow	Derbyshire	*Heah hlaw* 'high barrow'
Horninglow	Staffordshire	*Horning hlaw* 'horn-shaped barrow' or 'barrow of the horn-shaped land'?
Hounslow	Middlesex	*Hundes hlaw* 'hound's barrow' either a dog or a man named *Hund*. The barrow was the meeting place for the hundred, but its site is unknown.
Hunesberge	Dorset	*Hunes beorg* 'Hun's barrow'
Huxloe	Northamptonshire	*Hoces hlaw* 'Hoc's barrow', the moothill for the hundred.
Kearsley	Northumberland	*Cenheres hlaw* 'Cenhere's barrow' or 'Cynehere's barrow'
Kelloe	Durham	*Cealf hlaw* 'calf barrow'
Kenners Barrow	Oxfordshire	*Cenewardes berge* 'Cyneward's barrow', an alternative name for Shipton Barrow in Shipton-under-Wychwood (p.176). Once the site of the hundred moothill.
Kirkley	Northumberland	*Cruc hlaw* 'hill barrow'; perhaps originally known by the British name *cruc* 'hill' to which hlaw was added by the English-speaking population for clarity.
Knap Barrow	Dorset	*Cnæppede beorg* 'flat-topped barrow'
Knightlow	Warwickshire	*Cniht hlaw* 'warrior barrow'. Knightlow Cross was the meeting point for the Dunsmore hundred.
Lawshall	Suffolk	*Hlawsele* 'barrow-hall', a dwelling by a mound

Lowe	Staffordshire	*Hlaw* 'barrow'
Lew	Oxfordshire	*Hlaw* 'barrow' (p.174)
Lewes	Sussex	Perhaps *hlawas* 'barrows'? (p.117)
Lowton	Lancashire	*Hlaw tun* 'barrow estate'
Ludlow	Shropshire	*Hlud hlaw* 'loud (stream by a) barrow'; a mound of unknown date and purpose was destroyed when the town was expanded in 1199[588]
Moorsley	Durham	*Morwulfes hlaw* 'Morulf's barrow'?
Munslow	Shropshire	*Munseles hlaw* 'Munsel's barrow'?
Orslow	Staffordshire	*Horsan hlaw* 'Horsa's barrow' or *horsa hlaw* 'horses' barrow'
Osmotherly	Lancashire	*Asmundar hlaw* 'Asmund's barrow'; Asmund is a Norse personal name
Oulton Lowe	Cheshire	*Aldtun hlaw* 'old estate barrow'
Pathlow	Warwickshire	*Pæðan hlaw* 'barrow by a path'? or 'Paða's barrow'? An OE *paða* 'traveller, wanderer' is possible from *pæppan* 'journey'. Once the site of the moothill.
Pentlow	Essex	*Pentan hlaw* 'Penta's barrow'. The personal name Penta resembles Mercian Penda; there was a period of intense East Saxon contact with Mercia in the 7th c. during which a King Offa is known in Essex records. However, a connection to *Pant*, the local name for the River Blackwater, cannot be excluded.
Ploughley	Oxfordshire	*Pohhahlaw* 'bag barrow' perhaps named from its shape. It was a bell-barrow standing near the Bear Inn at Fritwell, but is no longer in existence. Once the site of the hundred moot.
Publow	Somerset	*Pubban hlaw* 'Pubba's barrow'
Queen Low	Staffordshire	*Cyne hlaw* 'royal barrow'? (p.206)

---

[588] Ellis Davidson, 1950, p.175

Rowball	Wiltshire	*Ruwan beorh* 'rough barrow'; on the Anglo-Saxon boundary of Coombe Bisset[589]
Rowbarrow	Dorset	*Ruh beorg* 'rough barrow', site of the hundred moothill.
Rowley	Buckinghamshire	*Ruh hlaw* 'rough barrow'; the mound may be Rowley Hill which was once the site of the hundred meetings.
Rue Hill	Staffordshire	*Ruh hlaw* 'rough barrow'
Sawley	Derbyshire	*Salh hlaw* 'willow barrow'
Slingley	Durham	*Slinge hlaw* 'trap barrow'?
Seckloe	Buckinghamshire	*Secgan hlaw* 'warrior's mound'? The hundred moothil was on Bradwell Common.
Shardlow	Derbyshire	*Sceard hlaw* 'barrow with a cleft'?
Softley	Durham	*Softe hlaw* 'soft barrow'
Stanlow	Cheshire	*Stan hlaw* 'stone barrow'
Tadlow	Cambridgeshire	*Tadan hlaw* 'Tada's barrow'
Taplow	Buckinghamshire	*Tæppan hlaw* 'Tappa's barrow' (p.168)
Thornley	Durham	*Þorn hlaw* 'thorn barrow'
Thriplow	Cambridgeshire	*Þryppan hlaw* 'Þryppa's barrow'? There is a Bronze Age barrow near the church. The hundred meetings were held at Mutlow, from *gemot hlaw* 'meeting mound'.
Throckley	Northumberland	*Þroc hlaw* 'barrow with a post'?
Thunderlow	Essex	*Þunor hlaw* 'Þunor's barrow'? Meeting point for the half-hundred. Perhaps named for the heathen god, Þunor 'thunder'?
Tinsley	Yorkshire WR	*Tynnes hlaw* 'Tynne's barrow'
Tremelau	Warwickshire	*Þrim hlawum* 'at the three barrows', the hundred meeting point was Moot/Mutt Hill in Lighthorne.
Twemlow	Cheshire	*Twæm hlawum* 'at the two barrows'
Wardlow	Derbyshire	*Weard hlaw* 'watch barrow', look-out hill
Wardlow	Staffordshire	*Weard hlaw* 'watch barrow', look-out hill

---

[589] Acornley, 1999, p.56

Warslow	Staffordshire	*Weardsetl hlaw* 'watching-seat barrow'
Wenslow	Bedfordshire	*Wednes hlaw* Woden's barrow', presumably a holy site where the god was worshipped, no longer known; a half-hundred was named from its meeting here, later joined with Biggleswade
Wharles	Lancashire	*Hwerfel hlaw* 'wheel/circle barrow'?
Winslow	Buckinghamshire	*Wines hlaw* 'Wine's barrow' (OE *Wine* 'friend' is a common personal name element.)
Winslow	Herefordshire	*Wines hlaw* 'Wine's barrow'
Winterslow	Wiltshire	*Wintreowes hlaw* 'vine barrow' or *winters hlaw* 'winter's barrow' (p.194)
Wolferlow	Herefordshire	*Wulfheres hlaw* 'Wulfhere's barrow'
Worbarrow	Dorset	*Weard beorg* 'watching barrow' cf. Wardlow

Bibliography

AJ   *Archaeological Journal*

ASSAH   *Anglo-Saxon Studies in Archaeology and History*

BAR   *British Archaeological Reports*

Med. Arch.   *Medieval Archaeology*

WANHS   *Wiltshire Archaeological and Natural History Magazine*

Acornley, J. *The Anglo-Saxon Charter Boundaries of Coombe Bisset* in *WANHS*, vol.92, 1999

Akerman, J. *Remains of Pagan Saxondom*, London, 1855

Allan, T. *The Archaeology of the Afterlife. Deciphering the Past from Tombs, Graves and Mummies*, London, 2004

Andrén, A., Jennbert, K. & Raudevere, C. (eds.) *Old Norse Religion in Long Term Perspectives. Origins, Changes and Interactions.* International Conference in Lund, Sweden, June 3-7, 2004, Vägar till Midgård, Lund, 2007

Anthony, D.W., *The Horse, The Wheel and Language. How Bronze Age Raiders from the Eurasian Steppes Shaped the Modern World*, Princeton, 2007

Arnold, C.J. *Wealth and Social Structure: a Matter of Life and Death* in Rahtz, Dickinson & Watts, 1980

- *The Anglo-Saxon Cemeteries of the Isle of Wight*, London, 1982

- *Roman Britain to Saxon England. An Archaeological Study*, London, 1984

- *An Archaeology of the Early Anglo-Saxon Kingdoms*, London, 1997

Artelius, T. *The Revenant by the Lake. Spear Symbolism in Scandinavian Late Viking Age Burial Ritual* in Artelius & Svanberg (eds.), 2005

Artelius, T. & Svanberg, F. (eds.) *Dealing with the Dead. Archaeological Perspectives on Prehistoric Scandinavian Ritual Burial*, Stockholm, 2005

Aspeborg, B. *The Dead in the Hills. Reflections on the Cult of the Dead in the Late Bronze Age and Early Iron Age of Uppland* in Artelius & Svanberg (eds.), 2005

Augustyn, P. *The Semiotics of Fate, Death and the Soul in Germanic Culture: The Christianization of Old Saxon*, New York, 2002

Baker, J.T. *Cultural Transition in the Chilterns and Essex Region, 350 to 650 AD*, Studies in Regional and Local History, Volume 4, Hatfield, 2006

Barnish, S.J. & Marazzi, F. (eds.), *The Ostrogoths from the Migration Period to the Sixth Century: An Ethnographic Perspective*, San Merino, 2007

Bateman, T. *Ten Years' Diggings in Celtic and Saxon Grave-hills* (1861), reprinted Buxton, 1978

Bauschatz, P. *The Well and the Tree. World and Time in Early Germanic Culture*, Amherst, 1982

Becker, A. *Franks Casket. Zu den Bildern und Inschriften des Runenkästchens von Auzon*, Regensburg Arbeiten zur Anglistik und Amerikanistik, band 5, Regensburg, 1973

Bedwin, O. *The Excavation of Three Ring-Ditches at Broomfield Plantation Quarry, Alresford, Essex, 1984* in *Essex Archaeology & History*, vol. 17, 1986

 - *(ed.) The Archaeology of Essex. Proceedings of the Writtle Conference, Chelmsford, 1996*

Bietti Sesteri, A.M. & de Santis, A. (trans. E. de Sena) *The Protohistory of the Latin Peoples*, Milan, 2000

Bird, J. & Bird, D.G. *The Archaeology of Surrey to 1540*, Guildford, 1987

Blair, I. *Prittlewell Prince* in *Current Archaeology*, vol.XVII, no.3, 2007

Boyle, A., Dodd, A., Mills, D. & Mudd, A. *Two Oxfordshire Anglo-Saxon Cemeteries: Berinsfield and Didcot*, ThamesValley Landscape Monograph no.8, Oxford Archaeological Unit, Oxford, 1995

Boyle, A., Jennings, D., Miles, D. & Palmer, S. *The Anglo-Saxon Cemetery at Butler's Field, Lechlade, Gloucestershire. Volume 1: Prehistoric and Roman Activity and Anglo-Saxon Grave Catalogue*, ThamesValley Landscapes Monographs no. 10, Oxford Archaeological Unit, Oxford, 1998;

Brandon, P. (ed.) *The South Saxons*, Chichester, 1978

Briggs, G., Cook, J. & Rowley, T. *The Archaeology of the Oxford Region*, Oxford, 1989

Brown, D. *Swastika Patterns* in Evison, (ed.), 1981

Brubaker, L. & Smith, J.M.H. (eds.), *Gender in the Early Medieval World. East and West, 300-900*, Cambridge, 2004

Bruce-Mitford, R. *Aspects of Anglo-Saxon Archaeology. Sutton Hoo and Other Discoveries*, London, 1974

- *The Sutton Hoo Ship-Burial. Volume 1. Excavations, Background, The Ship, Dating and Inventory,* London, 1975

- (ed) *Recent Archaeological Excavations in Europe*, London, 1975a

- *The Sutton Hoo Ship-Burial. Volume 2. Arms, Armour and Regalia,* London, 1978

- *The Sutton Hoo Ship-Burial. Volume 3. Late Roman and Byzantine Silver, Hanging Bowls, Drinking Vessels, Cauldrons and Other Containers, Textiles, The Lyre, Pottery Bottle and Other Items,* London, 1983

- *The Corpus of Late Celtic Hanging Bowls*, Oxford, 2005

Buckley, D.G., (ed.) *Archaeology in Essex to AD 1500*, CBA Research Report no.34, London, 1980

Bull, E.J. & Hunt, J. *Rewalking the Tenth Century Perambulation of Winslow Manor* in *Records of Buckinghamshire*, vol. 38, 1996

Burrows,V., Richardson, R. & Hammond, J. *Early Bronze Age Barrows and Anglo-Saxon Cemetery at Wolverton, near Dover.* (forthcoming)

Carver, M.O.H. *Pre-Viking Traffic in the North Sea* in McGrail, (ed.), 1990

- (ed.) *The Age of Sutton Hoo: The Seventh Century in North-Western Europe*, Woodbridge, 1992

- *Ideology and Allegiance in East Anglia* in Farrell & Neuman de Vegvar, (eds.), 1992a

- *Exploring, Explaining, Imagining: Anglo-Saxon Archaeology 1998* in Karkov, (ed.), 1999

- *Burial as Poetry: The Context of Treasure in Anglo-Saxon Graves* in Tyler, (ed.) 2000

- *Reflections on the Meanings of Monumental barrows in Anglo-Saxon England* in Lucy & Reynolds, (eds.) 2002

- *Sutton Hoo: A Seventh Century Princely Burial Ground and its Context,* Report of the Research Committee of the Society of Antiquaries of London, no. 69, London, 2005

C.A.T. *North of Saltwood Tunnel, Kent. ARC SLT 98C Detailed Archaeological Works. Interim Report*, London, 1999

Chaney, W.A. *The Cult of Kingship in Anglo-Saxon England. The Transition from Paganism to Christianity*, Manchester, 1970

Châtelet, M. et al., *Trésors Mérovingiens d'Alsace. La Nécropole d'Erstein (6 – 7 siècle après J.C.)* Strasbourg, 2004

Chambers, R. & McAdam, E. *Excavations at Radley Barrow Hills, Radley, Oxfordshire, vol.2: The Romano-British Cemetery and Anglo-Saxon Settlement,* Thames Valley Landscapes Monograph no.25, Oxford, 2007

Clarke, B. *An Early Anglo-Saxon Crossroads Burial from Broad Town, North Wiltshire* in *WANHS,* vol.97, 2004

Collis, J. (et al.) *Wigber Low, Derbyshire: A Bronze Age and Anglian Burial Site in the White Peak,* Sheffield, 1983

Colte Hoare, Sir R. *The Ancient History of Wiltshire,* London, 1812

Cook, J.M. *Early Anglo-Saxon Buckets. A Corpus of Copper-Alloy- and Iron-Bound, Stave-Built Vessels,* Oxford University School of Archaeology: Monograph 60, 2004

Cook, A.M. & Dacre, M.W. *Excavations at Portway, Andover 1975,* Oxford University Committee for Archaeology Monograph no.4, Oxford, 1985

Crawford, S. *Votive Deposition, Religion and the Anglo-Saxon Furnished Burial Ritual* in *World Archaeology,* Vol. 36, 2004

Creighton, J.D. & Wilson, R.J.A. (eds) *Roman Germany. Studies in Cultural Interaction,* International Roman Archaeology Conference Series, no.32, Portsmouth, 1999

Crummy, P., Crummy, N., Jackson, R. & Schädler, U. *Stanway: An Elite Cemetery at Camulodunum* in *British Archaeology,* issue, 99, 2008

Davies Pryce, T. *Oldox or Hodox Camp, Oxton,* Thoroton Society Summer Excursion, 1908

Dickens, A., Mortimer, R. & Tipper, J. *The Early Anglo-Saxon Settlement and Cemetery at Bloodmoor Hill, Carlton Colville, Suffolk: A Preliminary Report* in *ASSAH,* vol. 13, 2006.

Dickinson, T.M. *Cuddesdon and Dorchester-on-Thames: Two Early Saxon 'Princely' Sites in Wessex* B.A.R. 1, Oxford, 1974

Dickinson, T.M. & Härke, H. *Early Anglo-Saxon Shields,* London, 1992

Dickinson, T.M. & Speake, G. *The Seventh Century Cremation Burial in Asthall Barrow, Oxfordshire: A Reassessment* in Carver, 1992

Doppelfeld, O. & Pirling, R. *Fränkische Fürsten in Rheinland. Die Gräber aus dem Kölner Dom von Krefeld-Gellep und Morken,* Schriften des Rheinischen Landesmuseums Bonn, Düsseldorf, 1966

Drinkall, G. & Foreman, M. *The Anglo-Saxon Cemetery at Castledyke South, Barton-on-Humber*, Sheffield Excavation Reports 6, Sheffield, 1998

Du Bois, T.A. *Nordic Religions in the Viking Age,* Philadelphia, 1999

- *Rituals, Winesses and Sagas in* Andrén, Jennbert & Raudevere (eds.), 2007

Effros, B. *Skeletal Sex and Gender in Merovingian Mortuary Archaeology* in *Antiquity*, vol. 74, 2000

- *Merovingian Mortuary Archaeology and the Making of the Early Middle Ages*, Berkeley, 2003

Ekengren, F. *Performing Death. The Function and Meaning of Roman Drinking Vessels in Scandinavian Mortuary Practices* in Andrén, Jennbert & Raudevere (eds.), 2007

Elliott, R.W.V. *Runes. An Introduction*, Manchester, 1959

Ellis Davidson, H.R. *The Road to Hel,* London, 1943

- *The Hill of the Dragon: Anglo-Saxon Burial Mounds in Literature and Archaeology in Folklore*, Vol. 61, No. 4. (Dec., 1950)

- *Myths and Symbols in Pagan Europe,* New York, 1988

Evison, V. (ed.) *Angles, Saxons and Jutes. Essays Presented to J.N.L. Myres*, Oxford, 1981

Farrell, R. & Neuman de Vegvar, C. (eds.) *Sutton Hoo: Fifty Years After*, Oxford, 1992

Fern, C. *Early Anglo-Saxon Horse Burial of the Fifth to Seventh Centuries AD* in *ASSAH*, vol.14, 2007

Filmer-Sankey, W. *A New Boat Burial from the Snape Anglo-Saxon Cemetery, Suffolk* in McGrail, (ed.), 1990

Filmer-Sankey, W. & Pestell, T. *Snape Anglo-Saxon Cemetery: Excavations & Surveys 1824-1992*, East Anglian Archaeology Report 95, Ipswich, 2001

Fischer, S. *The Continental Background of the Scandinavian Migration Period Chamber Graves* available at www. arkeologi.uu.se/ark/projects/Luciasymposion

Fitch, E. *Ancient Taplow* in *At the Edge*, vol.1, 1996

Fleury, M. & France-Lanord, A. Les Trésors Mérovingiens de la Basilique de Saint-Denis, Luxembourg, 1998

Franceschi, G., Jorn, A. & Magnus, B. *Ten Thousand Years of Folk Art in the North*: vol. 1, *Men, Gods and Masks in Nordic Iron AgeArt*, Köln, 2005a

- vol. 2 *Bird, Beast and Man in Nordic Iron Age Art*, Köln, 2005b

Fulford, M. G. & Rippon, S. J. *Lowbury Hill, Oxon: A Re-Assessment of the Probable Romano-Celtic Temple and the Anglo-Saxon Barrow* in *AJ*, vol. 151, London, 1994

Garmonsway, G.N. *An Early Norse Reader*, Cambridge, 1928

Garson, J. G. *A Description of the Skeletons Found in Howe Hill Barrow* in *The Journal of the Anthropological Institute of Great Britain and Ireland*, vol. 22, 1893

Geake, H. *Burial Practice in Seventh- and Eighth-Century England* in Carver, 1992

- *The Use of Grave-Goods in Conversion Period England, c.600-850*, BAR British Series, no. 261, Oxford, 1997

Geake, H. & Kenny, J. *Early Deira. Archaeological Studies of the East Riding in the Fourth to Ninth Centuries AD*, Oxford, 2000

Green, B., Rogerson, A. & White, S.G. *The Anglo-Saxon Cemetery at Morning Thorpe*, vols. I & II, East Anglian Archaeology Report no.36, Norwich, 1987

Greenwell, W. & Rolleston, W. *British Barrows*, Oxford, 1877

Grinsell, L.V. *The Ancient Burial-Mounds of England,* London, 1936

- *Some Aspects of the Folklore of Prehistoric Monuments* in *Folklore*, Vol. 48, No. 3, 1937

- *Dorset Barrows.* Dorchester, 1959

- *Barrow Treasure, in Fact, Tradition, and Legislation* in *Folklore*, Vol. 78, 1967

- *Hangman's Stones and Their Traditions* in *Folklore*, Vol. 96, 1985

- *Barrows in the Anglo-Saxon Land Charters* in *AJ*, vol. 71, 1991

- *The Folklore of a Round Barrow in Kent* in *Folklore*, vol. 103, no.1, 1992

Guillaume, J., Rohmer, P. & Waton, M.-D. *L'Architecture des Tombes* in Châtelet et al., 2004

- *Accesoires du Costume, Objets de Parure et da la Vie Quotidienne* in Châtelet et al., 2004a

- *Des Armes Prestigieuses* in Châtelet et al., 2004b

- *Une Tombe de Cheval (S.68)* in Châtelet et al., 2004c

Hadley, D. *Negotiating Gender, Family and Status in Anglo-Saxon Burial Practices, c.600-950* in Brubaker & Smith, (eds.), 2004

Hållans Stenholm, A.-M. *Past Memories. Spatial Returning as Ritualized Remambrance* in Andrén, Jennbert & Raudevere (eds.), 2007

Halsall, G. *Early Medieval Cemeteries: An Introduction to Burial Archaeology in the Post-Roman West*, Glasgow, 1995

Harrison, S. *William Greenwell and Uncleby I: A Recently Discovered Contemporary Account*, East Riding Archaeologist, vol. 9, Hull, 1997

Harte, J. *Hollow Hills* in *At The Edge*, vol.5, 1997

Haughton, C. & Powlesland, D. *West Heslerton. The Anglian Cemetery. Volume i, The Excavation and Discussion of the Evidence*, Yedingham, 1999

 - *West Heslerton. The Anglian Cemetery. Volume ii, Catalogue of the Anglian Graves and Associated Assemblages*, Yedingham, 1999a

Hawkes, S.C. *The Early Saxon Period* in Briggs, Cook & Rowley, 1989

 - *Bryan Faussett and the Faussett Collection: An Assessment* in Southworth (ed.), 1990

Hedeager, L. *Kingdoms, Ethnicity & Material Culture* in Carver (ed.), 1992

 - (trans. Hines) *Iron-Age Societies. From Tribe to State in Northern Europe 500 BC to AD 700*, Cambridge, 1992

Hedges, J.D. & Buckley, D.G. *Anglo-Saxon Burials and Later Features Excavated at Orsett, Essex*, 1975 in Med. Arch., vol. XXIX, 1985

Henson, D. *The Origins of the Anglo-Saxons*, Hockwold-cum-Wilton, 2006

Higgitt, J., Forsyth, K. & Parsons, D.A. (eds.), *Roman, Runes and Ogham. Medieval Inscriptions in the Insular World and on the Continent*, Donington, 2001

Hills, C. *Chamber Graves from Spong Hill, North Elmham, Norfolk* in Med. Arch., vol. XXI, 1977

Hills,C., Penn, K. & Rickett, R. et al., *The Anglo-Saxon Cemetery at Spong Hill, North Elmham, Part III: Catalogue of Inhumations*, East Anglian Archaeology Report no, 21, Dereham, 1984

Hinton, D. *The Fifth and Sixth Centuries: Reorganization Among the Ruins* in Karkov, (ed.), 1999

 - *A Smith in Lindsey. The Anglo-Saxon Grave at Tattershall Thorpe, Lincolnshire*, Society for Mediaeval Archaeology, Monograph no.16, London, 2000

 - *Gold and Gilt, Pots and Pins: Possessions and People in Medieval Britain*, Oxford, 2005

Huggett, J.W. *Imported Grave Goods and the Early Anglo-Saxon Economy* in Med.Arch., vol.XXXII, London, 1988

Inker, P. *The Saxon Relief Style,* BAR British Series 410, Oxford, 2006

Irwin, J.C. *The Sacred Anthill and the Cult of the Primordial Mound* in *History of Religions*, Vol. 21, No. 4. 1982

Jennbert, K. *The Heroized Dead. People, Animals and Materiality in Scandinavian Death Rituals, AD 200-1000* in Andrén, Jennbert & Raudevere (eds.), 2007

Jessup, R. *An Earthen Mound Near Rochester* in *Archaeologia Cantiana*, vol. 55, 1942

  - *Anglo-Saxon Jewellery*, Aylesbury, 1974

  - *Man of Many Talents. An Informal Biography of James Douglas, 1753-1819,* London, 1975

Jones, W.T. *Early Saxon Cemeteries in Essex* in Buckley, (ed.), 1980

Kaliff, A. *Fire, Water, Heaven and Earth. Ritual Practice & Cosmology in Ancient Scandinavia: an Indo-European Perspective*, Stockholm, 2007

Karkov, C.E. *The Archaeology of Anglo-Saxon England: Basic Readings*, London, 1999

Kazanski, M. *The Ostrogoths and the Princely Civilization of the Fifth Century* in Barnish & Marazzi, (eds.) 2007

Kerr, L. *Taplow Revisited*, (unpublished monograph, 2004)

Kershaw, K. *The One-Eyed God. Odin and the (Indo-)Germanic Männerbünde,* JIES Monograph, no.36, Washington, 2000

Knight, J. *Basilicas and Barrows: The Latin Memorial Stones of Wales and Their Archaeological Contexts* in Higgitt, Forsyth & Parsons (eds.), 2001

Kure, H. *Hanging on the World Tree. Man and Cosmos in Old Norse Mythic Poetry* in Andrén, Jennbert & Raudevere (eds.), 2007

Larrington, C. *Diet, Defecation and the Devil: Disgust and the Pagan Past* in McDonald, N. (ed), 2006

Leeds, E.T. *An Anglo-Saxon Cremation Burial of the Seventh Century at Asthall Barrow, Oxfordshire* in *Antiquaries Journal* vol.4, (1924)

Lethbridge, T.C. *Shudy Camps, Cambridgeshire. Report of the Excavation of a Cemetery of the Christian Anglo-Saxon Period in 1933*, Cambridge, 1936

Lincoln, B. *Discourse and the Construction of Society. Comparative Studies in Myth, Ritual and Classification*, Oxford, 1989

Looijenga, T. *Texts and Contexts of the Oldest Runic Inscriptions*, The Northern World, vol. 4, Leiden, 2003

Loumand, U. *The Horse and its Role in Icelandic Burial Practices, Mythology and Society* in Andrén, Jennbert & Raudevere (eds.), 2007

Lovecy, I *The End of Celtic Britain: a Sixth Century Battle near Lindisfarne* in Archaeologia Aeliana, 5th series, vol.4 1976

Lucy, S. & Reynolds, A. (eds.) *Burial in Early Mediaeval England and Wales*, Society for Medieval Archaeology Monograph 17, London, 2002

Lucy, S. *Early Medieval Burials in East Yorkshire: Reconsidering the Evidence* in Geake & Kenny, 2000

Lutovsky, M. *Between Sutton Hoo and Chernaya Mogila: Barrows in Eastern and Western Early Mediaeval Europe* in *Antiquity*, vol. 70, 1996

MacGregor, A. & Bolick, E. *A Summary Catalogue of the Anglo-Saxon Collections (Non-Ferrous Metals)*, B.A.R. British Series 230, Oxford, 1993

Major, A.F. *Ship Burials in Scandinavian Lands and the Beliefs That Underlie Them* in *Folklore*, vol. 35, 1924

Malim, T. & Hines, J. *The Anglo-Saxon Cemetery at Edix Hill (Barrington A), Cambridgeshire,* CBA Research Report 112, York, 1998

Mallory, J.P. & Mair, V. *The Tarim Mummies*, London, 2000

Mallory, J.P. & Adams, D.Q. *The Oxford Introduction to Proto-Indo-European and the Proto-Indo-European World*, Oxford, 2006

McDonald, N. (ed.) *Medieval Obscenities*, Oxford, 2006

McGrail, S. (ed.), *Maritime Celts, Frisians and Saxons. Papers presented to a Conference at Oxford in November 1988*, CBA Research Report 71, Oxford, 1990

Meaney, A. *A Gazetteer of Early Anglo-Saxon Burial Sites*, London, 1964

Meaney, A. & Hawkes, S.C. *Two Anglo-Saxon Cemeteries at Winnall*, Society for Medieval Archaeology Monograph no. 4, London, 1970

MoLAS *Cuxton Anglo-Saxon Cemetery Archaeological Excavation Interim Report*, London, 1999

Mortimer, J. R. *"Kemp How" Cowlam* in *The Journal of the Anthropological Institute of Great Britain and Ireland*, Vol. 9, 1880

   - *An Account of the Exploration of Howe Hill Barrow, Duggleby, Yorkshire* in *The Journal of the Anthropological Institute of Great Britain and Ireland*, vol. 22, 1893

Mortimer, P. *The Sutton Hoo Warriors*, forthcoming

Musty, J. *The Excavation of Two Barrows, One of Saxon Date, at Ford, Laverstock, near Salisbury, Wiltshire* in *Antiquaries Journal*, vol. 49, 1969

Newman, J. *New Light on Old Finds – Bloodmor Hill, Gisleham, Suffolk* in *ASSAH*, vol. 9, 1996

Noble, T.F.X. (ed) *From Roman Provinces to Medieval Kingdoms*, London, 2006

Nordin, P. *Wealthy Women and Absent Men. Gender in Early Iron Age Burial-Grounds in Östergötland* in Artelius & Svanberg (eds.), 2005

O'Brien, E. *Post-Roman Britain to Anglo-Saxon England: Burial Practices Revealed*, BAR British Series, no.289, Oxford, 1999

Orchard, A. *Pride and Prodigies. Studies in the Monsters of the Beowulf Manuscript*, Cambridge, 1995

Parfitt, K. & Brugmann, B. *The Anglo-Saxon Cemetery on Mill Hill, Deal, Kent,* Society for Medieval Archaeology Monograph Series no. 14, London, 1997

Parsons, F. G. *A Round Barrow at St. Margaret's Bay* in *Man*, Vol. 29, 1929

Parker Pearson, M. *The Archaeology of Death and Burial*, Stroud, 1999

Parker Pearson, M., van der Noort, R. & Woolf, A. *Three Men and a Boat: Sutton Hoo and the East Saxon Kingdom* in *Anglo-Saxon England*, vol.22, London, 1993

Pedersen, A. *Ancient Mounds for New Graves. An Aspect of Viking Age Burial Customs in Southern Scandinavia* in Andrén, Jennbert & Raudevere (eds.), 2007

Penn, K *An Anglo-Saxon Cemetery at Oxborough, West Norfolk: Excavations in 1990,* Norwich, 1998

- *Excavations on the Norwich Southern Bypass, 1989–91 Part II: The Anglo-Saxon Cemetery at Harford Farm, Markshall, Norfolk,* Norwich, 2000

Plunkett, S. *Suffolk in Anglo-Saxon Times*, Stroud, 2005

Points, G. *Yorkshire. A Gazetteer of Anglo-Saxon & Viking Sites*, King's Lynn, 2007

Pollington, S. *Rudiments of Runelore*, Hockwold-cum-Wilton, 1995

- *Leechcraft - Early English Charms, Plantlore and Healing*, Hockwold, 2000

- *The English Warrior from Earliest Times till 1066*, 2nd edition, Hockwold, 2002

- *The Mead-Hall – Feasting in Anglo-Saxon England*, Hockwold, 2003

- *Wayland's Work,* forthcoming

Potter, J.F. *The Occurrence of Roman Brick and Tile in Churches of the London Basin* in *Britannia*, vol. 32, 2001

Poulton, R. *Saxon Surrey* in Bird & Bird, 1987

Price, N. *The Archaeology of Shamanism*, London, 2001

- *The Viking Way. Religion and War in Late Iron Age Scandinavia*, AUN 31, Uppsala, 2003

Puhvel, M. *The Ride around Beowulf's Barrow* in *Folklore*, Vol. 94, 1983

Rahtz, P., Dickinson, T. & Watts, L. (eds.) *Anglo-Saxon Cemeteries, 1979* BAR British Series 82, Oxford, 1980

Ramqvist, P.H. *Högom*, Malung, 1990

Rauer, C. *Beowulf and the Dragon. Parallels and Analogues*, Cambridge, 2000

Read, H. *A Saxon Grave at Broomfield* in *Proceedings of the Society of Antiquaries*, London, 1894

Reaney, P.H. *The Place-Names of Essex*, Cambridge, 1969

Rhodes, M. *Faussett Rediscovered: Charles Roach Smith, Joseph Mayer and the Publication of Inventorium Sepulchale* in Southworth (ed.), 1990

Sawyer, P. *Anglo-Saxon Lincolnshire*, Lincoln, 1998

Schutz, H. *Tools, Weapons and Ornaments. Germanic Material Culture in Pre-Carolingian Central Europe 400-750*, Leiden, 2001

- *The Prehistory of Germanic Europe*, London, 1983

Semple, S. *A Fear of the Past: The Place of the Prehistoric Burial Mound in the Ideology of Middle and Later Anglo-Saxon England* in *World Archaeology*, vol. 20, 1998

Semple, S. & Williams, H. *Excavations on Roundway Down* in *WANHS*, vol.94, 2001

- *Searching for a Lost Barrow: Excavations of Roundway Down North Wiltshire* in Excapades, vol. 1, 2006

Sherlock, S.J. & Simmons, M. *The Lost Royal Cult of Street House, Yorkshire* in British Archaeology, vol, 100, 2008

Shook, L.K. *The Burial Mound in "Guthlac A"* in Modern Philology, Vol. 58, 1960

Sigvallius, B. *Sailing Towards the Afterlife* in Artelius & Svanberg (eds.), 2005

Simek, R. *Dictionary of Northern Mythology*, Cambridge, 1993

Smith, R.A. *British Museum Guide to Anglo-Saxon Antiquities,* London, 1923 (reprint, 1993)

Smith, M. & Brickley, M. *Boles Barrow – Witness to Ancient Violence* in *British Archaeology,* no.93, 2007

Southworth, E. (ed.) *Anglo-Saxon Cemeteries: A Reappraisal,* Stroud, 1990

Speake, G. *Anglo-Saxon Animal Art and its Germanic Background,* Oxford, 1980

- *A Saxon Bed Burial on Swallowcliffe Down. Excavations by F. de M. Vatcher,* HBMCE Report no. 10, London, 1989

Stearne, J. *Oxfordshire,* London, 1996

Svanberg, F. *House Symolism in Aristocratic Death Rituals of the Bronze Age* in Artelius & Svanberg (eds.), 2005

Theune-Grosskopf, B. *Krieger auf der Leier* in *Archäologie in Deutschland,* no.3, 2004

- *Die vollständig erhaltene Leier des 6. Jahrhunderts aus Grab 58 von Trossingen, Ldkr. Tuttlingen, Baden-Württemberg. Ein Verbericht,* Mainz am Rhein, 2006

Thomas, J. *Monuments, Memories and Myths in the Early Bronze Age and Beyond* in *Current Archaeology,* vol.216, 2008

Thorvildsen, K. *The Viking Ship of Ladby,* Copenhagen, 1975

Todd, M. *The Early Germans,* Oxford, 2004

Tyler, E.M. *Treasure in the Medieval West,* York, 2000

Tyler, S. *The Anglo-Saxon Cemetery at Prittlewell, Essex: An Analysis of the Grave Goods* in *Essex Archaeology and History,* vol.19, 1988

- *Early Saxon Essex. AD 400-700* in Bedwin (ed.), 1996

Valk, H. *Cemeteries and Ritual Meals. Rites and their Meaning in the Traditional Seto World-View* in Andrén, Jennbert & Raudevere (eds.), 2007

van der Noort, R. *The Context of Early Medieval Barrows in Western Europe* in *Antiquity,* vol.67, 1993

Vince, A. *Saxon London: An Archaeological Investigation,* London, 1990

Walton Rogers, P. *Cloth and Clothing in Early Anglo-Saxon England, AD 450-700,* CBA Research Report 145, York, 2007

Watson, J. *Laid to Rest – Two Anglo-Saxon Chambered Graves Reconstructed* in *Research News,* no.2, 2006

Welch, M. *Late Romans and Saxons in Sussex* in Britannia, vol. 2, 1971

- *Early Anglo-Saxon Sussex: From Civitas to Shire in Brandon, (ed.),* 1978

- *Anglo-Saxon Kent to AD 800* in Williams (ed.) 2007

Wellendorf, J. *Homogeneity and Heterogeneity in Old Norse Cosmology* in Andrén, Jennbert & Raudevere (eds.), 2007

Weston Wyly, B. *On Wind and Waves* in Andrén, Jennbert & Raudevere (eds.), 2007

Wigg, A. *Confrontation and Interaction: Celts, Germans and Romans in the Central German Highlands* in Creighton & Wilson (eds), 1999

Williams, H. *Monuments and the Past in Early Anglo-Saxon England* in World Archaeology, Vol. 30, 1998

- *Ancestral and Supernatural Places in Anglo-Saxon England* in At The Edge, vol.9, 1998

- *Death and Memory in Early Medieval Britain*, Cambridge, 2006

Williams, J.H. (ed.) *The Archaeology of Kent to AD 800*, Woodbridge, 2007

Wilson, D. *Anglo-Saxon Paganism*, London, 1992

Wymer, J. *Barrow Excavations in Norfolk, 1984–8*, Norwich, 1996

Wymer, J.J. & Brown, N.R. *Excavations at North Shoebury: Settlement and Economy in South-East Essex 1500BC – AD1500*, East Anglian Archaeology Report no.75, Chelmsford, 1995

Yeates, S.J. *The Tribe of Witches. The Religion of the Dobunni and Hwicce*, Oxford, 2008

Some of our other title

Please see www.asbooks.co.uk for current availability and prices

The English Warrior from earliest times till 1066
Stephen Pollington

This is not intended to be a bald listing of the battles and campaigns from the Anglo-Saxon Chronicle and other sources, but rather it is an attempt to get below the surface of Anglo-Saxon warriorhood and to investigate the rites, social attitudes, mentality and mythology of the warfare of those times.

> "An under-the-skin study of the role, rights, duties, psyche and rituals of the Anglo-Saxon warrior. The author combines original translations from Norse and Old English primary sources with archaeological and linguistic evidence for an in-depth look at the warrior, his weapons, tactics and logistics.
>
> A very refreshing, innovative and well-written piece of scholarship that illuminates a neglected period of English history"
>
> *Time Team Booklists* - Channel 4 Television

Revised Edition
An already highly acclaimed book has been made even better by the inclusion of additional information and illustrations.

£16.95 ISBN 1–898281–42–4   245 x 170mm   over 50 illustrations Hardback   304 pages

The Mead Hall The feasting tradition in Anglo-Saxon England
Stephen Pollington

This new study takes a broad look at the subject of halls and feasting in Anglo-Saxon England. The idea of the communal meal was very important among nobles and yeomen, warriors, farmers churchmen and laity. One of the aims of the book is to show that there was not just one 'feast' but two main types: the informal social occasion *gebeorscipe* and the formal, ritual gathering *symbel*.

Using the evidence of Old English texts - mainly the epic *Beowulf* and the *Anglo-Saxon Chronicles*, Stephen Pollington shows that the idea of feasting remained central to early English social traditions long after the physical reality had declined in importance.

The words of the poets and saga-writers are supported by a wealth of archaeological data dealing with halls, settlement layouts and magnificent feasting gear found in many early Anglo-Saxon graves.

Three appendices cover:
- Hall-themes in Old English verse;
- Old English and translated texts;
- The structure and origins of the warband.

£16.95 ISBN 1-898281-30-0   9 ¾ x 6 ¾ inches   245 x 170mm   Hardback   288 pages

First Steps in Old English
An easy to follow language course for the beginner
Stephen Pollington

A complete and easy to use Old English language course that contains all the exercises and texts needed to learn Old English. This course has been designed to be of help to a wide range of students, from those who are teaching themselves at home, to undergraduates who are learning Old English as part of their English degree course. The author has adopted a step-by-step approach that enables students of differing abilities to advance at their own pace. The course includes practice and translation exercises, a glossary of the words used in the course, and many Old English texts, including the *Battle of Brunanburh* and *Battle of Maldon*.

£16-95   ISBN 1-898281-45-9   248 x 173mm / 10 x 6½ inches   Hardback   272 pages

Old English Poems, Prose & Lessons   2 CDs
read by Stephen Pollington

These CDs contain lessons and texts from *First Steps in Old English*.

Tracks include: 1. Deor. 2. Beowulf – The Funeral of Scyld Scefing. 3. Engla Tocyme (The Arrival of the English). 4. Ines Domas. Two Extracts from the Laws of King Ine. 5. Deniga Hergung (The Danes' Harrying) Anglo-Saxon Chronicle Entry AD997. 6. Durham 7. The Ordeal (Be ðon ðe ordales weddigaþ) 8. Wið Dweorh (Against a Dwarf) 9. Wið Wennum (Against Wens) 10. Wið Wæterælfadle (Against Waterelf Sickness) 11. The Nine Herbs Charm 12. Lǣcedomas (Leechdoms) 13. Beowulf's Greeting 14. The Battle of Brunanburh 15. A Guide to Pronunciation. And more than 30 other lessons and extracts of Old English verse and prose.

£11.75   ISBN 1–898281–46-7   2 CDs - Free Old English transcript from www.asbooks.co.uk.

Wordcraft: Concise English/Old English Dictionary and Thesaurus
Stephen Pollington

This book provides Old English equivalents to the commoner modern words in both dictionary and thesaurus formats. The Thesaurus presents vocabulary relevant to a wide range of individual topics in alphabetical lists, thus making it easily accessible to those with specific areas of interest. Each thematic listing is encoded for cross-reference from the Dictionary. The two sections will be of invaluable assistance to students of the language, as well as to those with either a general or a specific interest in the Anglo-Saxon period.

£9.95   A5   ISBN 1–898281–02–5   256 pages

An Introduction to the Old English Language and its Literature
Stephen Pollington

The purpose of this general introduction to Old English is not to deal with the teaching of Old English but to dispel some misconceptions about the language and to give an outline of its structure and its literature. Some basic knowledge of these is essential to an understanding of the early period of English history and the present form of the language.

£4.95   A5   ISBN 1–898281–06–8   48 pages

Anglo-Saxon Food & Drink
Production, Processing, Distribution, and Consumption
Ann Hagen

Food production for home consumption was the basis of economic activity throughout the Anglo-Saxon period. Used as payment and a medium of trade, food was the basis of the Anglo-Saxons' system of finance and administration.

Information from various sources has been brought together in order to build up a picture of how food was grown, conserved, distributed, prepared and eaten during the period from the beginning of the 5th century to the 11th century. Many people will find it fascinating for the views it gives of an important aspect of Anglo-Saxon life and culture. In addition to Anglo-Saxon England the Celtic west of Britain is also covered.

This edition combines earlier titles – *A Handbook of Anglo-Saxon Food* and *A Second Handbook of Anglo-Saxon Food & Drink*.

Extensive index.

£19.95   10" x 7" (245 x 170mm)   ISBN 1–898281–41–6   Hardback   512 pages

English Heroic Legends
Kathleen Herbert

The author has taken the skeletons of ancient Germanic legends about great kings, queens and heroes, and put flesh on them. Kathleen Herbert's extensive knowledge of the period is reflected in the wealth of detail she brings to these tales of adventure, passion, bloodshed and magic.

The book is in two parts. First are the stories that originate deep in the past, yet because they have not been hackneyed, they are still strange and enchanting. After that there is a selection of the source material, with information about where it can be found and some discussion about how it can be used.

£9-95   A5   ISBN 0–9516209–9–1   292 pages

Peace-Weavers and Shield-Maidens: Women in Early English Society
Kathleen Herbert

The recorded history of the English people did not start in 1066 as popularly believed but one-thousand years earlier. The Roman historian Cornelius Tacitus noted in *Germania*, published in the year 98, that the English (Latin *Anglii*), who lived in the southern part of the Jutland peninsula, were members of an alliance of Goddess-worshippers. The author has taken that as an appropriate opening to an account of the earliest Englishwomen, the part they played in the making of England, what they did in peace and war, the impressions they left in Britain and on the continent, how they were recorded in the chronicles, how they come alive in heroic verse and riddles.

£4.95   A5   ISBN 1–898281–11–4   64 pages

Anglo-Saxon Runes

John. M. Kemble

Kemble's essay *On Anglo-Saxon Runes* first appeared in the journal *Archaeologia* for 1840; it draws on the work of Wilhelm Grimm, but breaks new ground for Anglo-Saxon studies in his survey of the Ruthwell Cross and the Cynewulf poems. It is an expression both of his own indomitable spirit and of the fascination and mystery of the Runes themselves, making one of the most attractive introductions to the topic. For this edition new notes have been supplied, which include translations of Latin and Old English material quoted in the text, to make this key work in the study of runes more accessible to the general reader.

£4.95   A5   ISBN 0–9516209–1–6   80 pages

Looking for the Lost Gods of England

Kathleen Herbert

Kathleen Herbert sifts through the royal genealogies, charms, verse and other sources to find clues to the names and attributes of the Gods and Goddesses of the early English. The earliest account of English heathen practices reveals that they worshipped the Earth Mother and called her Nerthus. The tales, beliefs and traditions of that time are still with us in, for example, Sand able to stir our minds and imaginations.

£4.95   A5   ISBN 1–898281–04–1   64 pages

Rudiments of Runelore

Stephen Pollington

This book provides both a comprehensive introduction for those coming to the subject for the first time, and a handy and inexpensive reference work for those with some knowledge of the subject. The *Abecedarium Nordmannicum* and the English, Norwegian and Icelandic rune poems are included in their original and translated form. Also included is work on the three Brandon runic inscriptions and the Norfolk 'Tiw' runes.

£4.95   A5   ISBN 978 1 898281 49 8   Illustrations   88 pages

Anglo-Saxon FAQs

Stephen Pollington

125 questions and answers on a wide range of topics.

Are there any Anglo-Saxon jokes? Who was the Venerable Bede? Did the women wear make-up? What musical instruments did they have? How was food preserved? Did they have shops? Did their ships have sails? Why was Ethelred called 'Unready'? Did they have clocks? Did they celebrate Christmas? What are runes? What weapons and tactics did they use? Were there female warriors? What was the Synod of Whitby?

£9.95   ISBN 978 1898281-50-4 30 128pages

Anglo-Saxon Attitudes – A short introduction to Anglo-Saxonism

J.A. Hilton

This is not a book about the Anglo-Saxons, but a book about books about Anglo-Saxons. It describes the academic discipline of Anglo-Saxonism; the methods of study used; the underlying assumptions; and the uses to which it has been put.

Methods and motives have changed over time but right from the start there have been constant themes: English patriotism and English freedom.

£9.95　A5　ISBN 1–898281–39-4　9 ¾ x 6 ¾ inches　245 x 170mm　Hardback　64 pages

The Origins of the Anglo-Saxons
Donald Henson

This book has come about through a growing frustration with scholarly analysis and debate about the beginnings of Anglo-Saxon England. Much of what has been written is excellent, yet unsatisfactory. One reason for this is that scholars often have only a vague acquaintance with fields outside their own specialism. The result is a partial examination of the evidence and an incomplete understanding or explanation of the period.

The growth and increasing dominance of archaeological evidence for the period has been accompanied by an unhealthy enthusiasm for models of social change imported from prehistory. Put simply, many archaeologists have developed a complete unwillingness to consider movements of population as a factor in social, economic or political change. All change becomes a result of indigenous development, and all historically recorded migrations become merely the movement of a few hundred aristocrats or soldiers. The author does not find this credible.

This book has three great strengths.

> First, it pulls together and summarises the whole range of evidence bearing on the subject, offering an up-to-date assessment: the book is, in other words, a highly efficient introduction to the subject. Second – perhaps reflecting Henson's position as a leading practitioner of public archaeology (he is currently Education and Outreach Co-ordinator for the Council for British Archaeology) – the book is refreshingly jargon free and accessible. Third, Henson is not afraid to offer strong, controversial interpretations. The Origins of the Anglo-Saxons can therefore be strongly recommended to those who want a detailed road-map of the evidence and debates for the migration period.

Current Archaeology 2006

£16.95　ISBN 1–898281–40-8　9 ¾ x 6 ¾ inches　245 x 170mm　Hardback　304 pages

A Departed Music – Readings in Old English Poetry
Walter Nash

The *readings* of this book take the form of passages of translation from some Old English poems. The author paraphrases their content and discuses their place and significance in the history of poetic art in Old English society and culture.

The author's knowledge, enthusiasm and love of his subject help make this an excellent introduction to the subject for students and the general reader.

£16.95　ISBN 1–898281–37-8　9 ¾ x 6 ¾ inches　245 x 170mm　Hardback　240 pages

English Sea Power 871-1100 AD
John Pullen-Appleby

This work examines the largely untold story of English sea power during the period 871 to 1100. It was an age when English kings deployed warships first against Scandinavian invaders and later in support of Continental allies.

The author has gathered together information about the appearance of warships and how they were financed, crewed, and deployed.

£14.95   ISBN 1-898281-31-9   9 ¾ x 6 ¾ inches   245 x 170mm   Hardback   114 pages

Anglo-Saxon Burial Mounds
Princely Burials in the 6th & 7th centuries
Stephen Pollington

This is the first book-length treatment of Anglo-Saxon Barrows in English. It brings together some of the evidence from Sutton Hoo and elsewhere in England for these magnificent burials and sets them in their historical, religious and social context.

The first section comprises the physical construction and symbolic meaning of these monuments. The second offers a comprehensive listing of known Anglo-Saxon barrows with notes on their contents and the circumstances of their discovery. The five appendices deal with literary and place-name evidence.

£14..95   ISBN 978 1898281-51-1   272 pages

Leechcraft: Early English Charms, Plantlore and Healing
Stephen Pollington

An unequalled examination of every aspect of early English healing, including the use of plants, amulets, charms, and prayer. Other topics covered include Anglo-Saxon witchcraft; tree-lore; gods, elves and dwarves.

The author has brought together a wide range of evidence for the English healing tradition, and presented it in a clear and readable manner. The extensive 2,000-entry index makes it possible for the reader to quickly find specific information.

The three key Old English texts are reproduced in full, accompanied by new translations.

Bald's Third Leechbook; *Lacnunga*; *Old English Herbarium*.

£25 ISBN 978-1-898281-47-4   240 x 170mm   paperback 28 illustrations   544 pages

Anglo-Saxon Riddles

Translated by John Porter

Here you will find ingenious characters who speak their names in riddles, and meet a one-eyed garlic seller, a bookworm, an iceberg, an oyster, the sun and moon and a host of others from the everyday life and imagination of the Anglo-Saxons. Their sense of the awesome power of creation goes hand in hand with a frank delight in obscenity, a fascination with disguise and with the mysterious processes by which the natural world is turned to human use.   This edition contains **all 95 riddles of the Exeter Book in both Old English and Modern English.**

£4.95   A5   ISBN 1–898281–13–0   144 pages

Tolkien's *Mythology for England*
A Guide to Middle-Earth
Edmund Wainwright

Tolkien set out to create a mythology for England and the English but the popularity of his books and the recent films has spread across the English-speaking world and beyond.

You will find here an outline of Tolkien's life and work. The main part of the book consists of an alphabetical subject entry which will help you gain a greater understanding of Tolkien's Middle-Earth, the creatures that inhabit it, and the languages they spoke. It will also give an insight into a culture and way-of-life that extolled values which are as valid today as they were over 1,000 years ago.

This book focuses on *The Lord of the Rings* and shows how Tolkien's knowledge of Anglo-Saxon and Norse literature and history helped shape its plot and characters.

£9-95 ISBN 1-898281-36-X approx. 10 x 6½ inches (245 x 170 mm)   Hardback 128 pages

Ordering

Order online at www.asbooks.co.uk

See website for postal address, prices and availability.

If ordering by post please enclose a cheque or postal order payable to Anglo-Saxon Books

UK deliveries add 10% up to a maximum of £2-50

Europe – including **Republic of Ireland** - add 10% plus £1 – all orders sent airmail

North America add 10% surface delivery, 30% airmail

Elsewhere add 10% surface delivery, 40% airmail

Overseas surface delivery 5–8 weeks; airmail 5–10 days

See website for details of North American distributor.

Anglo-Saxon Books
www.asbooks.co.uk   tel: 0845 430 4200

Organisations

Þa Engliscan Gesiðas

Þa Engliscan Gesiðas (The English Companions) is a historical and cultural society exclusively devoted to Anglo-Saxon history. Its aims are to bridge the gap between scholars and non-experts, and to bring together all those with an interest in the Anglo-Saxon period, its language, culture and traditions, so as to promote a wider interest in, and knowledge of all things Anglo-Saxon. The Fellowship publishes a journal, *Wiðowinde,* which helps members to keep in touch with current thinking on topics from art and archaeology to heathenism and Early English Christianity. The Fellowship enables like-minded people to keep in contact by publicising conferences, courses and meetings which might be of interest to its members.

For further details see www.tha-engliscan-gesithas.org.uk or write to: The Membership Secretary, Þa Engliscan Gesiðas, BM Box 4336, London, WC1N 3XX England.

Regia Anglorum

Regia Anglorum was founded to accurately re-create the life of the British people as it was around the time of the Norman Conquest. Our work has a strong educational slant. We consider authenticity to be of prime importance and prefer, where possible, to work from archaeological materials. Approximately twenty-five per cent of our members, of over 500 people, are archaeologists or historians.

The Society has a large working Living History Exhibit, teaching and exhibiting more than twenty crafts in an authentic environment. We own a forty-foot wooden ship replica of a type that would have been a common sight in Northern European waters around the turn of the first millennium AD. Battle re-enactment is another aspect of our activities, often involving 200 or more warriors.

For further information see www.regia.org or contact: K. J. Siddorn, 9 Durleigh Close, Headley Park, Bristol BS13 7NQ, England, e-mail: kim_siddorn@compuserve.com

The Sutton Hoo Society

Our aims and objectives focus on promoting research and education relating to the Anglo Saxon Royal cemetery at Sutton Hoo, Suffolk in the UK. The Society publishes a newsletter SAXON twice a year, which keeps members up to date with society activities, carries resumes of lectures and visits, and reports progress on research and publication associated with the site. If you would like to join the Society please see website: www.suttonhoo.org

Wuffing Education

Wuffing Education provides those interested in the history, archaeology, literature and culture of the Anglo-Saxons with the chance to meet experts and fellow enthusiasts for a whole day of in-depth seminars and discussions. Day Schools take place at the historic Tranmer House overlooking the burial mounds of Sutton Hoo in Suffolk.

For details of programme of events contact:-
Wuffing Education, 4 Hilly Fields, Woodbridge, Suffolk IP12 4DX
email education@wuffings.co.uk   website www.wuffings.co.uk
Tel. 01394 383908 or 01728 688749

Places to visit

Bede's World at Jarrow

Bede's world tells the remarkable story of the life and times of the Venerable Bede, 673–735 AD. Visitors can explore the origins of early medieval Northumbria and Bede's life and achievements through his own writings and the excavations of the monasteries at Jarrow and other sites.

Location – 10 miles from Newcastle upon Tyne, off the A19 near the southern entrance to the River Tyne tunnel. Bus services 526 & 527

Bede's World, Church Bank, Jarrow, Tyne and Wear, NE32 3DY

Tel. 0191 489 2106; Fax: 0191 428 2361; website: www.bedesworld.co.uk

Sutton Hoo near Woodbridge, Suffolk

Sutton Hoo is a group of low burial mounds overlooking the River Deben in south-east Suffolk. Excavations in 1939 brought to light the richest burial ever discovered in Britain – an Anglo-Saxon ship containing a magnificent treasure which has become one of the principal attractions of the British Museum. The mound from which the treasure was dug is thought to be the grave of Rædwald, an early English king who died in 624/5 AD.

This National Trust site has an excellent visitor centre, which includes a reconstruction of the burial chamber and its grave goods. Some original objects as well as replicas of the treasure are on display.

2 miles east of Woodbridge on B1083   Tel. 01394 389700

West Stow Anglo-Saxon Village

An early Anglo-Saxon Settlement reconstructed on the site where it was excavated consisting of timber and thatch hall, houses and workshop. There is also a museum containing objects found during the excavation of the site. Open all year 10am–4.15pm (except Yuletide). Special provision for school parties. A teachers' resource pack is available. Costumed events are held at weekends, especially Easter Sunday and August Bank Holiday Monday. Craft courses are organised.

For further details see www.stedmunds.co.uk/west_stow.html or contact:

The Visitor Centre, West Stow Country Park, Icklingham Road, West Stow,

Bury St Edmunds, Suffolk IP28 6HG   Tel. 01284 728718